G000300633

One Boy's War

One Boy's War

Anthony Rudd

An Anthony Blond Book

First published in Great Britain by Quartet Books Limited 1990
A member of the Namara Group
27/29 Goodge Street
London W1P 1FD

A catalogue record for this title is available from the
British Library

ISBN 0 7043 2760 0

Typeset by MC Typeset Ltd, Gillingham, Kent
Printed and bound in Great Britain by
BPCC Hazell Books
Aylesbury, Bucks, England
Member of BPCC Ltd.

Acknowledgments

Almost anyone who writes a book like this, depends on other people. This particularly applies to me because I am, in the jargon, 'partially sighted': I can't see very much at all, let alone to read. This has placed heavy burdens on three people: on Karen Searle who typed the manuscript with unfailing patience and good humour; on my wife Ethne, who read the manuscript to me at every stage; and, most important, on Hugh Bredin who, in editing the book, played a crucial role in pulling it together and presenting it in a form which will, I hope, find favour with the reader. I am most grateful to all three individuals.

Contents

If you haven't got a sense of humour,
you shouldn't sign on

Introduction

Coming of Age 1939–47

People old enough to have fought in the Second World War, however briefly, are in a class apart from those too young to have shared the experience. Going to war didn't make that generation superior but, as I'm continually reminded, it did give them values and attitudes which set them aside from their successors.

Someone once commented, during one of the many financial crises in the City, that it must be the worst time of my life. I looked at him with surprise. The idea that any City upheaval could possibly rank with a severe wartime setback was grotesque. The events were simply not in the same league: no money matter could ever be half as upsetting as getting killed.

Professor Norman Stone recently gave his views on Thatcherite Britain. He said that, for the first time in years, when he went abroad, he felt proud to be an Englishman and was able to hold up his head. He should have been in RAF uniform, walking down the Champs Elysées on 14 July 1945. In that year, to be British and wearing air-force uniform put one squarely into the Superman bracket.

In the years that followed the war I was aware of being only an insignificant member of a majority that had had wartime experience. Then, at last year's Remembrance Service in our local church, I realized for the first time that I had become a member of a minority. The handful of men – nearly all with rows of medals, some with decorations for valour amongst the NAAFI gongs – had disappeared. My collection may have been third rate by earlier standards, but it was now the only one there. I was the last survivor of that group.

True, there are still many other survivors around; but amongst the working population to which I still belong, they are now very few indeed. There is, of course, no risk of their vanishing without a trace. The Second World War continues to spawn an enormous literature including quantities of memoirs; but these are mostly written by and about heroes, not everyday people. This memoir is an account of everyday life in the last war as experienced by a very ordinary mortal.

1 3 September 1939

The day war was declared, my aunt and I were temporarily lodged in a small family hotel facing Southampton railway station. We had arrived there the previous morning, having travelled on the overnight ferry from St Malo, our summer holiday in Brittany brutally cut short by the imminent threat of hostilities.

The day was memorable only for the event. Nothing happened. The sun shone. We went for a long walk in the country and watched a cricket match for a while. In the evening, I helped Major Webb, a long-term resident of the hotel vaguely connected to the management, a portly but kindly middle-aged lady, to put up the blackout; a process that largely consisted of hanging old blankets over the curtains.

We were stuck in the hotel because my aunt had let our house in Tiverton until the end of the third week in September. Always a keen traveller, she had first taken me along for a winter in Switzerland; then for six months in a rented villa in Alassio; and, for the last four or five summer holidays, to various beaches in Belgium and France. The economics of these arrangements were based on two factors: the amazing strength of the pound against all the weak currencies, particularly the French franc; and second, our ability to let our accommodation in England while we were away. There were further refinements. We usually took off for the Continent late in August to take advantage of off-season rates. By the same token, we always hung on well into the third week in September. This usually involved my aunt in complex negotiations with management: these she conducted with a frenzied fluency born of great experience.

The outbreak of war on that particular day irritated her because it threw all her calculations for our summer holiday out of kilter. Instead of staying on in our nice hotel, the Hôtel Chateaubriand in Dinard, until 18 or 19 September at a comfortably low tariff, the war bundled us out of France and into Britain where low rates for September were seemingly unheard of. Furthermore, my aunt didn't care for Mr Chamberlain.

My aunt's age was a mystery. I put it at about sixty-five. She was a small, self-educated Scotswoman; extremely well read and an accomplished pianist. As she didn't like politics, she only read of such matters in J.L. Garvin's leaders on Sundays in the *Observer*, turning with great relief to James Agate's play reviews in the *Sunday Times*. She hated political arguments and when, on a rare visit, her daughter Suzanne brought politics into the house, she got angry. This time, however, it was Mr Chamberlain who had provoked her. She thought his behaviour over Czechoslovakia, waving a piece of paper in the air and claiming 'Peace in our time', was quite disgraceful. She was that rare bird, a fervent pro-Conservative who was just as fervently anti-Chamberlain; a stance that did not make her popular in Tiverton. Her mood that Sunday morning when Mr Chamberlain's voice came over the wireless was, once again, one of irritation. As far as she was concerned, Mr Chamberlain had a lot to answer for.

When we broke up for the summer holidays at the end of my first year, the housemaster of the day boys' house at Blundell's School, Tiverton, had addressed the house on the issue of peace and war. The Reverend Major Abigail, to give him his full title, thought war was extremely unlikely. However, it was not to be ruled out entirely. He just wanted to say that, if it did begin during the summer holidays, he wanted no nonsense; no one was to rush off and enlist.

The war would be absorbed into Blundell's timetable. Our involvement in it would start in an orderly manner with names carefully listed in the Reverend Major's round hand; with a roster on the house noticeboard. So off we went on our holidays, clear in our minds about that eventuality if nothing else.

Not that war hadn't been on Blundell's peacetime curriculum, anyway. Once you were fifteen, you could volunteer to join the OTC (Officers' Training Corps). And no one, while I was at Blundell's, had ever failed to volunteer. There were three noticeboards in the main lobby of the central buildings, one each for academic matters, sport and the Corps. The latter was the largest and, appropriately, the most orderly; with everybody's weekly duties outlined in Abigail's neat but florid hand.

Corps activities took up time on at least two days a week, sometimes three. Behind every parade there was a lot of spit and polish. The Corps uniform was First World War vintage. The tunics twinkled and flashed with brass buttons so that, on sunny days, the wearer could be picked off by a notional German sniper all of a mile away. Tunics were worn with khaki breeches ending just below the knee; and joining breeches to boots were puttees: yards of khaki cloth some six inches wide which, starting at the knee, wound in spiral stages each of one-and-a-half inches down the leg to the boot; the final yard or so was turned round and round and securely fastened. With the emphasis firmly on the word 'securely'. Those unversed in the art of putting them on, often found their puttees slowly unreeling, leaving an ever-lengthening bandage behind them as they marched; a dire humiliation, always followed by punishment.

The only way to avoid this was to abandon the issue of puttees altogether because they were hopelessly inelastic, flaccid, already stretched, often warped and always resistant to easy winding around the leg. For true security, you had to spend 7/6d on a pair of Fox's Puttees; magical garments that came in neat packs featuring a fox with a pronounced smile.

The puttees overlapped boots of a sort that kept Kipling's soldiers movin' up an' down again, sloggin' over Africa. With new boots, you didn't know which would be broken in first, the boot or your foot. But once the agony was over, they never let you down. The metal in them clinked and clanked on every stone and road surface; and in dry weather, sparks flew. Furthermore, if you burnished your boots sedulously for weeks, you could see your face in them.

Over the tunic came webbing: shoulder straps that criss-crossed over the back to link with a webbing belt and support a whole series of webbing pouches for storing loose ammunition. For ceremonial purposes, we took a tuppeny block of blanco and applied it to the webbing with a cloth or brush. In theory, once dry, it gave the webbing a matt khaki surface. In practice, our efforts were frequently compromised by black smudges, unwelcome by-products of our attempts to shine up with Brasso the buckles that kept our webbing together; reciprocally, blanco often sploshed on to and smeared the brass fittings. The solution was dexterity with a button stick, a slither of slotted brass which you slipped under the button or buckle to be shone.

Last but not least was the hat. Just above the peak, this had a horizontal leather band which had to be bulled to a shade of deep mahogany.

Above the band was the cap badge of the Devonshire Regiment: a sniper's aiming point we Brasso'd and buffed to dazzling brilliance. Like most boys in their first year of the Corps, I was still a fag so I had to blanco and Brasso, press and polish two complete outfits. Being in the Corps at Blundell's could very easily have been a full-time occupation.

During the summer term, the Corps had two full-day set-pieces: the annual inspection and the field day. In summer 1939, the annual inspection was carried out by a colonel sent by the War Office to do a round of public schools; probably slotting us in between Clifton and Sherborne. The parade took place on the main playing field. We marched past, platoon after platoon of 1914-

style boy soldiers. The whole process took an hour and a half and was a horseless, miniature version of the Trooping of the Colour.

When we had all been inspected by the War Office colonel, the Reverend Major Abigail and their respective retinues and when the band had played, marched and counter-marched, we fell out and gathered informally by the pavilion steps to hear a few words from the colonel. He looked most impressive. Tall, dark, imperious, he had flashing eyes and a black moustache bristling blackly above white teeth that bit off brusque martial phrases. 'Dress, good,' he said. 'Better posture,' he advised, 'but recruits, good.' This meant that the recruits, including myself, had stood straighter than the rest. The colonel, although ostensibly in the same army as our own officers, cut a very different figure from them. Alongside him, the Reverend Major Abigail looked rounder than ever and the rest of us felt hopelessly vulgar.

Although some loathed them, I thoroughly enjoyed field days. For a start, they meant a full day out in the Devon countryside away from schoolwork. I was also greatly diverted by the make-believe war manoeuvres that took place between Red Force and Blue Force. The venue for the field day that summer was Woodford Common, a large stretch of moorland inland from Exmouth and Sidmouth, an area ideal for the purpose. We were taken there in a convoy of hired buses. We were all in full 1914 territorial battle gear complete with Lee Enfield rifles. We also wore side packs bulging with provisions that included bottles of lemonade as our water bottles were only for decorative purposes. They had been made during the First World War from blue enamelled metal in a skin of specially sewn khaki cloth to mask them from the eyes of enemy snipers. Inside, they rattled with decades of rust. Unstoppered, they smelt of the Somme. Nobody was unwise enough to drink from them.

That summer, a refugee from Czechoslovakia had arrived at the school, a boy called Fleichmann. Amongst his paraphernalia was a German soldier's water bottle. This stimulated much interest: made of light clean aluminium, it had rounded edges and strong corrugated sides. Around its centre ran a leather strap embedded in a special indentation: string held the stopper to the bottle. It was a very impressive, thoroughly modern object; an index of the up-to-the-minute way in which the Wehrmacht was equipped – in marked contrast to our pathetic 1914 equipment.

As a recruit, I was one of three runners attached to the Reverend Major Abigail, the lead umpire in the day's manoeuvres. Map in hand and binoculars at the ready, he perched on a shooting stick, steadily reddening under the midsummer sun. When it was my turn, he suddenly pointed: 'See that section over there? Tell them they're dead!'

Being one of the few who actually enjoyed cross-country running, I gladly charged down the hill, across a brook at the bottom and up the other side through the ferns. I approached the section head warily. It was Brown whom I'd seen one Sunday afternoon at the Palmerston Hotel, saying to his Russian mother, 'Don't be silly, mother.' He was short, blond and ferocious. After a very active war, he went to Oxford and despite having only one leg, made quite a name for himself; with two, he was truly formidable.

'What d'you want?' he snapped, tapping his thigh with his swagger stick as though tuning it up for the punishment of a runner bearing the wrong message.

'Major Abigail has asked me to tell you, Sergeant Brown, that you're all dead.'

As he lurched towards me, his seven-man section leapt up from the bracken behind him and fired their rifles. As I knew that a blank .303 discharged at short range can leave a painful scorch mark, I had turned to shout my last word, 'dead', over my shoulder; that way, I'd be well away before the fusillade rang out. Luckily for Brown and his section, the Reverend Major was some way away, pronouncing another small body of troops dead; otherwise, Brown and the rest would not only have been technically dead, they would also have been physically punished as Abigail didn't hold with his runners being attacked.

Our 1939 field day conformed to pre-1914 manoeuvres in its total failure to acknowledge fighting vehicles such as bren-gun carriers or tanks, let alone any form of aerial combat. Sometimes we compounded its air of unreality by contriving to get lost in the Exe Valley; to get our bearings, we used to ask the way at local farms which plied us with massive jugs of home-brewed cider; a wonderful drink for a hot summer's afternoon but fatal to any attempt to pinpoint the whereabouts of the enemy Red Force. So it was left to Fleichmann's water bottle to be the only material contact between our 1914-style charades and the real world: sooner or later, we would all have to jump the chasm between acting and actuality.

Talk aside, the only aspect of war that impinged on my aunt and myself was the scheme to evacuate children from London and the eastern counties. Some time before the war, a lady had asked my aunt whether she'd take two evacuees. As my aunt didn't think hostilities would ever break out she said, 'Yes, of course,' and we got a little window-bill to show we were part of the scheme.

In the event, we were spared having to have 'vaccies' because my aunt let our bungalow – with its six rooms, bathroom, kitchen and rich array of antiques and pictures – to two quiet, thin, middle-aged ladies in Liberty prints. They arrived at the beginning of July, thereby pushing us out into the Lorna Doone Hotel, Tiverton, for the three weeks until the end of term when we could get away to the Continent.

This year, we were going to France for eight weeks. I was the only boy in the house to go abroad that summer. No one else in Tiverton took holidays abroad; my aunt and I were regarded as rather odd. We planned to go to Trouville for two weeks and hoped to find somewhere in Brittany, probably Dinard, for the remaining six.

We travelled light, with just a valise and a little cabin

trunk. In theory we could just about carry them between us but, in practice, we didn't have to as in those days there were always porters. We didn't even have to book rooms as a queue of hoteliers invariably met us at the station.

Our hotel at Trouville had a season of about six weeks. It was pretentious and rather dirty. As always, my aunt started by spending a whole day cleaning out our rooms. That done, and the trunk installed, we set out to enjoy the amenities.

Two weeks later, we went by bus to Brittany with the trunk perched on the roof amongst suitcases and local produce. After several hot hours driving down dusty roads, we arrived at one o'clock in the main square at Avranches. Once the bus had left we were the only sign of life as everyone else was indoors having lunch. I sat on the trunk and my aunt, as always, went to find the first house with an open door; never mind whether shop, hotel or private home. It turned out to be a shop and after what seemed a long time, she returned. A taxi would come. And so it did, at a very decent interval after lunch, at two-fifteen. The trunk was loaded on to the roof, and we were off to the railway station about two miles away, far below on the plain.

When the train reached St Malo, we still had to cross the estuary to reach Dinard. Various porters helped us to get the trunk down to the water's edge, on to one of the little *vedettes* which plied back and forth, and on to the small jetty on the Dinard side. While I sat on the trunk, my aunt wandered slowly up the street trying to recognize the small hotel where she'd had a cup of tea some years ago. It turned out to be the Hôtel Chateaubriand. Up the hill we went, this time with another porter and the trunk, to install ourselves in the cleanest, brightest and best-run French hotel we'd ever seen.

God bless my aunt. An excellent cook herself, she could sniff out quality and value anywhere. While my schoolfellows continued to tuck into Bird's Custard and Cornish pasties, I was developing a *tendresse* for *langouste* followed by chocolate soufflé of unparalleled lightness and texture.

Small wonder then, that my aunt was so cross at the sharp deterioration in international relations. There we were, comfortably housed, eating magnificently, enjoying the panoramic sweep of Dinard's uncrowded beaches; enjoying films such as *Stagecoach* in the open-air cinema, when up cropped a crisis in Danzig of all places.

We went to the little Anglican church where the vicar said a special prayer for peace, adding that if this was done in every small church in the Anglican community, the power of prayer would surely deter Herr Hitler and his henchman Herr Forster, the Nazi bigwig in Danzig, from going to war. We duly added our mite of prayer before returning to a superb Sunday lunch at the Chateaubriand.

Our orisons were to no avail. A depression settled on the hotel and on the resort as a whole. Madame promptly went into a decline. Instead of bossing everyone about from a vantage point commanding a sweeping view of the restaurant and ground floor, she grew morose and silent and glued herself to an enormous wireless set that resonated to bad news in French. The English people began to leave. My aunt was determined not to follow suit, given the wonderfully low average cost of our holiday. By the last week in August, there were only a few guests left. In contrast to the subdued but practical English, the French had become dour and surly. They assumed that the war was inescapable and remembered the deaths of millions of Frenchmen in the First World War while, with typical optimism, the British still thought that Mr Chamberlain might pull off another miracle.

At first, this discrepancy in national viewpoints was puzzling. Then large placards appeared with fine print announcing the official call-up for each class of reservist. Overnight, the male population began to melt away. One day, there had been waiters, cooks, farmers and fishermen; the next, they were French soldiers in a dirty blue uniform, looking very scruffy and sad, milling about in hundreds along the quay. It was the general mobilization.

We had to leave the hotel because it was shutting down for the duration. The staff were on the way out and Madame had given up. Getting away was a problem as there were now no porters. We had to manhandle the trunk down the jetty and then, with much pushing and shoving, get it on to one of the remaining *vedettes*.

On the other side, I had to sit on the trunk for hours while my aunt got tickets and a passage on the night ferry to Southampton. Although the shipping agent said it was probably the last for many weeks, it was surprisingly uncrowded.

When we left, France was already at war so we travelled blacked-out. When we arrived next morning in Southampton, threading our way past the Union Castle liners lying at anchor, Britain was still at peace. But only for one more day.

2 The First Years at War

When school reassembled, everyone was back, present and correct; no one had disobeyed the housemaster's orders. The war brought about two changes straight away. Dover College was evacuated on to us so that every facility had to serve almost double the number of pupils. And there was the blackout, offering limitless scope for mischief. The school carpentry shop put heavy black cardboard into wooden frames which fitted into window apertures. At blackout time, the frames were put up to save us from enemy bombers. Putting up these frames gave a great deal of innocent merriment especially in the classes of masters who were poor disciplinarians. Boys kept slipping behind the frames to cries of, 'Please, sir, Smith Minor is missing.' It was great fun.

One or two of the senior boys in the house decided to leave at the end of the Christmas term as they had managed to get themselves into this or that regiment. On the last day of term, just before Christmas, there were a few goodbyes along the lines of 'See you in France.'

Meanwhile the concert party side of the war added an extra dimension to festivities, with everybody buying the sheet music for *We're Gonna Hang Out the Washing on the Siegfried Line* and other patriotic hits. I first experienced the full force of this new 'joining in' spirit at the Devonshire Arms in Dulverton, a hotel run by the parents of one of my friends.

Because of the war, it was enjoying a bumper Christmas season so, for the entertainment of the guests, Mr and Mrs Nelder put on a special Christmas concert party in which I had a part. The hotel glowed with goodwill and excellent English food, complete with clotted cream made in the hotel dairy in basins big enough to wash in.

There were limitless supplies of salmon from the Exe and venison from the moors. It was a Christmas of plenty that lodged in my memory as the years went on and that kind of richness vanished from the land.

1940 got off to an exceptionally cold start. The canal which began just below our house on the aptly named Canal Hill, froze. The reassembly of school was postponed because the pipes had also frozen. So all the day boys and a fair number of others got together every morning on the canal and skated down it all day for miles; often on fen skates screwed to the soles of our long-suffering Corps boots. Some householders tried to stop their water tanks from freezing by means that produced outbreaks of fire; these kept the Fire Brigade busy in hopeless, indeed waterless attempts to contain the conflagrations. Amongst the notable houses to burn in this way was that of our headmaster, the Reverend Neville Gorton, later Bishop of Coventry. It was, in Arthur Marshall's phrase, all part of life's rich tapestry.

Up till the spring, the war seemed to be largely promoted by newspapers trying to sell wall maps with little flags. We all bought them. Except for great excitement over the sinking of the *Graf Spee*, nothing much happened. Then the invasion of Norway ushered in an onslaught of great events: the downfall of Chamberlain, the invasion of the Low Countries and France. It suddenly seemed as though the whole country was hurtling towards a real conflict.

At home, my aunt's attitude to the war changed. During the winter, she hadn't treated it very seriously. She had even got into the irritating habit of switching on the verandah light every evening just to defy the blackout. But with the phoney war behind us, her flippancy gave way to serious interest in the war's dramas, especially the naval campaign in and around Narvik.

In time the news got nearer home. As France was falling, a telegram arrived announcing the imminent arrival of her daughter Suzanne. This received mixed reactions. Suzanne had been living in Toulouse, teaching English to university students, and the prospect of her emerging from the turmoil of France to tell all was very exciting. On the other hand, Suzanne always put her mother on edge. She talked politics which my aunt hated. She also adopted a patronizing air towards our steady, middle-class way of life. She liked to think that she came from the world of the arts. Her first husband had been the novelist, Leo Walmesley, and she had lived in Robin Hood's Bay in Yorkshire while he'd been writing the books set in that village. The village also featured in the pretty little watercolours over my aunt's Bechstein; they had been painted by her father-in-law who was a professional artist.

Later, when she left Walmesley, Suzanne had fallen in with a group which, amongst others, included Jack Skeaping and Barbara Hepworth. During our six months at Alassio, when I was eight, she and her second husband came to stay; they overflowed with stories of the evil government in Vienna and the vicissitudes of the workers there. When the Spanish Civil War started, she contrived to show up in Barcelona. So it was entirely typical of her to appear now in the midst of all the upheavals that resounded from the wireless.

When we went down to the station, we found her behind a rampart of baggage. She was dressed in a neat black suit of a cut never seen before in Tiverton; a cheeky black hat enclosed her nice blonde hair. Like her mother, she was small. The overall impression was that of Tallulah Bankhead in miniature. My aunt's spirits visibly sank. But mine soared.

Once settled in the single guestroom, Suzanne held forth. She had escaped from the Germans by the skin of her teeth and was lucky to be with us. She had only managed to get away with a few things, but there it was. We looked at the three large suitcases and marvelled at Suzanne's limitless capacity to get other people to carry her luggage. The French, she said, had been wonderful: poor darlings, they'd been badly let down and had, accordingly, succumbed to the Axis powers. Suzanne warmed to the thought that next time it would be our turn. At least the French had a proper army in the field; we hadn't – so how could we hope to resist?

It was true that there was still no general mobilization in Britain of the kind we'd seen in Dinard during the last days of peace. We had conscription but it was very slow to draw people into the services – which, judging by the rumours that reached Tiverton, were anyway quite incapable of absorbing them at more than a snail's pace.

As it was, the Expeditionary Force was straggling back from Dunkirk. As the weeks wore on, Suzanne continued in her critical vein and my aunt grew increasingly concerned. Whenever she put her views to tradesmen, Suzanne highlighted the vast difference between her thinking and the views then current in Tiverton. The situation came to a head when my housemaster, the Reverend Major, came to tea one Sunday afternoon; rather a formal affair with, as its gastronomic highlight, one of my aunt's magnificent cakes. Her skills were not lost on a trencherman as robust as Abigail.

Suzanne was swift to introduce her views on Soviet Russia, which she had visited for a few weeks in the late thirties with some arty friends. She had returned an ardent supporter of the USSR. To make matters worse, she then held forth on the valiant efforts of the French army – at which the Reverend Abigail disappeared in favour of Major Abigail. But no lasting damage was done as he had long categorized my aunt as an eccentric; thus pigeon-holed, she had considerable social and intellectual latitude – especially as she saw to it that I always turned up at school properly dressed at the right time.

So when Suzanne announced that she was a Communist, my housemaster just helped himself to another slice of orange cake. For all that, Suzanne's outburst, as always, appalled my aunt. Fortunately, Suzanne also knew the rules. After some six weeks, she was off to get back into the swim in London. She promised to write.

It was now late June, and a real crisis hit my aunt. Her fragile finances hinged on about six rents from shop properties and residential houses in Kingston-upon-Thames, Southend and Margate. When her tenants in the latter two considered evacuation, her rental income came under serious threat. The little contribution that came from my mother in South Africa was safe for the time being. But our days at The Chalet, as the bungalow was called, were clearly numbered. As yet, the economy of Tiverton seemed to be quite unaffected by the war but, due to our own links with the South-East, we were less happily placed.

Meanwhile, at Blundell's there were various comings and goings. An Australian master suddenly decided to return home. A boy called Cross left in midterm to join his parents in South Africa. To fill vacancies left by masters who'd joined the forces, the headmaster began to recruit some strange new staff. A former Austrian professor of linguistics who wished to teach Russian was set to teach elementary French. Still more dramatic, the poet Stephen Spender arrived to teach history and English. Over the following year, I got to know him slightly, and was much struck by the fact that he seemed to have been in the same party as Suzanne in Barcelona. I was also dazzled by his glowingly artistic clothes. He was a great success as a master and enjoyed the full approval of the headmaster; somehow, though, Abigail never quite got around to inviting Spender into his circle.

In many ways, the school was loosening up: its formal structure, typical of a minor public school, was adjusting to new ideas, to the new comradely spirit spread by Churchill's speeches and the fact that the country was now alone in its great struggle.

Nowhere was change more evident than in the Corps which, in the winter of 1940–1, officially became part of the Home Guard. This organization had started earlier in the summer with people walking around with armbands and painted tin helmets. A little later, it had acquired its name. Our Great War uniforms were replaced by battledress which, although badly cut, at least brought us into the Second World War. Our puttees went, of course, and so, to our immense relief, did our wretched webbing.

To Abigail's delight, some Second World War armaments turned up too: a pair of Thompson sub-machine guns in specially made boxes, all the way from Chicago, USA; the ammunition took a little longer. Major Abigail also got in step with the times. He took to leading the school on route marches of several miles in the early evenings. He too wore battledress but without the top, his shirtsleeves rolled up to the elbow. We even had a flying squad of three or four cars. It included a splendid Railton, driven by one of the directors of the Tiverton brewery, and the best taxi in town, a 1937 Packard.

The first time these vehicles turned out to a field day, we had a special briefing in the library. It was taken by a brigadier whose ill-fitting battledress sported three rows of medal ribbons. He spoke in a high-pitched voice and compared the approaching operations with some of his First World War experiences in the Balkans fighting the Bulgarians in the valley of the River Vardar. He spoke at length about the wily Bulgar's endless capacity for deceit, seemingly uninhibited by their likely absence from the Exe Valley. It was a colourful but useless briefing. In the event, the flying column flew so fast and so far that we, the foot sloggers, never caught up with the cars; we only saw them when they sped past us, flinging mud in our faces – as may well have been the way in the valley of the River Vardar.

The war now set in. The more established the Home Guard became, the less likely invasion seemed. The Battle of Britain had been won, and the island was safe; but the war was evidently very far from won. There was a brief flicker of success in the Western Desert, which led the more enthusiastically patriotic masters to forecast an early victory, but this was succeeded by monumental reverses. Then Russia came into the war.

I now felt that it was time to make plans: to get to the war before it got to me; that way, I could retain at least some sort of control over my destiny.

With hindsight, I realize that there were three categories of people who came of age in the war. For a tiny minority, the war was an amazing career opportunity; it provided the perfect arena in which they could display their skills and fulfil their destinies. These were the potential heroes, the boys who ended up with medals for valour: the naturals for war, the combat men. Casualties amongst them were no higher than for the rest; as a friend of mine observed, the first people to hit the beach and race across it often had the lowest casualties: on the rugby field, tackle really low and you won't get hurt.

The second category, a rather larger minority, comprised those who were quite unfit for war either mentally or physically or sometimes, both. A typical case was one of the boys next door, the elder of the two Sedgwick brothers. He had won an open history scholarship to Oxford but, instead of squeezing in a term or two, he was called up into the infantry. On his last leave that first freezing winter, we skated together on the canal. He had a slight stammer and a chalk-white face under a thatch of lavatory-brush hair. He looked dreadful in uniform. He would have made an exceptional historian but he vanished, drowned when his troopship was torpedoed in a convoy. This group comprised the war's true victims.

I was in the third category, the majority, that aimed to ride the war like a surfer on a board riding the waves. Although the war was our only career option, it offered numerous different opportunities. Eventually, they might all lead in the same unsatisfactory direction but at least there was some scope for exercising initiative.

So in the autumn of 1941, I settled down to a full and

careful examination of my options. I ended up by choosing aircrew duties in the RAF. At the time, I couldn't tell the difference between an ME 109 and a Spitfire; mathematics was far from my strongest subject and, unlike many boys, I had never dreamed of becoming a pilot. All the services offered a route into their training programmes through the universities. Presumably this was because the latter already had training facilities. For the candidate, it ensured two free terms at university before having to disappear into the forces. And, assuming survival, it also meant he would have a head start in the great post-war rush for university places.

It had to be one of these training courses – but which? Practically all of them required the candidate to spend the two precious terms studying physics and engineering or related subjects. Only the RAF, with amazing liberality, allowed the study of arts subjects. At Oxford, it could be a mix of politics and history. That clinched it. I filled in all the papers and got them supported by appropriate recommendations including, of course, that of Major Abigail who while doubting my choice gave it his loyal support. Within two weeks, I was given a date for an interview in early February 1942. I was on my way and absolutely delighted. As a wartime schoolboy, I couldn't wait to move out into the dangerous world that awaited me.

3 Attestation

I was called to the Air Ministry for interview in mid-February 1942. Perhaps, like all wars, this war increasingly felt like a team game in which one ought to be playing one's part. But the war and the feeling seemed to have bypassed Tiverton, leaving the little Devon town complacent, self-contained, even cosy. As such, it was almost unbearably claustrophobic.

Although I had little idea of what I was letting myself in for, I was glad to be off to London. The RAF was far from being the unanimous choice of my peers; most of them were opting either for the army or the navy. Abigail had no advice concerning prospects in the junior service. In his idea of war, as represented by field days and the newly introduced night operations, the air arm had practically no role. The Home Guard was neither bombed nor bombing; this was despite lurid news of aerial bombardment in France as relayed to us by Blundell's old boys who, by joining up before Dunkirk, had experienced the real thing.

I put myself up at the Regent Palace in the Strand. I had formed a strong liking for its strange mix of marbled grandeur and Corner-House cosiness when my aunt used to take me there before the war for four-day stays after Christmas. Moreover it was a massive structure that was probably as safe a place as anywhere in the event of a stray bomb. And it was near the Air Ministry, just around the corner at the foot of Kingsway, where I was due to present myself next day at ten o'clock.

My tax-demand-like letter on buff Air Ministry paper told me to ask at reception for the sergeant who would direct me to the interview room. He was a dapper man with short dark hair and a toothbrush moustache.

'Good morning sir,' he said, the 'sir' being almost unprecedented in my experience. An airman in a little hutch at the back of the hall was detailed to take me upstairs to the third floor and the interview room. So far, so good. At least I hadn't gone to the wrong place and inadvertently joined the wrong service. My piece of paper had been recognized and I had been nodded through. After a minute's wait in the small interview room, I was summoned by the same airman down the corridor to an office where there were two officers. They sat on either side of a desk by a window with a view of Bush House. They got up and welcomed me, motioning me to a chair placed between them. My interview had begun.

They were both flight lieutenants, both pilots with the diagonal blue and white striped ribbon of the DFC neatly sewn below their pilot's wings. One was fair and dashing; the other dark and deeply disfigured. I had read about the flash burns which so often maimed pilots whose aircraft caught fire suddenly when the fume-laden atmosphere of the cockpit exploded; an experience unforgettably described in *The Last Enemy* by Richard Hillary. But this was the first victim I had met face to face. I shook hands with a black leather glove and saw the near-unbearable sight of a smooth, contourless mask of multi-coloured flesh; a taut sheet of shiny skin with apertures cut for nostrils and eyes. The smile was crooked but the voice normal. The pilot wore his wound as he did his medal ribbon. It was all part of the deal.

He started the interview by asking, 'What do you think of *F for Freddy*?' He was referring to the first full-length propaganda film made by the RAF. I said I thought it was terrific but perhaps slightly laboured. This provoked a three-cornered debate for the next ten minutes as to whether propaganda films were better understated or overstated. Interesting literary references were invoked, usually by the disfigured pilot who turned out to be a Wykehamist.

They then turned to the forms which I'd filled out. They noted that I wasn't a particularly good swimmer.

'That won't do,' the fair-haired officer smiled. 'If you bail out, we want you to be swimming around down there all ready for us to fish you out.' There was laughter all round, and he made a note saying I should have extra swimming instruction. 'Don't want to lose you in the briny, do we?' More polite laughter, another laboured point.

They'd put me down for the Oxford University short course starting next October, if that was all right by me. Meanwhile, what was I going to do? I said I thought I'd leave Blundell's and go to work in an aircraft factory for the summer, see how the aeroplanes were put together. A capital idea, they agreed, broaden the mind, an interesting experience, jolly useful, too.

The interview was over. Of all my subsequent interviews, this was by far the most gentlemanly. I didn't realize it at the time but I had touched part of the pre-war RAF. These two men with their charming manners and delightful line in understatement were amongst the dwindling survivors who, as members of the pre-war RAAF (Regular and Auxiliary Air Forces), had gone to war in 1939.

The RAF that I was to join and get to know well was very different in style and content from the service represented by these two beautifully behaved warriors. They wished me every good fortune as a pilot – significantly, there was no question of my being anything else – and I was on my way.

The airman then took me down the corridor to the interview room. There a tall civilian came in with a Bible and a typewritten statement on a small board. This was the form of attestation, my vow to serve sovereign and country through thick and thin. Once I'd taken the oath on the Bible, I was 'in'. Soon I'd be receiving papers to say that I was 18051745 Aircraftsman Second Class

Riley Anthony Winton Rudd. Promotion to leading aircraftsman would follow once I'd been posted to the Oxford University squadron, to which I'd report in October when I took up residence at University College, Oxford. A few minutes later, I was out in the fresh air of Kingsway. In two months' time, I'd be eighteen. Meanwhile I was an Aircraftsman Second Class; despite being the lowest of the low, I had at least got my hand if not my foot on the bottom rung of the ladder.

4 Joining the Royal Air Force

In opting for the RAF, I was joining the most popular, morale-boosting and sought-after of the three services. This was partly because the RAF consisted, in the public imagination anyway, of 'knights in the sky'; romantic, heroic pilots who 'diced with death' in the air.

Then, in winning the Battle of Britain, the RAF had scored the first major victory of any Allied service. This triumph was particularly impressive because until then the Germans had seemed unbeatable. They had, after all, invented an entirely new, frighteningly effective and seemingly irreversible form of warfare: the Blitzkrieg, a combination of Teutonic efficiency and ruthlessness linked to the very latest technology.

Moreover the success of the Blitzkrieg was brilliantly exploited by another German innovation, modern propaganda, which soaked the world in the fact of German invincibility. So by the time the Nazis turned on Britain, the psychological stage was set for a walkover. Churchill could make his speeches and *Punch* churn out cartoons of comic krauts dressed as nuns but the man in the street had a good idea of what was in store for him.

Then a miracle happened. In the preliminary air battle, the RAF refused to be beaten. Day after day, the public watched the RAF knock the stuffing out of the Luftwaffe against a September sky of the brightest blue. Furthermore, the British made the most of the victory in propaganda terms: exaggerated claims were allowed to stand and to everyone's satisfaction, hugely inflated figures were proclaimed for the number of Germans shot down.

In practical terms, the victory prevented an invasion which most people thought the army incapable of repelling. It also shattered the myth of German invincibility: true, they might win subsequent battles but, having resoundingly lost one, they could now lose many more.

The Battle of Britain also showed that the British were just as resourceful and clever as the Hun. As it watched cinema newsreels, the public realized that, behind the ops room scenes with WAAFs pushing markers across huge maps, there must lie a remarkable system. And it was right: since 1936, the RAF together with some gifted scientists had evolved an air defence system, based on radar, which by 1940 was unmatched anywhere.

With radar 'eyes' that could see miles beyond any human vision, the RAF could garner information through landlines laid just pre-war to a command structure acting as brains. This nerve centre plotted counter moves and used other landlines to order fighter stations into action. These stations were equipped with another technical breakthrough, VHF (Very High Frequency) radio through which it could direct pilots in the air. As a result, RAF fighters could swoop out of the blue at just the right moment and annihilate the enemy; just as though they were guided by some unseen hand, as indeed they were. The Germans could hardly believe that the British, of all people, had completely outwitted them in what was ultimately a technological struggle. From the British point of view it may well have been the most satisfactory moment in history since the longbow had won the Battle of Crécy.

The RAF's popularity was also due to its bearing the burden of the war. At the start, the Germans had everything going for them in the air war. In Spain, they'd got their hand in by obliterating Guernica. Then their air arm had knocked other parts of Europe to pieces, reducing the cities of Warsaw and Rotterdam to smouldering ruins, demoralizing France by strafing refugees. Next, they moved on to the East End of London, to Liverpool, to Southampton and so on.

When the RAF's Bomber Command hit back, the public cheered. It could hear the aircraft taking off; it could sometimes see them amassing in the sky before a long flight over the North Sea; and it could hear the bombers returning.

At last, the Boche was getting a generous dose of his own medicine. This bombardment of German cities kept British morale going until we could develop the strength to mount the D-Day invasion in 1944. Bomber Harris never got a peerage but he was amongst the most popular of all our war leaders, up there with Churchill, far above Montgomery.

This, then, was the service I was joining.

5 Workers' Playtime

As far as I know, I was the only one of my year at Blundell's to volunteer for work in a factory while waiting for the next stage. The rest of my peers pursued activities which involved collars and ties. From early April to mid-September 1942, I was tieless and my collar very far from white.

The only aircraft factory in Exeter was an offshoot of the Southampton-based firm of Follands. It employed shifts of just over a hundred people by day and night, and was situated in what had been a foundry used by the local council for casting manhole covers and the like.

I called at the factory one Thursday afternoon and Mr Bennett, the tall lean man who ran the works, said I was to start on Monday at seven-thirty in the morning. He added that the shop worked two shifts a day: the first started at seven-thirty and finished at five-thirty in the afternoon, with two hours overtime running through to seven-thirty when the night shift came on for a twelve-hour stint until seven-thirty in the morning.

I was taken on as a worker, role unspecified, for 9⅜d per hour. Overtime and the night shift were paid time-and-a-half, and Sunday was double-time.

My aunt had moved from The Chalet on Canal Hill, Tiverton, into one half of a spacious farmhouse a mile and a half south of Thorverton and almost exactly seven miles from the factory; this was in a small industrial suburb at the foot of the hill covered by the city of Exeter.

My aunt used her gleaming antique furniture to make her side of the farmhouse as comfortable as the bungalow at Tiverton. The hard-working couple next door, a farmer and his wife, occasionally supplemented our rations and themselves ate very well.

The wife had a tight glowing skin that derived from regular recourse to the bowl of clotted cream that dominated their kitchen table at meals. The only lavatory was outside in a clean, rather ramshackle hut with ample supplies of pages from *Farmer's Weekly* torn into four. The garden was bright with lupins and Michaelmas daisies.

As I cycled off on the first morning at six-thirty, I thanked my lucky stars that I wasn't starting in October; at this time of year the mornings would get lighter and getting up would be easier.

Follands was then mainly a sub-contractor. It had made its own aeroplanes in the past and after the war was to produce the famous Gnat Trainer. Most of its work consisted of making or patching up Bristol Beauforts and Beaufighters. At Exeter, we made the tailplane for Beaufighters. We also took old tailplanes, sliced them in two, put in a flat section and stuck on the two original parts at an angle sloping up fifteen degrees; a shape that lent the aircraft more stability than had the original flat tail.

Most of the work was skilled or semi-skilled. There were two brown-coated boys who swept the place out. As I was unskilled and knew nothing, I should have been one of them. But it was decided that I was to learn a job instead. This wasn't a universally popular decision as everyone was paid a productivity bonus on top of the basic salary. Most of the workforce worked in teams of two with – and this was to be my role – the occasional hanger-on.

My only previous experience – a nodding acquaintance with Meccano – was only a little better than nothing. So I was lucky that my induction into factory life happened in kindly, non-industrial Devon. As a greenhorn in the Midlands, I would have sustained the rigours so memorably described in Alan Sillitoe's *Saturday Night and Sunday Morning*.

As it was, I wasn't even sent to the stores for a rubber hammer or a pot of striped paint. I never had any trouble from anyone; all the workers were remarkably good-humoured and tended to laugh with me rather than at me.

During the Second World War, aircraft and their sections – such as tail planes – were built on jigs; these not only supported the structure while it was being built but also guaranteed the accuracy of its dimensions. Once the metal framework was in place on the jig, teams of two or three fitters started cladding the framework with a metal skin. This was precut in panels drilled with the requisite holes so that they could be pinned to the structure with metal clips. All the hole drilling was done by air-driven hand drills. These and the riveting machines were driven by a spaghetti of airlines. If an airline shed its drill, it would snake round the floor in a frenzy, hissing and howling until someone could turn it off at the base. I soon became inured to the incessant hiss of escaping air broadcast from equipment that all seemed to be American in origin.

Once the structure was fitted with its metal skin – up to two days' fast continuous work by a skilled team – it was the turn of the riveters. All rivets were countersunk: a pre-war breakthrough achieved by Howard Hughes who when he made it had all the rivets drilled out of his current aircraft and new rivets drilled in so that his aircraft had smooth surfaces instead of skins bobbing with rivet-heads standing proud of the metal. The rivets themselves were first placed in a steaming chemical bath operated by girls with impressive sang-froid. An electric charge passed through the liquid to soften the rivets and so make them much easier to push home with a rivet gun; a miniature replica of those used for shipbuilding by Clydeside riveters. But the riveter could only do this effectively when his mate held a metal block the size of a pack of playing cards against the back of the rivet. As the blows rained on to the head, so the metal slab at the back pressed the back of the rivet absolutely flat against the metal, thus securing a tight hold. A team of two took about a day and a half to complete one of these assemblies.

The tail assembly involved several other jobs. The fairings into which the flaps slotted included certain wooden end pieces. These had to be carefully finished, rubbed down with no rough edges, by the 'chippy', probably the most skilled man in the factory. During its progress, each assembly was inspected twice by a completely separate department with the initials AID (Aircraft Inspection Department); its members were sealed off, socially and professionally, from everybody else. If they didn't pass a piece of work, it had to be done all over again.

There were odd jobs too, one of which finally devolved on me. The system of riveting with the second man holding the block, wouldn't work if there wasn't room for the block; for instance near the edge of the tail assembly where the two sides came within two inches of each other. So we had to find another way to rivet. The clever Americans, whose technology we used most of the time, had invented the pseudo-rivet. It was the normal shape but with a hollow axis so it could be threaded on a long piece of wire. This had a head with a diameter large enough to contain the rivet. Made of extra-strong metal, it was inserted into a kind of gun with a nozzle. The operator threaded a dozen or so rivets on to his spindle and fitted them into the holes, turning the handle to pull the spindle through each rivet – with the gun enlarging the rivet to lodge it firmly in place. The rivets were made of a special metal which didn't have to be dipped into the fuming tank. To complete the seal, a little pin was tapped through the hole in the rivet.

This amazing contraption, called the Schobert riveter, became my baby. I wielded this tricky but clever little US device and because there was a certain knack to it everybody was very happy to let me get on with it. Thanks to the Schobert riveter, I was established, working on every assembly and no longer a dead weight compromising the chances of a bonus for some otherwise high-performing team.

Although I fitted into this culture fairly easily in some ways, I stood out in others. For instance, I had volunteered for aircrew. Although everyone in the factory was in a reserved occupation and therefore couldn't be drafted, there was nothing to stop them from volunteering in the same way. Indeed that was the only escape route from a reserved occupation open to aircraft workers or, say, policemen. Aircrew volunteers got top priority but this simply wasn't appreciated in the factory.

Many joked about why, now that I'd seen how aeroplanes were put together, I could possibly want to fly in them. And it was a good point. Every now and again some over-large hole disguised by thick paint got past the AID inspectors. One day, a tail plane went out and at the last moment someone noticed a knocking noise just as it was being lifted. This proved to be a massive screwdriver which was duly extracted.

It was accepted that while I could go off and fight my little war, they would continue with their way of life. They were not unpatriotic. They all mourned Flight Lieutenant 'Paddy' Finucane, the famous ace, when he was shot down over Dieppe. But nobody rushed to fill his place. I didn't comment on this at the time, but I became aware that there were two Englands, the one that made things and the other that drove them. Not, of course, that all the 'drivers' came from Blundell's or other public schools. On the contrary, I was to find that aircrew came from all walks of life and that once the original RAF had been killed off, they came more often than not from grammar schools.

Physically, I had never been so tired in my life. As well as getting up early and going for a long bike ride, I worked extended hours in the factory. If a worker was moved from 'days' to 'nights', he had to stay at the end of the day shift and then work the next night; this meant a full twenty-four-hour shift. Keeping awake at around two and three in the morning was one of my worst difficulties.

Our factory was a small unit with a lowish noise level and, for those days, excellent food in the canteen. But it was still exhausting. Because – and this truth dawned only gradually – most people in factories are exhausted, whatever they do. This can never be grasped by anyone who hasn't worked in a factory. Professional people think they work hard, and they do, but they develop a different sort of fatigue from the overwhelming weariness that afflicts the factory-worker. He is always on his feet, always trying to concentrate on something physical, always trying to avoid mistakes. Conditions are far from clean and quiet. There are fumes from some tank or other and airlines hiss all the time. And there are aggravating little divisions and irritations between workmates. My five months at Follands taught me these home truths. It was altogether a valuable lesson.

Sheer pressure drove out all but the simplest pleasures. First, there was drink. While the aircraft industry was too technical to allow the heavy drinking traditional in some industries, we eagerly anticipated the odd pint or two with great relish. Sex was an active subject in the factory as there were a number of single men around and some wives whose husbands had become prisoners of war. And there were girls whose morals were no better than they should have been.

Apart from the cinema, which didn't fit easily with factory hours, and *ITMA* and other radio favourites, sex was the only leisure pursuit available. Our little factory was too well laid out for on-site activity – in marked contrast to the main factory on the Hamble at Southampton where I was sent as a temporary Schobert gunner for a week: there, in the great hangar, there was almost infinite scope for illicit activity on 'nights'. There were a number of Beaufort fuselages in for repair, to have jagged shrapnel holes made good. These commodious air frames furnished an ideal setting for nightly couplings of fitters with girls from the draughtsman's office and so on.

But most of the activity was off-site, with couples libidinously tearing off on Triumph or Norton motor-bikes. For all that, the place was decorous apart from the language. Like any public schoolboy, I knew the words but was surprised by the frequency of their use. Fundamentally, the atmosphere was cheerful because the money was good. In fact many of these people were having the time of their lives.

War came to Exeter in the form of one of the so-called Baedeker raids in the summer of 1942. At Thorverton, we had a ringside seat. The raid began at midnight and lasted two hours. It was like a giant firework display spread across the horizon. We could hear the bombs land, sometimes with an immense 'crump' as they detonated a landmine. It was safe, but frightening. The farmer's wife made tea for everyone.

'I can't remember, Mrs Rudd, do you take two lumps?' Crump.

'Thank you so much.' Crump, crump.

Then further noises from an aircraft which sounded as though it was going to land on the roof of the farm. There was a searchlight battery a quarter of a mile down the lane. The beam was racing about the sky, ineffectively trying to join up with the others. But it only served to make us all rather nervous that a German fighter might decide to snuff out the wavering light with a well-aimed burst of fire. But nothing so dramatic happened. As the raid drew to a close, we all agreed how dreadful it had been, finished our last cup of tea and went to bed.

Next morning, as I rode to the factory, I encountered evidence of the raid in the road near the station at Exeter St David's; a great deal of glass and a very strong smell of burning. My road skirted the main devastation in the city centre and like everyone else I arrived on time. The factory hadn't been damaged.

At midday break, some of the workers went across the bridge over the river and uphill to survey the damage. They came back shaken. The centre was a shambles. That afternoon, just after the day shift when hundreds of cyclists were pouring out of the factories, a police car led an old-fashioned upright Daimler along the road to the bridge. It was the King and Queen. The King looked pale and the Queen distressed. There were a few desultory cheers as they progressed to the scene of destruction. As so often after these raids, they'd come on their train to visit the stricken city.

It must have been distressing for them, having to go on a round-Britain itinerary determined by random hit-and-run raids on unlikely targets of minimal military significance. The scene must have been roughly the same every time. The only encouragement for us was that the great British air ace, 'Cats' Eyes' Cunningham, had himself shot down two of the German raiders that very night. But it was probably make-believe.

That evening I went up to Heavitree on the other side of the cathedral to see what had happened to the girls' school. Only two days before, on Sunday, I had cycled to the school and taken out a girl, then my current date in Exeter. I was still at Blundell's when I first met her – at a gathering in Exeter of representatives from several Devon schools, eager to discuss 'The Post-War Society'. The future lay in our hands, so what were we going to do about it?

I had spotted and immediately fancied this girl, Jane, who had been nominated as co-chairman by her school. As there were to be two chairmen, one male and one female, I worked on the fairly malleable Blundell's brigade to secure for myself nomination as the school's candidate for the male role. Putting my all into an adoption speech, I won and duly took my joint chair next to Jane.

This was very satisfactory except that, in those days, it was almost impossible to conduct a wild romance in the midst of an officially sponsored and carefully monitored school activity such as a debate on 'The Post-War Society'. For all its modern tendencies, there was tea and scope for nothing beyond a walk in the garden, a quick kissless hug and, from her, a muttered 'I'll write.' A modest success, but a success all the same.

I got the letters; they were full of quotations from John Donne, a factor that suggested that an acquaintance with the Metaphysicals was vital to progress with Jane. The society met a second time, and we met again in the holidays. Like many girls, she looked far better in uniform than in her other clothes.

I got my kiss one Sunday in May during a picnic on the banks of the Exe. I wanted to make love to her, but didn't know how to set about it. Anyway, the beautiful patch under the beeches near the bridge at Thorverton was far from private. And the chances of her letting me do so were, I suppose, about a million to one against.

So, as the bombs crumped down that night, I was worried about her. When I got to the school, I found that, apart from a few blown-in windows, there was no real damage. But everybody had vanished.

A week later I got a letter, written from her home near Kingswear, describing the girls' night in the shelters and assuring me that she was safe.

6 Oxford and the Air Squadron

The next October, when I arrived in Oxford at the old station, I immediately participated in the ritual of sharing a decrepit taxi with at least three other undergraduates. We were dropped at our various colleges – in my case University College.

Univ was then half empty, despite playing host to Keble which was occupied for the duration by the navy; in fact, by a large gaggle of Wrens engaged on cypher work. I announced myself at the lodge, and was told that my room was on 'Ninety High'.

To me, Oxford was magic from the word go. I was addressed by the porter as 'Mr Rudd'. What a thrill: not plain Rudd, or, worse still, Tony, but 'Mr Rudd'. This beguiling formality instantly added cubits to my stature. At last I was going to be a person in my own right; no one was going to push me around.

I found the correct staircase down past the Shelley memorial and there was my name again: 'Mr Rudd', lettered white on black, amongst those of the others resident on the staircase. 'Mr Rudd' was also one of two names over the door of the room I was to share, up and along the winding passages. And what a room! It was completely panelled and had a huge bow window; when I sat in its window seat, I felt as though I were sitting in the aft part of an old galleon, except that I looked, not at the heaving main, but across the High Street and into Queen's College just opposite.

Further excitements awaited me that evening. Beer,

the only drink on offer, was served in glinting tankards of early Georgian silver which shone down the length of the tables. As yet, rationing had hardly touched the college catering arrangements. There were none of the little pots of jam and smudges of marge that were such a feature of post-war Oxford life.

There was even a fire in the grate of our room in Ninety High. The coal was always kept in wooden bunkers like storage cupboards on the staircase and although we got no deliveries of coal that winter there was so much embedded on the staircase from years of generous deliveries that we virtually mined it and kept the fire in all the time we were there.

Like myself, my room companion was about to spend two terms at Univ as part of his initial aircrew training. He came from Barrow-in-Furness and had been to a grammar school there. He was tall, tough and a product of the industrial wasteland of the inter-war period. But he was also the product of a first-class grammar school and in consequence gave me much intellectual stimulation and my first real introduction to left-wing views.

For the dozen of us in college at the RAF's expense, there was a notice directing us to report to the University Air Squadron in two days' time. Meanwhile, we were to be sorted out academically. Those who wanted to do a couple of terms out of the full three-year PPE (philosophy, politics and economics) degree course had to report at ten o'clock the next morning to 'Schools', as the examination rooms were called, just down the High Street towards Magdalen Bridge. As far as we were concerned, the system of pupils going to college tutors had been abandoned. Instead we were allotted to one or other of the tutors available in the university. When my room-mate and I were farmed out to A.J.P. Taylor and Agnes Headlam-Morley, we knew that we'd done well; but just how well, we didn't at first appreciate.

The air squadron occupied a series of spacious single-storey buildings. During the thirties it had offered opportunities to fly for anyone so inclined; these were free of charge just so long as you joined the reserve afterwards. However, as industry and commerce didn't recruit very vigorously in the thirties, many members had committed themselves further by volunteering for an auxiliary squadron or even becoming regulars. Even in late 1942, the squadron still had a relaxed, almost opulent atmosphere. The mess was excellent and the food good. And although we were only lowly leading aircraftsmen, we were treated like officer cadets.

By that time, the air squadron had a full complement of regulars to look after us and see to our training. In that first term of the 1942–3 academic year, the staff was still largely drawn from officers of the pre-war RAF. Along with their professionalism, they all had a light touch; a witty elegance which totally entranced me.

On the first day, we were issued with our uniforms and kit. Because we had yet to join the RAF proper, we were technically deemed to be members of the ATC (Air Training Corps). This was an organization which had grown up along the lines of the venerable OTC, to give schoolboys training in elementary RAF lore. The only outward and visible sign of our modest status (for practically nobody had been a member of the ATC) was that we had to replace the proper brass service buttons on our tunics with the silver ATC buttons. With one exception, we sat on the second evening, sewing on the wretched buttons. The exception was a Repton boy who whisked his uniform off to the dry-cleaning and quick-mending shop just up the High, and got his buttons switched for only half a crown. The rest of us viewed this manoeuvre with envy and disapproval. It was our first introduction to the power of Midlands money.

The major event at Univ that term was the unveiling of the Beveridge Plan by the master, Sir William Beveridge, in College Hall. He looked very benign, with a wide smile and an even wider forehead capped by an unruly mop of white hair. He was one of the great men of the day; fully on a par with, say, Lord Reith or J.B. Priestley.

Although not in the government, Sir William, being

the author of this plan – which virtually laid the foundations of the Welfare State – almost instantly became a national, indeed, international celebrity. For a government short on war aims, other than the obvious one of preventing Hitler landing and turning us all into soap and lampshades, Beveridge's plan became within days a positive goal; a goal for which everyone could now work and fight. It was exactly the sort of programme we who had debated the post-war society in Exeter needed to prevent us from waffling around a number of pious hopes. Beveridge had channelled the yearning for a 'Better Britain' on to a practical agenda. And he had done it brilliantly.

It was all very exciting. We felt that we were in at the beginning of something very different. And so we were. For it was Beveridge who forced the government to adopt a welfare state as its post-war goal. It was hardly surprising that Labour won the 1945 election. The people, particularly the armed forces, didn't trust the Tories to implement a report which it had been forced to accept in 1942. Since then, historians such as Corelli Barnett have argued that this spirit of the time, the yearning for a 'new Jerusalem', his phrase, contributed to a lack of realism and practical application in the country's post-war planning. And he's right: Beveridge suggested how money should be spent but nobody had any ideas about how we were going to earn it. This was because so much had gone to waste before the war that it was now felt that as long as the nation's wealth was distributed more cleverly, all would be well.

Corelli Barnett misses a point all the same. The atmosphere of the war itself from 1942 onwards was, in my experience, always positive and hopeful; spirits were comradely and to a great extent this was Beveridge's doing. It was an idealistic war in which sacrifices were being made by all so that, when it was over, Britain would be a better place.

This may sound very naïve, especially in the context of today's materialistic culture, but it explains why the Second World War escaped the horrific element which had been such a feature of the First. The difference wasn't just trenches in the First and more mobility in the Second; it was that, in the Second, the Beveridge element made the whole conflict seem morally tolerable.

The other major public incident that term was the visit of a very distinguished woman sniper from Russia. She was on a propaganda trip to the United Kingdom, the aim being to demonstrate the prowess of our gallant Russian allies and, at the same time, to encourage their equally gallant, but, as yet, not fully engaged British allies in the struggle against the fascist hordes.

In Oxford, the main ceremony was the presentation to the lady sniper of a specially wrought 'Sword of Stalingrad'. It was in this beleaguered city, now thankfully relieved, that the formidable lady had rung up a personal score of three hundred and fifty-nine German soldiers, all caught in the telescopic sights of her rifle. For the presentation, there was a gathering in the Balliol senior common room of about thirty or more dignitaries and hangers-on like myself.

Throughout the short ceremony, the object of our admiration had kept her greatcoat on. She was a big woman, but the coat made her seem vast. She also wore riding breeches and shiny black boots. She had a fixed, menacing smile and a faintly sunburnt face which seemed incompatible with Stalingrad.

Someone very like Lord Halifax made the presentation, taking up the sword – which looked like a prop from a Wagner opera – and presenting it to the lady. As he held the gleaming weapon, he intoned some formal words about the friendship between our two great nations and added a laudatory reference to the three hundred and fifty-nine victims of the lady sniper. The sniper then showed some animation for the first time. She seized the sword from the hands of the bent figure, seemingly bowed down by its weight, and holding it as though it were as light as a feather, swept the blade round in a wide arc. Luckily, the pseudo Lord Halifax had stepped back a pace or he would certainly have been decapitated.

The deadpan smile on the Russian woman's face gave way to a grin showing each of her teeth and the tiny but perceptible gaps between them. An elegant Welsh Guards captain stepped forward holding the open case, ready to receive the sword, and after a tiny pause, the Russian warrior surrendered the weapon. It seemed to me that if she had had the chance, she would have preferred to have beheaded, rather than shot, the three hundred and fifty-nine Germans. Heaven knows what she made of the ceremony. To us, she seemed a figure from another world; perhaps the world of the real war.

Apart from the air squadron, we were involved in only one other war-related activity: air raid precautions. In fact, Oxford was to escape bombing altogether but we were hardly to know that at the time. In the garden behind the senior common room, Univ boasted its own static water tank complete with a brand new Coventry Climax pump driven by a petrol-engine. This could throw a high-velocity jet of water several hundred yards. It was under the control of the domestic bursar, the Reverend John Wilde, a quiet and charming clergyman who subsequently became master of the college. We hugely enjoyed operating the Coventry Climax and throwing powerful jets of water round the fellows' garden in the hope of drenching a passing fellow. Less fun was an exercise that had all of us climbing over what seemed like every inch of the college fabric. Steel ladders and rungs had been inserted in the sheer walls of the college so that young men could swarm up and clamber on to the roofs, there to grasp a long-handled spade and toss any incendiaries that might have fallen from German planes into the street below.

The only people who enjoyed all this were the few undergraduates who had taken to the Oxford equivalent of mountaineering, namely, climbing in and out of college. Most of us did this out of necessity as all doors were locked at eleven at night, but for some it was a sport in its own right. ARP (Air Raid Precaution) exercises gave these enthusiasts a legal excuse to do what they really enjoyed and find new and even more hazardous routes. For the rest of us, climbing up and around these dizzy heights was far from pleasant although, as intrepid aviators in the making, we kept our doubts to ourselves.

Our training at the air squadron turned out to be pretty boring as it was almost entirely theoretical. We were allowed practically no flying, and got no instruction in the air. Instead we were treated to endless lectures on navigation and other subjects such as meteorology and aircraft recognition. Meteorology was accompanied by pre-war films of staggering tedium with voice-overs seemingly speaking through a mile-long tube, droning on about the 'adiabatic lapse rate' while an unfocused glass of water turned opaque in very slow motion. The only relief was the occasional sight of a Hawker Hart biplane, taxiing to a halt and disgorging a pilot in immaculate flying overalls. He was then saluted by an Erk (an ordinary aircraftsman) to whom he handed a piece of paper, his meteorological report. The Erk ended the scene by running dutifully off screen to deliver the report, presumably in a cleft stick. Even then, the scene was very dated.

Aircraft recognition was dauntingly difficult as it meant identifying up to a hundred different enemy and allied aircraft, each shown on the screen in one-second flashes. We had to get their profiles right as our lives depended on it; so did success in forthcoming exams.

We also had to come to grips with morse, a technique which only aeons of practice made perfect. It was soon obvious that for beginners like us to achieve even a modest level of competence would take years, so we all devoutly prayed that we wouldn't end up as wireless operators. Visually transmitted morse was far worse than the aural variety: little dots and dashes ringing in the ears were bad enough but interpreting them from an Aldis lamp blinking some hundreds of yards away was infinitely worse.

So, as the end of the first term came near, most of us were depressed at the prospect of how much we had to learn and how little we had achieved during the first couple of months. We were entering a world filled with techniques and to master them was going to take all our ingenuity and then some. But our instructors stayed calm and impeccably well-mannered. We attended little lectures filled with hints about how to comport ourselves in our future service life. Never, a lecturer told us one evening, volunteer to be the mess treasurer. We might not believe it, but in his experience more than half the people who had become mess treasurers had ended up fiddling the books, being found out, and then cashiered.

Unfortunately, only a few of the talks were about actual war experience. We hung on each word of these treats which were rationed by modesty and characterized by understatement, both typically British traits. There was no hope, for instance, of getting a pilot to tell us what it had been like during the Battle of France or what it had been like flying Blenheims in Two Group.

One of the few occasions when an aircrew member opened up was when a flight sergeant air gunner was detailed to take us for the Aldis lamp exercises. He was the first man I ever saw with a really marked 'twitch'. He would screw up his right eye as though taking aim and then blink, sometimes a dozen times a minute. He also gave us the longest smoking breaks, about five minutes during which he would light and partly smoke three cigarettes. He inhaled them with such force that we almost expected smoke to issue from his boots.

He had started off as a gunner in a Defiant, a fighter with a four-gun Boulton-Paul turret just behind the pilot. The first time this aircraft was in action on any scale was over Dunkirk when it caught the Germans unprepared. But after that the enemy was ready for them and always knocked the Defiants out of the sky the moment they appeared. Our gallant air gunner, an early victim of this treatment, had bailed out over Dunkirk. He had gone on to be a gunner on Blenheims flying on daylight shipping strikes, an unbeatably hazardous occupation. He was now having a rest but said he was looking forward to going back on 'ops' – next time on a Bomber Command tour, with luck on the new 'Lancs', as he called the Lancaster Bombers then coming into squadron service. We marvelled. We wondered whether the brave air gunner's charmed life would last right through the war; we already knew that the life expectancy of this particular member of aircrew was short.

The staff at the squadron didn't neglect our social graces. Guest nights were laid on to familiarize us with the cut and thrust of a formal mess dinner. There were very particular rules about proposing and responding to the loyal toast. Despite drinking slightly too much, we paid careful attention because in due course we were each of us bound to be in the hot seat. We may have been children playing at it, but we took it seriously enough.

The academic side of life was leisurely. 'What is your opinion, Mr Wudd, of the Versailles Settlement?' asked Professor Agnes Headlam-Morley. My room companion and I bicycled up the Woodstock Road to have our occasional tutorial with the distinguished professor, an attractive person, always slightly dishevelled but invariably smiling. Tutorials with Mr Alan (A.J.P.) Taylor were very different. While he was the most stimulating lecturer and teacher I had ever come across, he was also quite terrifying. When he dissected my essays I felt like someone undergoing an operation without anaesthetic. It was an unforgettable experience. At his suggestion, I bought a slim volume of essays by Professor Lewis Namier and gradually got to appreciate the point of the course.

One of the most stimulating aspects of these tutorials was the way in which past events were linked to current politics. Vichy France, the events in North Africa during 1942, the differing views of General de Gaulle held by the various Allies, were all explained in terms of what had happened in France during the Dreyfus Affair, whilst the events in the war itself were compared with events of the First World War. I also went once a week to the hall of Magdalen College to hear Alan Taylor lecture. He would walk in, mount the platform at the end of the hall and, putting his hands behind his back, start on the dot of nine: 'Ladies and Gentlemen, this morning I am going to look at the seven causes of trouble in Bosnia-Herzegovina in 1907.' And off he would go into the tangled web of Austrio-Hungarian politics in the decade before the First World War, finishing right on time, fifty-nine minutes later, with the end of his seventh point. It was a *tour de force* I have never seen equalled anywhere. John, my room-mate from Barrow-in-Furness, clearly found it as enthralling as I did.

Some of the work prompted the two of us to engage in animated political wrangling. In these evening sessions we were only rarely joined by other undergraduates and once we went right through the night. John's left-wing views were difficult to counter as they were based on his own experiences. When I heard about his childhood in Barrow-in-Furness, I could easily understand how he had arrived at his views. His father had been continuously unemployed for ten years as there had been no work in the shipyards. However, he had driven John to learn, reading to him to develop his taste for English literature and generally encouraging him to try for grammar school entry. Worn out by the struggle, his mother was no help. But his father more than made up for this, concentrating all his attention on John, pushing him through to success.

Until then, the political debate had for me been mainly intellectual. Spain had been the burning topic in the last few years of peace. We had even heard about it in Tiverton. My enthusiasm for the Republicans had been shared by the jobbing gardener, Mann, who came to The Chalet to cut the lawn and help my aunt tend the rose bushes. I didn't see how it was possible to be against Hitler and sympathetic to Franco all at the same time. So on this point at least my credentials were satisfactory. As for domestic issues, my aunt, who was always a sturdy individualist, had drummed into me a form of proto-Thatcherism which stemmed from her own background of having to fight for herself; she had been on the stage for over ten years, always a matter of the survival of the fittest. Being a Scot and a natural hard worker, she had no time for what she saw as the feather bedding of modern labour. Whenever she saw workmen leaning on their shovels, her very audible expletive was 'Rascals!' All that was light years from John's world. Her view on Barrow-in-Furness was that there was quite enough work, but people simply didn't want it. Like many middle-aged or elderly people of her generation, she didn't realize that the depression of the late twenties and thirties was quite unprecedented. Her memories harked back pre-1914 when there had, indeed, been jobs, if badly paid, for everyone. Unemployment in industry was something which very few people in the South of England ever understood. But for John it was the central fact of life, so he couldn't understand the totally unsympathetic attitude he came across once he got south of Manchester. He put it down to the Labour Party's failure to get its views across, something which would be put right directly the war was over. His experiences and ideas certainly affected my thinking; whether I had any impact on him, on the other hand, I never really knew.

That winter, university social life was busy. There were numerous societies devoted to this or that activity, many of them political. They were usually run by earnest people who seriously believed in what they were doing. The greater part of those attending, however, were, like myself, only there for the fun – to meet people, especially girls, and get free food and drink. Hence our visits to the Yellow JCR at St Hilda's, to play-readings in LMH and little gatherings in other women's colleges. Eventually, after weeks of reading plays, listening to poetry, debating the question of Indian independence and attending chamber music recitals, I and three others from Univ managed to pick up girlfriends so that at full strength we were a party of eight.

We then did something very daring. I, as leader of the band, went and called on the dean, Kenneth Wheare, later professor of political economy in the university. Kenneth Wheare was a charming, slightly frail man, who even in his early forties adopted the stance of a man in his seventies. I approached him for permission to hold a 'mixed' party in college in the evening. Members of the opposite sex were allowed within the college precincts only up until six o'clock. Any infringement was treated as a serious crime so the rule was never broken. In those days nobody ever thought of smuggling a girl into college and letting her out next morning; we may have dreamt of doing so but the idea was hopelessly unrealistic. I applied for permission to have our mixed party in college until the daringly late hour of ten. Happily, Kenneth Wheare found the idea quite charming and asked about our plans for refreshments. 'Well,' I said, 'we thought a glass of sherry followed by a little cold buffet, washed down with a glass of white wine if we could find some, otherwise coffee, and possibly a glass of beer for the chaps.' 'How very nice,' the dean said. He was so positive that I almost asked him to join us, but then thought better of it. On the night of the party, my room looked marvellous with glowing panelling and a flickering fire. We had found a loo for the girls: a clever touch, as up till then all the loos and baths we knew had been communal, an arrangement which would hardly have gone down well with our young guests. The whole evening would seem pretty tepid these days, but for us it was a daredevil affair: women in college! And after six in the evening! Our depravity remained unequalled for the rest of term.

When we went down for Christmas, I was taken to London as the guest of John Warburton, a Christ Church man and a fellow trainee on the short course. His father was an air commodore and his mother was a queen bee in the VAD. When the former took us to lunch at the RAF Club overlooking Piccadilly, I was very impressed. In those days the Schneider Trophy was in the entrance hall. A real-life air commodore was the most senior RAF officer that I had ever met. At lunch, he waved his hand to call over the 'booze girl', as he called her. What fascinated me was the broad band around his sleeve, far wider and much more distinguished even than a group captain's tight row of thin little rings. In the evening we went to the Arts Theatre where we were joined by John's mother, very smart in her beautifully cut uniform. Afterwards we had dinner at a little French restaurant nearby. The air commodore passed me the wine list and said, 'Choose.' It was my first wine list. The only name on it I knew was 'Chablis'. 'Excellent choice,' said the air commodore; I couldn't have felt more pleased if I'd shot down an ME 109.

Next day, I was off to Paddington and the West Country. During the war, main-line termini were exciting places seething with a great diversity of uniforms and nationalities: there were Free French sailors with red pompoms on their hats and a few Polish aircrew, wearing extraordinary swooping eagles instead of pilot's wings. Loudspeakers always blared with 'music while you work', rather like the music in the factory at Exeter. Strangely, immediately after the war the music was switched off at every station except Waterloo.

I joined my aunt in the comfortable boarding house in Painswick in the Cotswolds to which she'd moved from the farmhouse in Thorverton. She was no stranger to Painswick because before moving to Tiverton she had had a house there in Friday Street called The Gables. My bedroom ceiling there had sported a '1609' worked into the moulding. We had spent five happy years in Painswick but to be there on her own in wartime was very different for my aunt. While a group could just about manage on the steadily diminishing rations of the time, they were both meagre and awkward for single people. That's why the small hotel and boarding-house business flourished during the war, catering as it did for elderly people, singles and couples taking refuge from the rigours of the time.

Painswick was perfect for Christmas. If Tiverton was

cosy, Painswick was beautiful. When we had lived there before, in the mid-thirties, there had been no new developments in or around the village. The first new houses were built in 1938 on the western fringe overlooking the road to Stroud. Miss Howard, who rented The Gables to my aunt and lived just below the church in a house looking across the valley to Boar's Hill, very much disapproved of the new building. My godfather, Herbert House, a partner in the respected Stroud firm of solicitors, Winterbottom, Ball & Gadstone, was not popular with Miss Howard because he lived in one of the new houses that detracted from the beauty of the village.

There was only a handful of us in the guest house. There was a large, tall lady who was head of the Gloucestershire Red Cross who, by day, wore a very severe uniform appropriate to her rank. There was Mr Stratton, a former actor almost in his eighties. And there were two middle-aged ladies, both of them timid and self-effacing who had come from London for the duration. We had our turkey and trimmings on Christmas Day. The large Red Cross lady swept into the dining room in a flowing gown which prompted Mr Stratton to mutter 'Priestess of Baal!' This was only meant for our ears, but the old actor's stage-whisper rang throughout the house. Being of impeccable breeding, the lady herself took no notice. After dinner, we all went into the drawing room where a fine log fire flickered. Mr Stratton drew a slim volume from his pocket and volunteered a complete reading of Dickens's *A Christmas Carol*. It proved the ideal showcase for his considerable professional skills and rounded off a memorable evening for our little group, comfortably collapsed in the dancing firelight.

Not counting the first four months of the 'phoney war' in 1939, this was the end of the third year of war. By now, I was thoroughly accustomed to 'the duration'. Perhaps it would stop at some point, but not for a long time yet. 1942 had got itself off to an abysmal start but was ending more hopefully. The collapse of our empire in the Far East seemed quite horrific. Newspaper pictures of Rear-Admiral Sir Tom Phillips, a small trim figure in white uniform on the Singapore quayside, were very sad. Even sadder was the fact that, by the time they appeared, he had gone down with his two ships off the coast of Malaya, taking with him any future for Britain as a power in that part of the world. It was all very well for us back in the United Kingdom, we had become democratic. The war in which everybody was caught up was now almost classless. Looking back, it was as though Labour had already won its post-war election. Although the nation was right behind Mr Churchill, the pre-war British establishment had already evaporated. But in the Far East and India, it was still a major presence. Out there we were still an Imperial power right up until the Japanese came swarming through the jungle and knocked us off our perch. The final picture of General Percival, a thin humiliated figure, in knee-length shorts walking with the white flag towards his Japanese conquerors, was too much to bear; it brought a stab of ignominy to everybody that saw it.

Then, during the summer and autumn, we had endured reports from the Western Desert of the Eighth Army being forced back to the gates of Cairo while, in Russia, the Germans were putting a ring of steel round Stalingrad: a seemingly interminable siege charted on maps by an ever-thickening mass of Axis arrows pointing into the Russian defences. Our Allies looked doomed. In mid-summer the Dieppe Raid was a catastrophe for the Allies. So by the time General Montgomery won his famous victory in the Western Desert, people were slow to generate much enthusiasm. We had heard about desert victories time and time again, and they had usually turned to dust. So we reserved our judgement. But by Christmas our scepticism had melted. Perhaps we were poised for a new phase after all.

When we got back to Oxford, the air squadron had changed. There was an entirely new complement of permanent staff. This was an unwelcome development.

A new broom had disposed of our easy-going group of instructors and the old relaxed, gentlemanly atmosphere. Two people had engineered this revolution. Replacing our genial CO was a tight-faced wing commander straight from Bomber Command where he had been under considerable strain commanding a squadron. He now needed a rest but was far too committed to let himself take it easy. So instead of relaxing, he channelled all the tension and frenzy from the front line to the non-operational life of the air squadron, quickly generating an atmosphere of panic in the once happy-go-lucky buildings at Manor Road. His mission was furthered by a squadron leader who assumed responsibility for good order and military discipline with particular reference to the aircrew trainees. He came from a smart unit in Training Command where things were, he told us, very spick 'n' span and he was going to ensure that they became equally spick 'n' span at the air squadron. He imported a series of NCOs to help him. Our marching was the first activity to be affected: we had been moving around at what he regarded as a snail's pace, probably a hundred and twenty paces or less a minute. He was mustard keen to see us cracking along at the rifle-brigade speed of a hundred and sixty paces or more. Our hearts pounded and our mouths got dry. We realized that the good times were over, an inevitable development as the old order made way for the 'new model' RAF.

The second term wasn't as exciting as the first. Our real service life was approaching fast. We still went to the meetings in the yellow JCR, had tea with Joan and discovered the Union where an honorary Univ man, a Barbadian called Cameron Tudor, was the elegant and eloquent President. The great and the famous still came down to Union debates. I took my aunt, on one of her visits, up into the gallery to hear Noël Coward. Afterwards, at the Mitre, we were introduced to the great man by Simon Eden, another aircrew trainee who was shot down and killed in Burma in 1945.

Near the end of term we had Collections which meant

facing the master and a few fellows. Agnes Headlam-Morley and Alan Taylor must have been quite kind because the master, smiling his wide smile and shaking his mane of white hair, said that he hoped I would return to the college after the war. In other words, if I survived, I could get educated.

We had our exams at the air squadron. These were essentially the ITW (Initial Training Wing) passing-out papers which, like most of the intake, I managed to pass; the one or two casualties had already emerged as non-aircrew material.

At our passing-out parade, a student of dazzling all-round aptitude stepped forward to receive a small piece of parchment, the wartime equivalent of the Sword of Honour. Our parade was in the road near the air squadron, but there was so little traffic in Oxford that a battalion could have paraded in the High Street with only the occasional bus having to run round it.

7 The First Rung

Service life proper started at the ACRC (Aircrew Receiving Centre) in Regent's Park. The night before we were due to report, several of us met in the bar at the Palladium. I was now in uniform with the proper brass buttons sewn back on and highly polished, reflecting skills nurtured in the OTC. As the others, all Londoners, had yet to put on uniform, I was the butt of much good-humoured banter. My friend John Warburton who had brought his parents, got quietly ticked off by his air commodore father, he told me later, for laughing at 'the uniform'.

This was the first of many 'holding units' which we would pass through over the next couple of years. But this one was different in that, to the permanent staff, we were the raw, the very raw, material which they had to mould into something that would pass for airmen. Their first task was to kit us out and smarten us up. They began by cutting our hair. If possible, they would have had our heads shaved like monks. But they stuck to exactly the regulations, a short matting on top and not a bristle below the line of our caps. The task took about three minutes per person. It was like sheep-shearing. The floor was deep in the hair of undergraduates. The drill corporals who had taken us in charge examined us critically and sent some back for a second shearing.

We were billeted in the blocks of flats around the north-west corner of Regent's Park. These had been commandeered from their owners or tenants, emptied of all furniture and equipped with iron bedsteads. Here we learned the drill of a kit inspection: how to lay out all our just-issued bits and pieces in a neat, pre-ordained array. Our day began at five-thirty and at six-fifteen we were marched off to breakfast. We did a great deal of marching around the Regent's Park area. I was very lucky in one way. Because of my lack of swimming skills I was nominated for special instruction at a nearby swimming baths with several other non-swimmers. All I had to do was learn to swim one length, so I took stock and reckoned to spin out my efforts to achieve this feat over a period of about two weeks; as we were held in ACRC for nearly four weeks, my judgement was about right – and many hours' drill were successfully missed.

My only problem was that I caught vaccine fever. Our jabs came on our third day. We formed a queue right round the block of flats housing the medical team. If our hair cutting had been sheep shearing, our jabs were pure veterinary medicine. One or two young men, soon to be the scourge of the Luftwaffe, fainted the moment they saw the double row of white-coated medical orderlies wielding their fearful weapons. They were carted off to revive and then started queuing at the back again. The rest of us shuffled reluctantly forward, sleeves rolled up well above the elbow, hands on hips, arms crooked at a nice angle and it was a jab on the right, shuffle, jab on the left, shuffle, scratch on the right, shuffle, a blood-sucking needle on the left for a blood specimen, and on and out.

Two days later I woke at five-thirty a.m. with a splitting headache, fevered brow and dry mouth. I knew I had to report sick. This was a grave decision because – as our drill corporal had explained with crystal clarity – reporting sick was designed to discourage all but the very ill. In today's idiom, it was a *Catch-22* situation. You had to be near to death's door to justify going on sick parade, and yet well enough to handle the parade; indeed, at that stage in our service career, we had to go on parade to do everything from drawing pay, to having a meal. Furthermore, when reporting sick, you had to parade with all your personal kit; presumably, just in case you never returned. Anyhow, on sick parade I went and marched, starting at six-fifteen with the rest of the halt and lame, some two miles to the appropriate medical centre. An hour and a quarter later, in a large bare room with no seating, I was hauled in front of a doctor. Then, once my temperature had been taken, I was whisked into an institution which could well have been started by Florence Nightingale. I was put into a small room with three other sick people and tended by ministering angels dressed in what looked like starched tennis clothes – complete with white shoes, white stockings and starched head-gear with embroidered RAF insignia on them. During three days there, I was treated with unprecedented politeness and consideration. A corporal came round with gifts of magazines and cigarettes together with writing paper and pre-addressed envelopes so that – good manners being at a premium in the RAF – we could write thank-you letters to the elderly ladies of the district, who had provided all these good things.

We of the Oxford Air Squadron had arrived at ACRC as a single intake. This was unfortunate because, although far from being an identifiably upper-class lot, we were demonstrably a group; something of the air squadron atmosphere clung to us and generated a cool response from some of the permanent staff. They in turn surprised us by making us turn out on parade after parade: first simply as we were; then in full kit; then very shortly after kit inspection. It seemed to be planned so that we could never be in the right place at the right time in the right order. Once we were meant to be on parade in full kit but the preparation time had been so short we were in rather a messy state. A fair-haired squadron leader went into a routine temper, ending up by saying: 'I'm not going to be insulted by nobody.' Luckily, no one tittered or there would have been trouble. On the other hand I'm sure that we looked a sloppy, far from airman-like lot. Once, when waiting in the hall of one of the blocks for something from the orderly room, I let my shoulders rest against the wall for a second or two. The next instant, a nasty-looking flying officer of the new breed materialized an inch from my left ear into which he hissed venomously: 'Get away from that wall.' I might have been engaged in some unnatural practice. He glared and was gone.

Amongst much else, service life meant learning to live out of the kit-bag which contained all your personal possessions. These included a sewing kit so we could sew on buttons, darn socks and effect other running repairs. Every week, the laundry absorbed one shirt, several collars, one set of underwear and one pair of socks; leaving only a few smalls to be washed during the week. We kept our soap in a container and had to be careful or it was nicked. There were the eating irons – the knife, fork and spoon we took to every meal – together with mugs for 'char', the serviceman's word for tea. Practically everything was supervised from start to finish, including meals: corporals hung around as food was dished up and eaten, dirty plates put away and irons rinsed.

Although I wanted to get out of the ruck, there was no scope for volunteering. I always put my hand up when a dance was offered, but they weren't always a success. The girls were sometimes pretty, but they didn't rate aircrew trainees. Wrens in particular gave us the cold shoulder. Apart from lowly rank, extreme youth and heavy boots, our dancing was less than polished. In those days, partners had to match their steps precisely or there were barked ankles and toes. As with flying, we needed more practice. Much more.

On Sunday afternoons, we went to pianoforte recitals during which I tended to doze off, what with reveille at five-thirty, church parade and a heavy lunch. Still, they were reminders of our previous Oxford identity. After some four weeks, the news of imminent postings came through. Later on, we found that postings were a surefire antidote to boredom. True, you might end up somewhere just as nasty or nastier but it was still a change and, who knows, you might combine the journey with a few days' leave.

We were on our way to an ITW, not for the full ITW course – we had done that at the air squadron – but to get a little more groomed, a little more airman-like before getting to the next stage. There were dozens of ITWs in the United Kingdom. At least half of us, including myself, were posted to the Cambridge ITW. We were going from one university city to the other.

Our group was billeted in Trinity Hall. Like Oxford, Cambridge University was much diminished in numbers with at least half of the colleges given up to the services. As at the ACRC, we spent most of our time on parade and having kit inspections but now in the most beautiful surroundings. My own problem was that, being a little over six foot tall and of slight build, I did not naturally assume the guardsman's stance so desired by the drill sergeant; indeed, he took my slight stoop as a personal insult and rigorously applied himself to straightening out my spine. He largely succeeded and, although I never became the apple of his eye, I at least ceased to be regarded as needing remedial treatment during drill.

Away from the parade ground, I developed my skill at punting, handling the pole with a rhythmical finesse that propelled the punt firmly on a straight course, with no water running down the sleeve. The 'backs' at Cambridge were an unsurpassed setting for practising this art. It absorbed so much concentration that I had no time to pick up a girlfriend. I either went punting alone, or ferried the reclining bodies of other former members of the Oxford air squadron as they whiled away the time eating cherries.

This idle existence lasted two months. We were then posted for about a month to Marshalls, a pre-war flying club just up the road, now an elementary flying training school. It consisted of a large grass field surrounded by a few small hangars, a number of huts for accommodation or administration and what were termed the 'flights': huts surrounded by aircraft, mainly De

Havilland Tiger Moth dual trainers. This was to be our grading school. By this point in the war, the provision of aircrew was no longer simply a matter of training everybody for pilots and then re-training the failures as navigators. Instead there was the PNB (Pilot Navigator Bomb-aimer) scheme, the training scheme that provided pilots, navigators and bomb-aimers; there were still separate arrangements for rear gunners and wireless operators. Rear gunners had completely different training and sadly a much shorter life-cycle; the reason for training wireless operators separately was more obscure.

The arrangements meant our intake had to be split between so many pilot trainees, so many navigators and so many bomb-aimers, the proportions between the three hingeing on the demands of the squadrons. In the event, there were enough of all three to go round, although by the end of the war there were far more surplus pilots than navigators or bomb-aimers; a factor which even reached down to me. It was remarkable that between them, the planners and the training system always continued to provide enough aircrew. At grading school, they were going to identify candidates suited to pilot training. Only those proven by a dozen hours' flying were to go on as pilots, as at this stage of the war the demand for navigators and bomb-aimers was rising fast; fast enough to catch me – so I became a navigator, allocated to training as an air gunner and bomb-aimer as well.

I was turned down as a pilot because, despite a nice 'touch', I hadn't sufficient judgement; for flying, you needed not just a sixth but a seventh sense. Without that, a pilot, though perfectly competent, was prone in times of stress to human lapses which could easily prove fatal.

Down at the flights on the first morning at Marshalls, I was allocated to a very singular sergeant pilot instructor. His deep, cultured voice and elaborate syntax could only have been acquired at a leading public school. He must have been in the RAF about twenty years because when he was teaching me to swing the propeller, an elementary lesson, he said that, in Aden, in the late twenties, they'd had to use camels to swing the propellers on the old Avros because the engines were so heavy. I marvelled and wished we had a camel at Marshalls. The sergeant was full of reminiscences of this sort but volunteered nothing about his provenance and education; no explanation for his current situation. He was a mystery to everyone at the flights; a respected but remote figure, very much set apart from his colleagues.

His flying was extraordinarily self-confident. On the first morning when he took me up to do a simple circuit and some turns, he spotted the tea wagon going round the perimeter just when he was about to show me a simple approach and landing. 'We'll leave that till next time,' he said through the voice tube, when we were still a few hundred feet up in the air and coming into our landing about one hundred yards from the perimeter. He immediately side-slipped down to starboard, dropping some hundred feet like a stone, stabilized the aircraft, and did the same down the portside. It was like sliding down a rope in a gym. We were on the ground in a flash; only a hundred yards into the airfield, he reversed the aircraft and taxied smartly back to ensure our prompt arrival at the tea van.

The beautiful midsummer days gave me the time to complete my allotted hours within a fortnight. My sergeant pilot liked my 'touch' and found my landings quite reasonable. But because I landed my little Tiger Moth amongst some Flying Fortresses on the far side of the field, my chief instructor noted down some adverse comments on my performance. I hadn't run into anything, let alone another aircraft, but that moment was, nonetheless, the moment I became a navigator. Officially I wasn't to know my fate until several weeks later but in my heart of hearts, I knew it then. As all my friends seemed to have done irritatingly well with their steep turns and other manoeuvres, I said nothing about my performance and crossed my fingers.

8 From Manchester to Monkton

I was now ready for training as aircrew, probably in Canada. Training the tens of thousands of aircrew needed for a long war could not be organized in the United Kingdom; not only because of lack of space and poor weather but also because a war might well have to be fought over the skies of Britain. Hence the Empire Air Training Scheme: the chains of flying schools set up across Canada, Southern Rhodesia and South Africa, countries with space, peace and fine weather. The planners also arranged for an overflow into the US, sending trainees as private pupils before the US came into the war and then, after Pearl Harbour, as seconded trainee airmen. By the time I was poised for the pipeline, this vast training system was in full swing. With hindsight it was one of the best organized and successful training schemes of the whole war, if not the best. It certainly made total victory in the air possible for the Allies.

Entry to the pipeline in the summer of 1943 was through the inevitable holding unit, this time in Heaton Park, Manchester. This large park – the municipal playground for the citizens of Manchester – had been taken over by the RAF and covered with the vast collection of huts always attendant on service life: huts for administration, accommodation and messes; for kitchens, classrooms and permanent staff quarters. By the time I got there, a large through-put was imposing an intolerable strain on accommodation and half the transit population was billeted out. Chance decided whether a trainee was in or out. As I passed through the administrative block on arrival, the WAAF clerk handed me a slip of paper; I was 'out' and my address was c/o Mrs Prince, 221 Elland Road. As most of my friends were 'in', my premonition of non-pilot status was consolidated.

Taking the bus from the park entrance, I got off ten minutes later only a few steps away from my destination. This turned out to be a neat, semi-detached house. I knocked on the door and was let in by Mrs Prince, a young-looking middle-aged woman, comfortably round though not fat. She had a jolly north-country accent, and a skin with the telltale bloom last seen on the cheeks of the farmer's wife at Thorverton; the bloom that can only come from good food. She showed me my nice little room and the shared bathroom next door. She explained the arrangements and showed remarkable confidence in me by giving me a key. There was always a bite of supper if I got in before nine o'clock at night and they would be very happy for me to join them for Sunday dinner. She told me that Mr Prince – whom I met that evening, a thin little man with a friendly smile and very false teeth – was driver to the Lord Mayor of Manchester. I knew straight away that I was on to a winner. And so it proved.

I returned to Heaton Park and the day's work. This consisted of our formal classification under the PNB scheme. For this, our intake assembled in a large hangar-like building. A flight lieutenant, flanked by aides, explained that he was going to read out everyone's name and classification; the individual was to respond with the words 'I understand.' It was like a management telling its workers what their job was going to be and getting them to agree in public. We were entering a contract. The names began to be called out. Just name and initials – no rank – after all, we were all LACs (leading aircraftsmen) – and no number. Eventually Rudd, R.A.W. was called; 'Navigator/Bomb-Aimer' came the category. I was disappointed, but not surprised. 'I understand,' I answered a little throatily. The next name was Rudge, and he was a pilot. So that was that. A few of us in the navigator/bomb-aimer category forgathered shortly afterwards. We were now a group and we would go forward as such.

Heaton Park was to be our base for just over two months that summer. Without instruction or facilities, the weeks dragged by. There were parades, of course, and we were marched about the park, a squad some thirty to forty strong, by the sergeant in charge. It was up to him to devise activities pleasant and unpleasant to while away at least half the day. The rest of the time was our own.

Our particular drill sergeant had, it was rumoured, been a meat porter down in the Manchester market. Hence his wiry fitness and aggressive attitude. He delighted in marching us all over the park, barking out unflattering comments on our bearing until we were ready to drop. One day, he marched us to an isolated part of the park where he produced boxing gloves. The colour drained from the faces of most of the thirty odd airmen. He formed us into a ring and selected his first victim. It was obvious that none of the trainees had ever indulged in the noble art.

My own boxing experience was limited. There hadn't been time for boxing at Blundell's but at my first prep school, in Chepstow, there had been an old pro who had taken a great deal of trouble with the boys. His technique smacked of Bob Fitzsimmons but he had been very thorough. Amongst much else he taught us youngsters the feint, a manoeuvre which I had used to some effect in bouts with older boys. As the moment approached for me to join the series of trainees knocked over by the sergeant, I imagined myself back in the ring at my prep school.

As it was, my rusty technique put the contest on to an equal footing. The sergeant was nimble, strong and aggressive but not a practised boxer. My feint soon connected with him and made him look foolish. I soon hit him again where he wasn't expecting a blow. Then, just as I was starting to enjoy myself, the sergeant decided he had had enough and held up my hand. I immediately became the squad hero. And made the great mistake of regarding myself as a fledgeling Tommy Farr. True, I had a little technique and a very long reach and the benefit of height, but I was thin, flimsily built and, much worse, lacked the true killer instinct. As I was to find out in due course.

My billet with Mrs Prince was superb. The first Sunday set a pattern which was to be repeated every weekend. We sat down at one o'clock to a succulent roast joint together with trimmings which included Yorkshire pudding risen in the pan a good six inches. Fruit pie and custard rounded off a meal that was gargantuan by wartime standards. After washing up, Mrs Prince dozed in front of the fire while Mr Prince and I sat quietly, trying not to rustle the newspapers. Tea at four-thirty was another large meal. Although it wasn't a high tea, it encompassed practically everything Mrs Prince could bake, and totally immobilized me for well over an hour. The Princes had no ration book for me – a very important consideration in those days – so it was extraordinarily generous of them to treat me in this way; in fact, I should have been eating at one of the mess halls.

A few days later, I chanced on a useful source of excellent meals for weekdays: the Kardomah Café, just off Piccadilly, in the centre of Manchester. One afternoon, I treated myself to a reasonably generous high tea and got a bill for sevenpence. The waitress was young, blonde and pretty; she may also have been bad at arithmetic – or perhaps I had made a hit? To find out, I went there again two days later. I asked for everything available on that wartime menu and there it was again; a bill for only sevenpence; the smallest bill possible, for a cup of tea and a biscuit. So I remained faithful to the establishment.

Culturally, the big bonanza that summer in Manchester was a two-week season by the Sadler's Wells Ballet Company – complete with Margot Fonteyn and Robert

Helpmann. I went to one of the first performances of the season. It was not my first visit to the ballet. I had been in London the previous year and had loved the experience so I was keen to see the much-vaunted Sadler's Wells Company as often as possible. In the afternoons I went off to read books on ballet at the central library, a large round building which had escaped the bombing which had flattened much of the city centre. I was entranced by accounts of the Imperial Russian Ballet and its break-up and the subsequent rise of Diaghilev.

One evening, four of us took a box right down near the stage. The company performed excerpts from classical ballets. They were wonderful. Afterwards, we went to dinner at the Midland Hotel and were only two tables away from a foursome which included Helpmann and Fonteyn. I was stage-struck. Next evening, I went to hear Ninette de Valois herself talk about the company at a small gathering. She reminisced about its wartime experiences: of how they had been on tour in Holland when the Germans had invaded and had only just managed to get back safely, losing all their scenery in the process. As there were only a few people there, we were all introduced. She was charming. It was an altogether unforgettable experience.

Over the tea and biscuits which followed, I talked to a well-informed middle-aged man of medium height whose English was excellent but accented. He could have been a Pole out of uniform or just a refugee. He said that he had been a financier before the war, dividing his time between several European capitals. Now of course all that was finished; he gave a little wave of his hand. He was called Alex and as he was interesting, I went and had a drink with him.

Alex became a friend. He took me to my first modern art gallery which must have been boring for him as my reactions were predictably negative. I couldn't see any point in all the blodges, squares and non-representational shapes. While at Blundell's, Stephen Spender had lent me a Henry Moore drawing of reclining figures which I'd liked very much (ever since I've regretted having to give that picture back to its lender). But at that stage the pictures Alex took me to see were too much for my untutored eye. Alex also taught me about German politics – who had been who before the rise of the Nazis, and who might be who after their demise. We met frequently. One day, however, he explained rather tensely that there could be more to friendship than met the eye; and, so saying, he pressed on me a slim volume; it was *Friendship* by Plato. I decided that as Alex might become an embarrassment, I had better not see him again. I have often wondered whether I misjudged poor Alex; but when I think of his porcine face with its gimlet eyes boring into me, I conclude that I was right. Of course, I could have misjudged Plato too – I was no classical scholar – but it much amused me when, in later life, I was married by a certain Canon Fox, the author of *Plato for Pleasure*.

Soon there loomed the prospect of being put on a draft for some far distant place like Southern Rhodesia or Canada. As the weeks had gone by, my name and those of my few remaining colleagues from the original air squadron intake were rising to the top. As happened several times in my RAF career, the posting was to resolve various matters.

I had asked the Kardomah waitress, Sally, to come dancing one evening. After so many gargantuan seven-penny meals, I thought it was the least I could do. Anyhow she was pretty – but she was too shy to say yes. When I went there again, just after I had been put on the draft, a tall, rather older waitress said, 'If you ask Sally again, she will come out with you.' But it was too late. I was off in a few days' time.

The next evening I stayed out too late with an air squadron friend and some of his cousins. As we walked back through the deserted Manchester suburbs, we had the misfortune to be picked up by an RAF police patrol van. We got a lift back to our billets at the cost of being put on a charge – except that I was due to be drafted in twenty-four hours' time. So the charge, Alex and the shy pretty waitress would all recede into the past as I moved on to the next stage of my career.

Even in Training Command, the RAF added drama to humdrum events. Going on a draft was treated ceremonially as a turning point in a trainee's career. We weren't told our destination, of course, we were given a number on parade; a number that meant we had to parade with all our kit in the evening at nine-thirty in the main mess hall. As so often in wartime, we were travelling overnight.

Having said goodbye to Mr and Mrs Prince, I took the bus down the hill for the last time and – complete with kit-bag, greatcoat, side-pack, gasmask, gas cape and wearing a uniform glinting with brass buttons – reached the mess hall at nine o'clock. There we were given supper with bacon and egg, a sure sign of a special meal, the weekly civilian ration then being one egg per person. Shortly after ten, the senior officers of Heaton Park drifted over to the dining hall from their mess. Their message to us was simple. Once abroad, we would represent our service and be ambassadors of our country. We must therefore behave properly so that overseas people would look with favour on Great Britain. One young man, overcome by many pints of beer consumed to celebrate his departure, clattered backwards off his bench. He then disappeared between two drill corporals. I often wondered what became of him.

The wing commander finished by wishing us every success. We would be off in one hour's time. Meanwhile, there was more coffee. There was also Holy Communion in the ante-room for anyone who wanted to attend. Two dozen from the biggish crowd moved towards the ante-room. I joined them, prompted less by religious fervour than a sense of occasion. The padre in vestments embroidered with RAF insignia was impressive; so was the ante-room, all done up as a chapel.

We were trucked to a suburban Manchester station where a train with dim lights awaited us. We piled in with our gear, and it shunted off with much hissing at about midnight, destination unknown. We woke to find ourselves passing through the outskirts of Glasgow, heading for the Clyde. When we arrived at the edge of a Scottish loch, we saw, looming enormously in the grey early morning, the Queen Mary, steam lazily escaping from her tall funnels; all set to take us across the Atlantic. Like everyone else, I knew this great ship as a pre-war symbol of regeneration, an emblem of hope that the country would eventually be free of the Depression. Now we were to travel in her.

In the middle of the last war, the Queen Mary was the equivalent of a sovereign state. She had her own virtually pre-war standard of living because she was provisioned in New York which was now her home port. So it was to a temporary paradise that we were ferried across the loch in a tender. We went up the gang-plank to the lower decks where we were sorted out and allotted bunks. Each cabin had about eighteen bunks in tiers of three. The ship was equipped to carry an American division of up to twelve thousand troops so, since there were only one thousand five hundred of us, we rattled like peas in a drum; one hundred of us were airmen, the rest were largely naval ratings on their way to Royal Navy ships completing refits in the American naval yards at Norfolk, Virginia.

In the afternoon, we slowly made our way down the Clyde into the open sea. We were followed by a huge cloud of screaming seagulls as the ship must, at that time, have had one of the richest bilges anywhere. The ship sailed without a convoy. Now that the turning-point in the Battle of the Atlantic had passed, U-boats and German aircraft were still a menace. All the same, we kept up a speed of over twenty knots. Our party was mustered on deck for boat drill. Once it was over, I volunteered to help in the stores and was one of six to be chosen. Then we had high tea, one of our two daily meals. The food was superb, unlike anything we'd experienced for four years: the purest white bread, lashings of butter, unlimited eggs and bacon, beans on toast, and fruit including oranges and bananas. We were in a world that knew nothing of Woolton Pie, points and rationing. No wonder we gorged ourselves stupid. For the troops, the ship was dry – but there was limitless Coca Cola. For recreation, there were wireless sets and a big saloon, normally for steerage passengers, at the stern. Here the major diversions were three 'crown and anchor' games run by hardened naval ratings.

The next morning found us out of sight of land, well into the Atlantic. The sea was choppy enough to give the ship some roll but only enough to unsettle the most queasy. The rest of us regarded these first casualties of life on the ocean wave with wry amusement. We didn't know what was to come.

Our volunteer detail reported to the cabin of one of the senior storekeepers, a man of some consequence who sat, clean and neat in white uniform, behind a large desk on which were photographs of young ladies, presumably one for each port of call, together with the sort of desk furniture which could have graced the desk of a business tycoon in a Hollywood movie. Behind him was a vast box piled high with two-hundred-cigarette cartons of Camels and Chesterfields.

'It would be nice if you boys could help us with a few of the stores,' the man said very graciously. 'Bill here will show you where, and when you have finished, drop in. I'll have some cigarettes for you.' He smiled briefly and we thought, what a world!

The courtly introduction was deceptive. We were each given a hand trolley to push down to one of the dry stores. There we loaded up with crates of tins or sacks of flour. In my case it was flour, in two heavy sacks which were all right if carefully balanced. From there we had to push our loads down a steel corridor running through the bowels of the ship towards the kitchens. We had never seen so much food. The cooks were big men, fourteen to fifteen stone, in rather discoloured chefs' trousers and singlets. Their faces and limbs shone with sweat which seemed to mix with the vapours coming off the boiling liquids and bubbling food. The sight, heat and smell of the kitchens were quick to take their toll; by the end of the morning, two of our number had retired hurt. However, I and the remaining five ate a hearty midday meal of excellent rissoles rolled between the ample hands of one of the gigantic chefs. We worked for only an hour in the afternoon, humping lighter delicacies for tomorrow's consumption; we then repaired to the storekeeper's office where we were delighted to find that we got a cup of tea and between us a pack of two hundred Chesterfields. Altogether, a very satisfactory day. It might have been healthier doing exercises under the eagle eye of a PT instructor on the top deck in the howling wind, but those of us with firm stomachs far preferred the sheltered existence down below.

The next day was different. A full-scale Atlantic gale was blowing from the west, and as we were going westwards it blew all the harder. The waves were gigantic. The ship had developed a corkscrew motion with a cycle of some twenty to thirty seconds for each full turn; a motion that combined pitching forwards and backwards as the vessel ploughed down into the chasms and up the other side, rolling all the while. Far from having stabilizers to help iron out the motion, the vessel had the equivalent of destabilizers in the form of substantial anti-aircraft gun platforms fixed fore and aft to the upper decks of the superstructure. As there was no slowing down, the vessel hurled itself at the elements with gusto. By mid-morning, several hundred ratings were clinging to the rails as they yielded up to the deep that which they had packed away with such relish the previous day. Only two of our detail, myself and one other, reported for work in the storekeeper's cabin. Yesterday's light task had become today's perilous assignment. The steel corridor through which I had to steer my two sacks of flour became alternately a steel mountain up which, panting, I had to push a heavier-than-ever load while the next moment it became a steel chute down which I had to guide my load, preventing it from accelerating to an uncontrollable pace. It was like working on a moving switchback, more dynamic and dangerous than any fairground feature. I was desperate to avoid being crushed under my two sacks as we went up or, as we went down, being in collision with a bulkhead at breakneck speed. I got little sympathy from the chefs who, as I shot past the kitchens on a downwards swoop, cheered me from positions of safety. I was an accident waiting to happen.

That afternoon I was the only representative of the detail still working, as my partner of the morning had turned a light shade of green at midday. Now it was my turn to have an accident. As I charged down the steel corridor with another bag of flour, my load now reduced to one for safety's sake, a lurch in the corkscrew motion threw me, my trolley and the sack against a bulwark. The truck and I bounced off unharmed. The sack split. Within a second I was engulfed in flour, and a farinaceous fog was spreading down the steel corridor both ways. One of the cooks emerged from the kitchens to see what had happened. He picked me up and dusted me down, checking to see nothing was broken. Miraculously, most of the flour had remained in the two halves of the broken sack. The cook and one of his colleagues carefully picked them up, and my day's work was over. The gale continued to blow for the next two days and I went on with my one-man detail. Because of the accident, I had achieved some notoriety and henceforward I was only asked to carry crates. As a result of my exploit, some fine white flour had been sucked into the ship's airducts and evenly distributed in minute amounts throughout the vessel. This worried the engineers – not because the Queen Mary was going to grind to a standstill with flour clogging the machinery and turbines turning into bread ovens, but because it would take a few weeks for the last traces of flour to blow out into the Atlantic. In the kitchens, they were sufficiently proud of me to reward me, on the third day, with a complete carton of Camels.

Eventually, the storm blew itself out. The ashen-faced sailors who had lined the rails returned to normal and the risk of spotting a spontaneous 'throw up' diminished. Numbers at meals rose and the 'crown and anchor' boards reappeared. Towards the end of our six-day voyage, some were blowing french letters into balloons and then releasing them for the diversion of the WAAF and WRNS officers taking the air on the upper decks. The American crews of the anti-aircraft guns chewed gum and looked bored; they had seen it all before.

The romantic way to arrive in America is to come up the Hudson past the Statue of Liberty; we did this slowly and majestically in our great liner painted in her wartime camouflage. We were aware that the unfolding panorama of the New York skyline that met our eyes was equalled by the dramatic spectacle presented by the arrival of the Queen Mary. Soon, the tugs were bustling around below, nudging us into a berth next to the *Normandie*, the pre-war pride of the French transatlantic fleet. Some months earlier, a fire had swept through this noble Blue Riband winner, leaving her a sad wreck listing thirty-five degrees to one side.

We were met in style. A military band played on the quay as the ship made fast and the gangplanks were run out. Earlier that morning, ever the volunteer, I had offered to help with the baggage of the airmen who had been told to put their kit-bags into a great pile; they would disembark empty-handed and meet up with their kit later. There were twelve of us baggage handlers, detailed to get the kit-bags off the ship and on to the train; a task that proved much easier than it sounded. A single crane swept up the kit-bags in a huge rope net and dumped them on the quay where we were waiting to meet them. We simply bundled them into a truck and, in half an hour, our stint was over. This left us ninety minutes to stroll around the quay and chat up American Red Cross girls dishing out coffee and doughnuts. These girls weren't prettier than average, but they looked better than their English equivalent because they all had the well-groomed healthy look that stems from money and peacetime conditions. Their clothes were well cut, their long legs clad in nylons. We liked what we saw, and they were kind enough to appear reciprocally impressed.

The train taking us to Canada was on the other side of the quay. Although it looked like a veteran of the Civil War, it was quite comfortable with plenty of room in the 'day coaches' that creaked and groaned when the train moved out. We burrowed through tunnels and culverts and eventually emerged on to a stretch of line running beside the Hudson. Our engine moved slowly, making the particular hoot so typical of American engines, so evocative of endless prairie and the pioneer days of steam.

We were now under RCAF (Royal Canadian Air Force) discipline. A flying officer in RCAF uniform, minus wings, came through the train, stopping in each coach to deliver a lecture on security. He explained that America was crawling with foreign agents and saboteurs who might well select this train as a target. He told us to be on our lookout at all times. If the train made an unscheduled stop, we were on no account to get out or let anybody in. There would be a scheduled stop the next morning when we had crossed the Canadian border and arrangements would be made for us to get off and stretch our legs then. For the time being, we would be train-bound. Never fear, we would be fed. He passed on down the train with his serious message which nobody took seriously. Indeed, we all felt very secure in this environment thousands of miles away from the wartime scenario we'd just come from. Outside Albany, the train slowed to a halt in a spaghetti of railway sidings. Soon there were several dozen children walking along the track shouting up to us: 'Any pennies?' So we threw down a hail of huge brown predecimal pennies. That was what they wanted. They were friendly but, unlike the Red Cross girls on the quay, they wore reach-me-down clothes, not quite ragged but pretty threadbare. Not all of America was prosperous.

During the night, we rattled our way up through the New England states, the RCAF flying officer ever watchful for saboteurs while we smoked too much, digging into our stockpiles of Camels and Chesterfields following an excellent meal from the kitchen car. Unless taking part in one of the card-playing schools, we lay around the day coach in various grotesque poses, uneasily sleeping in blankets distributed earlier.

Our promised stop was at the township of Megantic in Quebec, just north of the border; three hours to get off the train and stretch our legs. Megantic was a small farming town in a beautiful, fairly mountainous setting; a typical slice of rural eastern Canada. However, it was French so, to our surprise, we found ourselves in a hostile atmosphere: the shopkeepers were pleasant enough, but otherwise our reception was glacial. Nothing daunted, we bought ourselves excellent breakfasts; and some used their gains at 'crown and anchor' to buy flashy watches of dubious origin. We left on time and chugged north heading towards the Maritimes, to Monkton, New Brunswick, the next great holding unit in our slow progress along the path of aircrew training. The train crossed the St Lawrence by Montreal and then headed east, arriving at the little station at Monkton at about ten; after thirty hours of travelling we were all ready for a good night's sleep.

Through the Monkton holding unit were channelled aircrew trainees coming into North America for training. It was on the outskirts of Monkton, a medium-sized New Brunswick town which was a communications centre through which the railway from the west ran and fanned out to the various communities of the Maritimes. Most of the aircrew from North America sailed either to New York or Halifax, the Canadian port. They then travelled by train to and from the flying schools spread out across Canada and America. Given that the holding unit had to be on Canadian soil rather than in the US, Monkton was an obvious choice.

The barrack blocks of the camp were H-shaped and had two storeys. Well over twenty in number, they were light, wooden and reasonably spacious and flanked a wide, featureless road. There were also the usual administrative offices and messes.

Monkton was extraordinarily boring. The holding unit was too large for a place that at best had only been a nondescript provincial town sitting on a railway junction. It hadn't even got the sea, the saving grace of most maritime townships. History seemed to have bypassed it. As a result, its local scenery and culture couldn't begin to absorb the groups of airmen swirling around the street.

After a week of sitting in the early September sun, I started combing the classified advertisements in the *Monkton Gazette*, the local newspaper which was nine-tenths syndicated material from other newspapers. An advertisement in the personal column offered a ray of hope. The Monkton University Society was holding its next meeting at five o'clock next Saturday afternoon at an address in the better part of the residential district. So off I went. It might, after all, be a lecture on ballet. It wasn't, nor were the members of the Monkton University Society quite what I'd expected: once through the mosquito-proof outer door, I was confronted by a group of middle-aged ladies about to be addressed by a bearded clergyman.

'I'm so sorry,' I blurted out, making as if to go. 'I came because of the advertisement. I was up at Oxford for a term or so and . . . ' I had been interrupted by a chorus of, 'Come in . . . Sit down . . . How lovely.' The middle-aged female university graduates of Monkton, New Brunswick, were richly amused to find that I had wandered into their midst. Considering that there were some ten thousand airmen up at the holding unit just a few miles away, it was odd that I should be thought so extraordinary but this only confirmed my view that the war, the air force, and the holding unit in particular had had very little impact on the town of Monkton.

The first item on the agenda was tea; not a formality but a substantial meal, Canadian-style, complete with waffles and maple syrup, an extraordinary gastronomic delight, in near limitless quantities. I couldn't stop eating them until, half an hour later, I felt as though a small tyre had been inflated just under my chest. For a moment or two, I thought it was going to stop me from breathing and that I was about to die from internal asphyxiation. But this acute symptom was soon replaced by serious discomfort; the inevitable outcome of eating waffles to excess. On top of them, I had also devoured several pieces of triple-decker iced cake of that moist stodgy type so popular with North American women – who consume this delicacy at any time, even after the heaviest lunch or dinner. The more I ate, the happier were my hosts. Tea and all the attendant toing and froing between the large room and the house's ample kitchen was followed by everybody sitting down to listen to the Reverend.

His talk was my first experience of the widespread North American habit of showing holiday slides. The Reverend had been to Bermuda. All good Canadians eventually go to Bermuda as Muslims to Mecca. And there was the Reverend in Bermuda shorts to prove it. Here, he was in a boat with fishermen; that was his hotel and there was his bicycle. And there – thanks to some amazingly clever colour transparencies – were shoals of multi-coloured peculiarly shaped tropical fish with long trailing whiskers. The Reverend started his talk with reminiscences of his first visit to Bermuda as a young man with a moustache. Loud titters. Looking at me he said that he thought his moustache made him look older than he really was. The titters turned to good-natured laughter which, trying not to finger my moustache, I tried to take in good part. It was too late to shave it off, and if it gave them pleasure, what the hell? In fact I rather fancied myself with a moustache and although I never meant to turn it into a growth of handle-bar proportions, it was, at least, in keeping with service tradition. And the clergyman was right. Secretly, I felt it made me look older than my age – nineteen – an ambition most young men nurse until they're twenty-five.

The hostess for the function was a senior school teacher in Monkton, unmarried and over forty. She now befriended me. She was quiet, charming and slightly boring but, considering how excruciatingly dull Monkton was by local standards, she represented high excitement. And at least I now had somewhere to go on a Saturday afternoon and eat a restricted number of waffles.

My only other foray into self-entertainment occurred when I volunteered for yet another baggage detail. There was a daily train at the holding unit's railway spur which took drafts of airmen usually going west to a station in one of the prairie provinces or, alternatively, taking trained personnel down to Halifax or New York to catch a transatlantic troopship back to the UK. There were also regular smaller parties, often going to training stations down in the US; these travelled on cars attached to regular trains going through Monkton to the west. It was the baggage belonging to these parties for which my twelve-strong volunteer detail was responsible. We humped the kit-bags on to the trucks, drove with them to the station and unloaded them down there. We had an easy-going Canadian corporal who, before we drove back, let us have an hour or so off; this we spent hanging around the soda fountain in a little row of shops opposite the station, chatting up two girls whom we took to the cinema in turns.

About six weeks after our arrival we suddenly found ourselves posted. 'Our' group, first found in Manchester, was now down to just over a dozen. Only one of the group had come with me from the Oxford Air Squadron. He was 'Dixie' Barnes, fair haired, also with a moustache, also six foot one and a half. As we came from the same background, we naturally made common cause. Our destination was a bombing and gunnery school in Ontario called Mountain View where we were due to join a course starting in the third week of September. This time when the great big Canadian National locomotive drew slowly into Monkton's station, its brass bell clanging, it was our turn to head westwards.

9 Mountain View

Mountain View was an RCAF station a few miles away from the town of Belleville, Ontario, itself a mile or so from Lake Ontario. It was a bombing and gunnery school equipped with Blenheim aircraft, oddly named Bolingbrokes (by the Canadians) and Oxfords. The courses took three months, with one starting and another ending every two weeks. We were due to finish the week before Christmas.

The station had been going for about eighteen months when we got there. It was entirely staffed by Canadians. On the face of it, there was very little difference between an RAF and an RCAF station but, below the surface, they were poles apart. Although we had heard about the rugged individualism of the Canadians, we had never come across it. The administrative and teaching staffs which made up the Canadian equivalent of Training Command were geared to handle Canadian pupils, rather than those from the mother country – let alone hard cases from New Zealand and Australia. The young Canadian recruit was far more biddable than the rest. This was because Canadians and Americans were treated like children while we were independent adults who'd been treated as such from the moment we joined the RAF. In America, this had caused a real problem. So many RAF trainees had been thrown off courses for alleged ill-discipline that, to avoid wastage on an intolerable scale, the RAF had set up a special board at Windsor, Ontario, to reallocate them to Canadian schools. Several such cases on our course told us their experiences.

It was a convention that, when allowed into the local town, trainees in American flying schools got wildly drunk. As a result they could be let out only very occasionally, and only in the presence of numerous MPs who could knock them on the head and drag them back to camp. The more grotesque forms of American discipline had also caused trouble. One punishment was having to run round the perimeter wearing a pilot's parachute or having to eat a 'square meal'; the latter involved lifting food from a plate in a way that described a square: first the spoon came up nine inches; then it went outwards horizontally nine inches; then up another nine inches; then horizontally to the mouth; then followed the same pattern downwards. There had recently been a riot in one American unit where a number of New Zealanders had rebelled at this childish stuff. They had hit back where it hurt most, at the American flag. The Americans, they found, were sensitive to the point of being neurotic about their flag, so one of their number had typed out a vivid message to the American CO telling him and his staff what they could do with it, star by star and stripe by stripe, and had pinned it to the flag pole. They were posted the next morning.

The fourteen in our class included a veteran regular corporal, a forty-year-old fitter who had volunteered for aircrew duties. He was a small Welshman, Davis by name, who was naturally called Taff. He demonstrated the old campaigner's capacity to save energy. He spent all his leisure time in mole-like slumber on a lower-tier bunk cleverly 'bagged' in the quietest corner of the block. The rest of us were all about nineteen or twenty. The accommodation was adequate, with two-tier bunks reasonably well spaced in a single-storey building that was warm and draught-proof. Like the blocks at Monkton, they were H-shaped with ablutions in the cross part of the letter. Beyond the ablutions were Canadian airmen on the permanent staff, resourceful folk who made the best of the war by servicing itinerants – renting electric irons to anyone who wanted to press their trousers, running a private taxi service and such-like.

We found the Canadian conscription rules kept us apart from the locals: although they were conscripted they could not be made to serve overseas. For this they had to volunteer. French-speaking Canadians were far slower to volunteer than English-speaking Canadians; even so, plenty of the latter were 'zombies', as non-volunteers were called, and quite a few of them were at Mountain View.

Our course was divided between theory and practice. Practice involved dropping white one-and-a-half-pound practice bombs on targets on the foreshore of Lake Ontario; as they fell on the ranges, they exploded in puffs of white smoke; their accuracy was plotted by two operators in range-finding huts. We flew in the Oxfords. The trainee crawled forward into the bomb-aiming position and lay on his stomach in the nose of the aircraft. He looked down through a perspex panel at the inhospitable foreshore and identified the target. It was then his duty to 'talk' the bored instructor pilot into the right position. The trainee then tracked down the twin arms of the bomb sight until it reached the cross bar; he then pressed the button and away went the bomb.

Before setting off on his mission, the trainee bomb-aimer was given vital clues: the direction and the speed of the wind. As we learnt later, life in the air hinged on knowing what the wind was. Without that, nothing happened; people got lost; targets weren't spotted; bombs missed. While it was up to the navigator to find out what the wind was, he always started with a hypothetical wind supplied by the meteorologists; the Met. The given wind on these exercises was often wrong. In training terms, this hardly mattered. It was easy to plot the position of the theoretical target relative to the real one by substituting the given wind for the one blowing at the time. If someone dropped a spot-on cluster of six bombs, the 'plot' would show all six hits on top of each other in a bull's eye on the theoretical target. We were marked on tight grouping. Plots showing scattered bombs scored low, those showing tight-knit hits scored high – especially when accorded the 'right' wind. Every day, the best plot was prominently displayed in the corridor of the main administration block. One day I had a near-perfect group of five bombs, with one stray bomb right out at an angle of three hundred and twenty degrees.

We picked up our plots from a couple of WRCAF corporals at a little counter. One of them had light-blue eyes flecked with green. I looked at those eyes and back at my pencilled plot. Looking at me, she slowly but firmly rubbed out my errant bomb and re-sited it smack in the middle of the group. So that day my plot had pride of place.

On that bombing range, everything that could go wrong, went wrong. Residents along the lake complained of practice bombs dropping on their houses. A fisherman claimed that a bomb had narrowly missed his dinghy. Some bombs failed to go off and release their puff of smoke. Others wiped out plotters' huts. Yet more fell several at a time; a mistake I made myself on my fifth run. In getting down into the prone position, I pulled several switches into the 'on' position by brushing against them in my bulky flying suit. As a result, when I pressed the little plunger, away went four little white bombs. This prompted an immediate explosion over the intercom from my pilot; an angry reminder of just how much each practice bombing run cost the RCAF.

The practical in the air-gunnery course started on a firing range along the windswept lakeside beach. Anyone using a firearm for the first time always finds that the weapon is in charge, not vice versa. I experienced this when we fired a single Browning machine-gun. And the feeling was hugely amplified when we graduated to firing four at once, housed in an imitation Boulton-Paul turret. How I would ever take charge of this monster was beyond my imagination.

Once in the air on our first live-target practice, the difficulties were magnified a thousandfold by noise, discomfort and sheer cold. Trainees went up three at a time in rather battered Blenheims. At a given signal, a flashing green light and a deafening buzz in the middle of the aircraft, the first trainee was to clamber into the turret for firing practice. Once over, he got out and made way for the next trainee and so on. At first we scrambled about like chimpanzees in flying gear; banging into sharp objects, into each other, pressing the wrong knobs; generally making awful fools of ourselves to increasingly staccato threats on the intercom. We were further hampered by severe cold, the notorious Canadian winter having set in early that year. Temperatures had already plummeted to levels only comparable in our experience to the severe winter of 1939–40. On the ground it was very unpleasant; in the air it was almost unbearable.

Each trainee had to fire bursts of tracer at a drone, a long fifteen-foot strip of material, rather like a windsock, towed behind an aircraft. We flew so that the drone was above and behind our own aircraft. In theory the trainee gunner in the mid-upper turret was meant to fire off tracers coded by one of three colours. When my turn came, the drone looked like a tiny pocket handkerchief dancing about thousands of yards away in a bright blue sky. Hitting a fly with a ruler would have been easier. Once I pressed the trigger, the four Brownings took over in a wild, brain-numbing clatter. The guns bucked and the turret jumped around as though about to come apart from the airframe, so that it, guns and I, would cascade out into the sky, with luck hitting the drone on the way down. The first week of practical showed up our collective inability to control these weapons of war; we felt thoroughly humbled.

So much for practice. In the meantime, we were also immersed in theory. What governed the flight of a projectile? A regrettably complex mix of algebra and trigonometry. Bombs were dropped and bullets fired; otherwise they were projectiles that behaved according to an unimaginably intricate set of physical laws. We made heavy weather of it all. Our progress was further slowed by a cloud of sloth that clamped over the class. A man due to defend his life by sword or gun will concentrate during lessons on swordsmanship and marksmanship. Unfortunately the theory of projectiles didn't seem as relevant to our survival and effectiveness in European skies. We were further retarded by our instructor, a delightful corporal with regrettably little grasp of his subject. As the course progressed, and we didn't, it became obvious that unless he went, the entire class might well fail.

Trainees didn't have much time off at Mountain View. It was over ten miles to Belleville; there were no forty-eight-hour passes; and we were there to the end of the course. And during that time, we couldn't spend a night off the camp. Our only outside facility was a small YMCA house a few hundred yards from the main gate. Nicely furnished and run by the ladies of Belleville, it served coffee, doughnuts and like fare.

This put a premium on in-camp entertainment. There was a well-equipped, well-heated cinema with twice-weekly changes of fairly recent films. And once a fortnight there was a dance; a major multi-rank affair for which the whole station turned out. It was held in an enormous hangar that resounded to a Glenn Miller-type band. There was excellent food and drink and, sometimes, some attractive girls. The first time I went, I struck up with Belinda, a tall blonde in her mid-twenties. Her English mother lived in Toronto but her father's provenance and whereabouts remained a mystery. She had an English-Canadian accent, was well read and altogether quite different from the rest of the WRCAF girls. By trade she was a corporal fitter. I had sometimes seen her plying her trade, a white-overalled figure clambering about an Oxford. I introduced myself saying, 'Would you like to dance?' She smiled, and we did. My dancing, thank heavens, had improved from the early Oxford days. I had learnt from various incidents, including the humiliation at a London dance of having a Wren walk off the floor rather than take any more punishment. Dancing was much more fun in those days: you got hold of your partner and continued in unison; with luck, close unison. Anyway, Belinda and I made out at the dances, making for each other every fortnight.

Between times there was the cinema, now attended with Belinda. But there were still many blank evenings. Desperate for action, I even went with Dixie Barnes, my companion, to the large, well-equipped gym. He had been impressed by my prowess with the sergeant at Heaton Park. So we took to having an innocent fifteen minutes' sparring in the boxing ring. One evening, as we were finishing, the PTI (physical training instructor) stopped me. He was a tiny man with a close-cropped bullet head emerging from a white polo-neck jersey. Could I help him? He was in a fix. There was a boxing match coming up next Saturday and one of the chaps had dropped out with an injury. So the PTI desperately needed a substitute. Just a friendly little bout against a novice. He'd be so grateful. Innocent that I was, I allowed myself to be persuaded.

It was soon Saturday. My chums on the course promised to come and support me. So did Belinda. Early that evening, I had my shower, put on running shorts, singlet and gym shoes; and over them, in unconvincing imitation of a boxer's dressing gown, my RAF greatcoat. I then went across to the gym where I expected to find a few people, including my supporters, all set to watch the friendly bout.

The gym had been transformed in what I assumed to be an imitation of Madison Square Gardens. Huge arc lights hung from iron girders; a full-scale boxing ring stood five feet above the gym floor, its white canvas dazzling, reflecting the lights from above, its padded corner posts holding the ropes. Tiers of seating accommodated hundreds of spectators: not just all Mountain View, but numerous representatives from a nearby RCAF station. I realized with horror that this was an inter-station boxing evening. I walked around the back to the sounds of a fight in progress. A burly official in a polo-neck sweater asked me where my seconds were. 'Seconds? I haven't got any,' I said. He looked me up and down. 'No seconds, eh?' Wiping his mouth on the back of his hand, he seemed more put out by the sight of me than my lack of seconds. He went to consult one of the officers at the side of the gym, now partitioned off as a dressing room. From it emerged the little PTI. 'Lovely,' he said, nodding with approval. 'Good, good. We'll get you some seconds, don't worry.'

In the circumstances it was difficult to obey this injunction. It became impossible when I saw my opponent. He lay, a long lanky figure, on a table in the dressing room. He wore flashy silk shorts, topped by inch-wide elastic gathering round the waist, and athletic boots of shiny black leather laced over the ankles. His seconds were applying a final massage to his prone frame. The gym resounded to the announcement that the third bout was due to start. Mine. A figure from the group in the dressing room came over to me. 'I'm your second,' he said. 'We'll manage,' he added without much confidence. I turned to follow but then saw my opponent get off the massage table and stand up. He was about an inch taller than I was, with hands, now encased in thinly stuffed boxing gloves, hanging down to his knees.

We headed towards the ring between tiers of seats all seemingly occupied by fans of my opponent baying for my blood. My next problem was getting into the ring. My opponent caught the ropes in his gloved hands and neatly swung himself up, sliding his body between them. I tried to emulate him but for one nasty moment hung perilously swinging, wondering whether I was going to drop on to the floor. With a huge effort, I managed to slither between the lowest rope and the mattress floor, and finished up at the referee's feet. I got up, and retreated to my corner and the comfort of my single second. I now got a further look at my opponent. He had Neanderthal features with dark bushy eyebrows from which his forehead slipped back at an acute angle for about two inches before meeting his hairline. He scowled at me from under his matted black hair and chewed menacingly on a gum shield.

The bell rang, we advanced and met in the middle of the ring, our gloves touching in token friendship. We parted. He hit me. The blow landed in my solar plexus. I had never before been hit so hard. All the breath was knocked out of me and I sank to the floor, landing in a sitting position, arms outstretched. I struggled in vain to regain my breath but I felt as one flattened by a steam-roller, with the wall of my stomach pinned against my backbone. I was aware that the count had started. At the count of five, my deep-gurgling gulps had forced the first life-giving air down my gullet. I was going to survive. By the seventh count, I was breathing again. I got up. It was a three-minute bout, but I felt this initial experience must have absorbed well over five. I was wrong. Less than thirty seconds had elapsed. I had two and a half minutes more to go before I could get back to the safety of my corner and regroup.

This was going to be difficult. My Neanderthal opponent, sensing an easy victory, was after me immediately. For my part, I was determined to avoid another crashing blow; otherwise I'd be done for. Casting aside all pretence of public school spirit, I beat an undignified retreat. My nightmarish opponent came after me. But despite his enormous reach, he had trouble hitting my fast-retreating figure.

My desperation yielded footwork fully worthy of one of Dame Ninette's young men. I danced and I skipped and I wheeled backwards. I cavorted sideways and I punched the air. My opponent caught me one or two glancing blows. He grunted and chewed his gum shield. His supporters, which meant practically everybody in the gym, shouted encouragement and exhorted him to polish me off. But I lasted. Eventually I could hear that marvellous sound, the ringing of the bell tolling me back to my corner.

I had never been so breathless before. I panted as though I'd been on a ten-mile run. I was done for. My second was silent; events had gone beyond any comment. All I could think of was the advice of my prep-school boxing pro: feint.

The blessed intermission was soon over. The bell rang. Out into the ring I went to face the primitive man. So eager was he to finish me off that he had bounded across and met me when I was only a yard or two out of my corner. He lunged viciously and missed. I said a prayer and feinted. The next few moments consisted of a blurred commotion. My second led me back to my corner. Primitive man was over in his corner with both his seconds and the referee. Miraculously, the fight was over. I still couldn't see why. Then it became clear. I was declared the winner, my opponent having been forced to retire. Why? My feint had caught him a sharp blow on his protruding eyebrow; this, standing out like that of a gorilla from the rest of his forehead, had opened up like a ripe melon; it had split apart along a two-inch seam, and was now pouring with blood so that he was blinded. In the event, it needed twelve stitches. My eight supporters went wild. The hundreds poised to see me murdered sat silent. In a welter of blood, my persecutor climbed down from the ring and went back to the dressing room. My second couldn't stop smiling.

The prize-giving was the climax of the evening. The prizes – tokens worth several dollars redeemable for goods at the station shop – were handed out by the group captain who spoke a few well-chosen words to each successful competitor. Except, that is, for me. When it came to the third bout, he couldn't forbear mentioning the unsuccessful contender, 'who had been doing so well when ill luck overtook him'. Cheers resounded round the hall. For all that, I got the prize; and wild cheers came from my faithful eight, so much so that I feared for their lives. That was the end of my boxing career. I had been foolish, but luck had saved me. I had learned my lesson.

The course neared its end in December. Report of our class's slow progress must have filtered through to the administration because, without warning, our instructor was changed. In place of the agreeable corporal, we got a career-oriented sergeant who was himself angling to get on a course and thereby attain the longed-for status of commissioned rank. He took us in hand, starting with the classic approach of any professional NCO faced with a difficult group of trainees: 'You play ball with me, and I'll play ball with you.' In effect, he offered us good examination results on which we could build our futures.

The problem was that with only three weeks to go, few of us had grasped the theory of the flight of the projectile. So he immersed us in an intensive series of dummy runs. Numerous previous exam papers were produced, explained and analysed. I never knew whether later the others realized too that embedded amongst those dummy runs was a far-from-dummy run. Unknowingly, we had been put through the exam we were about to sit; as a result the class congratulated itself on its good fortune in finding a number of positively familiar questions in the actual examination.

So as a group, we sailed through: nobody failed and the more intelligent got excellent marks. It was all very satisfactory. Our sergeant instructor enhanced his reputation as a trouble-shooter and was shortly afterwards posted to an officers' training course at Kingston. Having completed the requisite number of practice bombing runs and air-to-air gunnery exercises, we graduated from the school, pasting into our log books the appropriate forms and getting them signed. We had achieved the first step towards gaining our wings, never mind how.

10 St John's, Quebec

The RAF did not need us again until the second week in January when we were due to join a navigators' course lasting six months at St John's, Quebec, some thirty miles south of Montreal.

Like all airmen, in our group at least, Dixie Barnes and I wanted to see New York. We got there by hitchhiking and train. We hitched along the Queen Elizabeth highway, going west, and ended up in Buffalo. The last person to pick us up worked in the aircraft factory there, turning out Airacobras. He took us to his nice suburban house and plied us with so many lethal Martinis that we slept for most of the train journey from Buffalo to New York. When we arrived, children pointed at us in Grand Central Station exclaiming to their mothers, 'Look, Canadian airmen!' As we hung about, collecting ourselves, a captain in the US Army Air Corps came over to us. He had the metal wings of the Air Corps on the left side of his tunic while on the right he had a smaller version of RAF wings. He had obviously been an American volunteer in the RAF who had transferred to the American service after Pearl Harbour. He chatted about his time flying Spitfires. He couldn't bear it back here at home in America. 'They don't know that there's a goddamned war going on.' He was homesick, not for home but for the war he had left behind.

We decided to make for the YMCA. We waited for a bus outside on the pavement. In a plate-glass window, behind us, there was a crack. A large piece of glass slithered to the ground and a man leant in to embrace the furs inside. Next moment he was running down the street. We gave chase. At the corner of the street he dived into a waiting car and was gone. Searching for someone to tell our news, we picked on a passing naval officer in white scarf and top coat and told him. He looked at us calmly and asked, 'You guys on furlough?' 'Yes sir.' 'If you guys don't want to spend your furlough down at the precinct, I'd advise you to forget all about it.' We saluted. It was disappointing, but we were in New York now and that was that.

New York was a great sight, but it was no place for non-commissioned trainee airmen. The hospitality provided by ordinary people in both Canada and the US during the war was legendary; unlike anything I'd ever experienced. But New York was an exception because it was too busy making its own fortune to subsidize airmen with only a few dollars a day; for them, picking up the bill for drinks – or worse, lunch – meant ruin. Perhaps the British reputation in New York for not paying, stems from those war years when so few British had the wherewithall to do so.

But Dixie and I had two lucky breaks. Once, at a charity lunch, we were adopted by a very chic, rather rich girl from up-state New York. She had just married an officer in the Royal Navy. He was currently stationed in Trinidad so she was trying to wangle a seat on Pan Am which was still running restricted services to the Caribbean. She was as amused by us as we were by her and insisted that we should visit the Stork Club that evening. She rang up the head barman and told him to give us as much drink as we wanted. He duly welcomed us as 'the two young British from Oxford University' and we propped up the bar for the rest of the night.

On another occasion, we got free tickets at the Stage Door Club to a broadcast radio show given by a celebrated big band, Fred Waring's Pennsylvanians. After the show, the band gave a supper for any service personnel in the audience. The bandleader's brother,

Jim, took a liking to us and for the rest of our leave showed us around town.

It was soon time to make our way back to Canada and resume our training at the next camp, St John's – or St Jean – Quebec. It was, and probably still is, pure French-Canadian. The French Canadians were not so much hostile as detached. They weren't interested in us or our war; their relationship with us was entirely commercial. The base was under the discipline and legal provisions of the RCAF so our instructors were RCAF. But the physical operation of the place – from the cleaning, victualling, right on through to the maintenance and flying – was handled by private contractors. The pilots who flew the Oxfords in which we trained were seconded from the RCAF to employment by the contractor. On the ground they wore blazers and grey flannel trousers.

Being stationed at St John's gave me an early experience of life as run by the private sector. We got the benefit of consumer choice. There was low-grade food in the canteen or far better food – including such delicacies as eggs and bacon – for a price in the private canteen. Clearly, our canteen had to be run on the minimum outlay to maintain profits. As a result, we trainees found ourselves forking out our pay to eat. The situation would probably have continued undisturbed during our six months on the station but for the management's zeal in maximizing those profits. The food in our canteen got so bad that eventually there was a riot. It flared up over spare ribs, a delicacy then unknown to practically all young Englishmen. The particular spare ribs which the contractor supplied were more spare than rib: they were all bone; large and disgusting. That evening, the murmurs in the canteen grew to a howl. Everybody stayed at their tables and banged their mugs. The compliant Canadians had never seen anything like it. Several hundred airmen, hungry and angry all at once. The cooks took refuge behind their stoves.

A spokesman was elected by the airmen and the cry

went up, 'Send for the orderly officer.' He turned out to be an Australian and was accompanied by a tall pilot officer with a pencil moustache who was responsible for discipline on the base. 'Take that man's name for smoking,' he snapped at someone who'd lit up during the wait. Luckily, the Australian chipped in, demanding to see the food. It was so demonstrably disgusting, he condemned it outright, ordered bacon and eggs all round and promised to look into the matter. This he did, and from then on the food improved a little. However, the administration of St John's impressed on us all the difference between private contractors and the public service.

At the start, there were twenty-eight on our course. Most of the Mountain View lot were on it apart from two or three who'd gone to be bomb-aimers. Six former pilot trainees joined the course; they had failed at American flying training schools and then regraded at Windsor, Ontario. The rest comprised trainee navigators who'd left the US after us. Two such courses of up to thirty pupils ran simultaneously with two new courses starting every fortnight. So at any one time there were about twenty-eight courses running with some thirty pupils on each – at the start anyway, they usually ended up with about ten or even less. But on our course, eighteen pupils graduated.

The theory and practice of navigation as taught in the RAF and the RCAF at the time was well within the capabilities of the numerate; but they presented difficulties to less mathematically minded people such as myself. Training and experience helped but I also needed far more time than was available. A good navigator trainee had to be fast, accurate and neat with logs and charts – and this not only in the classroom but also in an aircraft, in a dark, draughty and very confined space, and sometimes under fire. Navigation in the RAF was serious: it determined the safety and success of the mission. In the US Air Corps, navigation was a specialist art practised in one of every twelve aircraft. This was fine in daylight, but the RAF operated at night when every crew had to navigate on its own. With these factors and my own incompetence in mind, I started the course with considerable qualms.

Unfortunately Dixie Barnes had been posted on to the twin course so I found myself with a different colleague: Sam, a twenty-five-year-old from Birmingham, which he pronounced Bir-ming-gam. He called me Tone. 'Where you from, Tone?' Of several possible answers, I plumped for Oxford. And Sam asked, 'Do Oxford girls fuck, Tone?' We were a mixed bunch on that course. One chap had run a hand-made chocolate shop in Bond Street. One, an ex-metal basher in a small engineering works, was probably the best natural navigator in the class. Another was a massive ex-policeman in his mid-thirties. Early on, he explained to me that he'd been in the Grenadier Guards for some years before joining the police; he had volunteered for aircrew as it was the only way to go to war if you were a policeman; if I had any trouble from any of the rougher members of the course, I only had to let him know. In the event, I held my own but I appreciated the offer.

Our navigational exercises took us over the wild, lake-pitted country north of Montreal. Even from several thousand feet up, it was beautiful scenery. We also flew over the more populous parts of Quebec province, the small towns each dominated by a huge church. We did much night flying. This was when we practised the most esoteric aspect of our trade, astro-navigation. Navigation by the stars has long been one of man's accomplishments. It sounds romantic but is, in practice, a very demanding activity. It may be fine on a ship travelling at twenty or so knots an hour at the most, but aircraft, even in those days, went at over one hundred and twenty knots per hour. This meant that the use of the sextant, with which the navigator takes his 'shots' of the stars, had to be enormously speeded up to be effective. On top of that, our aircraft became unstable above a certain height; it wallowed and pivoted, rendering it almost impossible to take an accurate astro-shot.

Then the RAF came up with a solution: the Mark Nine Sextant. The user simply wound up its clockwork engine and, when the heavenly body was finally in his sights, he pressed a knob which caused the sextant to take a series of shots over a minute, with results far more accurate than any single shot. However, the navigator had a three-fold task. His main aim was to get a fix on his exact position. To this end, he maintained an air plot on his chart by drawing a neat line indicating the direction in true terms, corrected for deviation and variation, and speed against time; this plot showed him where he was in a world without wind. Once he'd got his fix, he could join it to the position on his plot and the difference would give him the direction and speed of the wind. A navigator's plot consisted of a continuous attempt to get the fixes, some of which would be by visual points, others by radio beams or, later on, by radar. Each fix would yield a 'wind'. With this wind he could plot forward and alter course to his target or his base. He could then give his pilot his ETA (estimated time of arrival).

The most difficult and demanding of fixes was the astro-fix. This was because his three position lines had to be made up of three separate star shots. When he plotted the three lines, it would give him a little triangle and in the middle of that triangle, theoretically, was his aircraft. The problem was that he had to identify each different star he was going to use and then, with the help of a book full of tables, work out his position line. Each position line took at least three minutes to calculate and draw. So at the end of the process, he had to transfer forward, allowing appropriate time lapses for each of the position lines so that they could represent a simultaneous three-position-line fix.

Training to use the sextant meant taking hundreds of star shots on the ground, standing in sub-zero temperatures outside our huts. We always knew the answer because we took these shots from one position; but we still had to work them out. We were trained in a kind of astrodome, an amazing machine which reproduced the night sky and which moved in exactly the same relationship to the earth as did the real sky. This advanced simulator included our navigation table which mirrored the movement of an aircraft through the sky. As it was a very sophisticated and valuable piece of machinery, it was operated on a twenty-four-hour, seven-days-a-week schedule so we sometimes found ourselves spending an hour in it at three in the morning or at two on a Saturday afternoon; it was just the luck of the draw.

The least demanding and most enjoyable navigation was low-level map-reading. It incapacitated my Birmingham friend because the thumping of the aircraft when flying at two hundred feet off the ground made him air-sick within ten seconds, leaving him prostrate until we landed an hour and a half later. That left the field clear for me. Anticipation was the key to successful low-level map-reading so I used to gear myself up in advance to spot all the key features as we went along.

Every three weeks we got forty-eight-hour passes. My godfather, Herbert House, who lived in Painswick, was married to a Canadian and part of her family lived in Montreal. Word was sent and a few days before a forty-eight-hour pass was due, I had a call from Elaine, the daughter of the house. The Markhams lived in Westmount, on Murray Hill, the English-speaking suburb above Montreal. Mrs Markham's only son had been in the Canadian navy, and had been lost at sea about a year previously. Her husband ran a substantial printing and publishing business. Elaine worked in the Met Office at Dorval, Montreal's international airport and then headquarters of RAF Transport Command. Mrs Markham was a kind, middle-aged family woman; she was a fervent monarchist, highly suspicious of Catholics, French speakers, politicians and anyone at all hailing from Toronto. Her house was immaculate and comfortable to a positively un-English extent: it was centrally heated, with crisp warm bed-linen; in the fridge there was always fresh grapefruit and orange-juice; the bacon was crunchy and brown in a way indigenous to Canada; the real coffee was unbelievably scrumptious.

Altogether, Mrs Markham looked after me like another son. I fell into the relationship of brother to Elaine.

The Markhams did everything for me and for several of my course mates. We wanted to ski? They would arrange it. Four of us, including the little Welsh corporal and Dixie from the other course, were sent off to the Mount Royal Hotel where we were handed some old skis of the type on which Amundsen and his Norwegian team had explored the Polar regions. Thus equipped, we set off for the Laurentians. Taff distinguished himself in the skiing lodge when, on being offered a Martini by a smooth Norwegian flight lieutenant, he replied: 'No thanks, I've had my tea already.'

As the course went on, trainees began to drop out. One moment, they would be striving with the rest of us and the next, they had given up, resignation written all over their features, and were off to be bomb-aimers. This was an attractive option – first, because most of them had been on the air gunnery and bombing course already; and, second, because by completing half of a navigator's course, they had already done more navigation than was taught on a bomb-aimer's course.

The aspect which most rankled with those who still clung precariously to the bottom half of the navigation course was that those who left for bomb-aiming were almost bound to get a commission; a privilege denied to those who stayed and just scraped through the navigator's course. This was because the commissions were granted to the top third of each graduating class in each discipline. The rest, if they had done reasonably well and behaved themselves, would be recommended for a 'commission in the field'. This meant that if you survived you might be commissioned from the squadron. At this stage in the war, commissions were handed out by the RAF strictly on the basis of competence; in retrospect, a very radical departure from normal service tradition.

At the end of this grinding course, exams faced us. Every exercise in the air formed part of the total on which we were assessed: each log was analysed; each area, criticized. However good we were in the air, we could still fail on theory. I scored sixty-two per cent, the pass mark was sixty per cent, so I was through by a whisker. As I contrived to pass meteorology, I wasn't disgraced. But I was headed for the rank of sergeant along with my brevet as a navigator. The best two were the panel-basher and the chocolate-maker; the first had a voice like tearing calico, the second a manner like a pantomime dame. But they both had neat nimble fingers and quick numerate brains; a combination which produced accurate fast-flowing logs and charts. And that was what the crew of an RAF Lancaster would need, never mind the accents.

I set up our farewell course dinner at a small hotel recommended by Mr Markham who printed the commemoration menu card with everybody's name and typically 'forgot' to send us a bill. The passing-out parade was organized by the tall thin-moustached pilot officer who, now that we were to pass out, was all good humour and smiles. We reflected this mood; here at last was the one parade for which we didn't mind falling in.

Mrs Markham travelled down to St John's for the ceremony. The moment came. A distinguished, but to us unknown, air vice-marshal pinned on our brevets one by one, the band playing throughout as we came up, stepped back, saluted and marched off. The names had come through for commissions and NCOs. Mrs Markham very kindly sewed on my sergeant's stripes for me. My envy of those who'd got commissions was mitigated by my success in getting through and passing out. Only I knew, given my lack of natural aptitude, what a struggle it had been; indeed I was very grateful to have achieved in Canada my objective of getting basic training as a member of aircrew. I remembered the old story: 'Was so and so a good pilot?' Answer: 'All pilots in the RAF are good.' So: was I a good navigator?

We had to report to Monkton in just under three weeks; meanwhile, the next step was leave. I now had several connections in Montreal, including a charming girl called Mary O'Toole whom I wanted to take dancing at the Mount Royale; and down in Toronto, there was Belinda. In those days Montreal was a fun city. With the start of transatlantic air crossings, it was cosmopolitan and almost seemed like the hub of the world. The time flashed by and all too soon I was back at boring Monkton. The weather was surprisingly warm for late May; we read about the excitement of D-Day in the local Monkton newspaper and felt very spare. Rumour suggested that we would have to wait weeks to get on a draft.

Eventually I discovered that there was a quicker, faster route out of Monkton. From time to time there were seats on transatlantic flights from Dorval to Prestwick in Scotland. There was a waiting list for these in the main orderly office of the administration block. My informant added that there were nearly forty on the list and only two or three seats available at infrequent intervals. Even though my chances were almost nil, I saw no harm in putting my name down.

So one hot afternoon in June, down to the orderly room I went. And, true enough, there was a list of nearly forty names, the last one having been added eight days before. I put my name down and left. Later that day, there was an announcement which, as luck would have it, absorbed the whole of the orderly office list. Next day as I lay in my bunk wondering what to do, a naval rating trainee marched through the hut shouting my name. I asked what he wanted and was told to report to the orderly office immediately. There I learnt that, in three days' time, next Saturday, there was an aircraft leaving Dorval and I had been allotted a seat; my name had been the only one left on the orderly office list after the forty above had been swept up in the draft. I was going with a certain Squadron Leader Jones whom I was to meet next day at noon at Monkton station. We were to travel to Montreal on the one o'clock express.

My only concern was that I had a $200 savings bond for which, like every other trainee, I had been practically blackmailed into subscribing by instalments. It had now come to hand in bearer form. So when I got my taxi next day, I rushed off to the bank and, with the taxi waiting, cashed my bond; then I ran out again, clasping my crip $200-worth of Canadian dollar bills – much to the amusement of the middle-aged lady teller. I met the squadron leader, surprisingly an air gunner, and off we went in the clanging train, dining in the stately restaurant car and sleeping in old-fashioned accommodation which doubled as day and night cars.

I was delighted to be back in Montreal, even for only twenty-four hours. The squadron leader and I shared a room in a very over-crowded Mount Royale. In the evening I took Mary out, and next day we went to Dorval for our transatlantic flight run by Imperial Airways, the predecessor of BOAC and British Airways.

We were packed into the fuselage of a Liberator in two rows of single seats. I was the only NCO on board and sat behind an elderly group captain. We set off at nine in the morning for Gander, the staging post and coastal command station on the coast of Newfoundland. The weather was perfect.

From the air, Newfoundland looked rather like the rugged land we had flown over north of Montreal on our navigation exercises. When we taxied to our parking place at Gander, we were met not only by a truck for the officers' mess but a jeep to take me to the sergeants' mess. Gander was busy. Once the aircraft had refuelled, my jeep promptly brought me back to the waiting aircraft. The captain was there; as it was hot, strangely hot for so far north, he had taken off his dark blue jacket but still looked neat and trim with his dark blue tie and his black Imperial Airways hat. 'At least, *you're* on time,' he greeted me from under his close-cropped steel-grey moustache. He was going round his aircraft, casting a practised eye over the flaps. At length, the rest of the passengers returned replete with lunch from the officers' mess. We climbed aboard the aircraft, spacious enough in those days but agonizingly cramped by today's standards. The engines started, we taxied round to the start of the runway and took off in a westwardly direction, soaring over the wild scrub that surrounded the base. Slowly we turned northwards and came back over the sea, picking up our Great Circle route. I had spent nearly a year in Canada; it had been a great experience.

11 Operational Training

The next port of call in my slow progress towards operational flying was Harrogate, my last holding unit before I went on operational training. It was felt that aircrew who had completed their training courses overseas needed flying experience in the theatre for which they were destined, in aircraft like those in their squadrons. So a series of AFUs (advanced flying units) had been set up to provide flying experience in the United Kingdom; the operational command to which aircrew were finally allotted provided the last link in the training in the form of operational training units. These were the units which had helped Bomber Command raise the crews for the one thousand aircraft which had bombed Cologne in 1942.

I reported to the holding unit at Harrogate; once a five-star hotel, it had been stripped of its former glory so that it could house thousands of airmen rather than hundreds of residents. Then I went on leave. It was early August and the English countryside was beautiful. I went by train to York and gave myself dinner at the Station Hotel. The hotel gardens had a well-kept appearance about them, surprising in wartime; even York station looked spick and span. But the inside of the trains had changed completely. The windows were filthy, the low-wattage bulbs few and far between, and the seats oozed horse-hair from torn covers. My train south had come from Edinburgh and by the time I got on there wasn't even a seat in the Pullman. Indeed what with all the kit-bags, rifles, tin helmets and gasmasks all over the place, there was hardly room to stand.

Next morning, I got to Oxford where my aunt had moved from Painswick. In those days, with domestic servants a newly extinct species, the women's colleges in Oxford had taken to recruiting middle-aged ladies too old for war work. My aunt, her circumstances further reduced by the cessation of rents from the south-east, had been introduced by a friend to the gentle team helping out at Lady Margaret Hall. As part of the arrangement, she had a very nice room where I found her comfortably set up.

That morning she told me that a close friend of my childhood had been killed in France, a few weeks after D-Day. The news had made a particularly deep impression on her because the young man concerned, Keith Douglas, had visited her only two weeks before D-Day, so his image had been very clearly in her mind when the news had come through.

Keith – we called him Billy – was some six years older than me. He and his mother had come to live with us, pre-Painswick, in a house in Sussex, a few miles outside Crowborough. We had shared the house for several years before we had moved on. But we had always kept in touch with the Douglases: I used to go and stay with them in Sussex and, from time to time, Billy and his mother used to come to us in Painswick. There had also been one or two holiday trips to France together. Billy Douglas was a very powerful character, physically strong and rather ruthless. When we played cowboys and Indians, I was always the Indian and he the cowboy and when he shot me clean between the eyes with his airgun, he made me explain to his grandmother that I'd scratched my forehead with a thorn.

We played long-drawn-out war games with model soldiers, incorporating train movements. We made a mountain railway through the rockery. We constructed a replica of Brooklands out of the drive on which we raced our Alfa Romeo models. Billy became a great modeller, particularly of sailing ships which he made entirely out of his own raw materials. From there he moved to lino cuts, drawing and painting. Soon, in his mid-teens, he was writing. In the end he became one of the outstanding poets of the Second World War. Even as a child, I knew that I was being exposed to raw talent of an exceptional kind. It wasn't a comfortable experience but it was certainly stimulating.

My aunt had not been surprised by Billy's death. She had always regarded him as somebody who courted danger. Indeed, his stories of his role in the Syrian campaign confirmed that he had as usual been taking every kind of risk. She had always felt that he was somehow doomed; somehow fated to find life difficult; destined to be in frequent awkward collision with events or people. She had always felt uncomfortable in his company. She had deplored the times when, in my compliant fashion, I had copied Billy's noisy way of eating soup and swallowing it from the front of the spoon instead of the side.

So there it was: poor Billy killed, we learned later, by a single shell splinter in the head. He and I had sat one Saturday morning in a field near Painswick painting in sepia the view before us. We were taught by a local artist, a Mr Kennedy, a veteran invalided out of the Royal Flying Corps in 1917. Compared with Billy's remarkable effort, my painting had seemed very dull. But I kept it all the same. I later found that the episode was enshrined in one of his poems in which he had perceived the essence of our crippled teacher in Kennedy's insistence that we paint in sepia, not colour.

Meanwhile my aunt and I walked in the Parks and had dinner at the Eastgate where I put up. It was nearly eighteen months since I had gone down but very little had changed. The colleges were still half empty. The same medical students continued their unending studies. Cameron Tudor was still in residence. Rudi Weisweiller, with whom I had fire-watched in the Union, had become president of the Union. My aunt's main intellectual excitement was the discovery of the novels of a Rumanian writer, Panait Istrati, which she gave me to read. Most were in French translation which I couldn't manage but there was one in English which I enjoyed.

Soon I was back in Harrogate waiting for a posting to an AFU. Harrogate was the least demanding of all my holding units because all the aircrew were technically qualified so there was almost no further instruction. I found diversion in the Harrogate Discussion Group which was lodged down a side street in a small shop. The front had been turned into a lecture room, complete with blackboard and about twenty-five uncomfortable school chairs. Behind the lecture room were the kitchen and a sitting area, where coffee and sandwiches were sometimes available for a few pence. Upstairs was shared territory; half discussion group, half living quarters for Alice West and her young Irish friend, June.

The discussion group was a lively affair, full of people in or attached to the RAF. As well as lectures, there were weekend outings: picnic expeditions, bus trips to beauty spots. Underneath the veneer of culture, there was a strong political commitment – naturally, to the left. The discussion group ran the gamut from social democrat to committed Communist and as usual in such circles it was the actively committed Communists who held most of the organizational posts. But not that of organizer because that was the role of Alice West who, unlike the rest of them, was there all the time.

Alice was a handsome, slightly gaunt woman of forty with prominent teeth which were inescapable because she laughed a lot, screwing up and almost shutting her eyes at the same time. She was thin, athletic and wore long brown corduroy skirts and brown leather jackets. She had been a student at the Slade but had got so worked up about the plight of the poor that halfway through her course she had left and gone to work for a mission in the East End of London. She was now devoted to painting and social work. At that time, the painting was being squeezed out by the social work and the burden of running the discussion group; this she had founded because there seemed to be so many unoccupied people hanging around Harrogate. Alice's two companions were her black labrador dog and June, an Irish girl who worked in some civil service department in Harrogate. Alice pretended to be very strict with the dog but when it failed to obey her commands she just collapsed into helpless laughter.

The Communist cadre had picked off the non-executive posts in the discussion group one by one so that its members – now installed as chairman, secretary, treasurer and librarian – dominated the discussions. They tore into speakers who clung to the social democrat line or were just old-fashioned Labour supporters. They wouldn't tolerate a Conservative speaking at all, and they clapped and cheered when one of their number or a Communist guest was speaking. This was all very stimulating and exciting. I had grown up with arguments generated by Suzanne and her fellow-travelling friends. I had been an early reader of Arthur Koestler's *Darkness at Noon*. I enjoyed nothing more than a brawling argument with the comrades. However, as a difficult case, I attracted a fair amount of odium. The secretary – a dark good-looking girl in her early twenties, married to the treasurer, a flight lieutenant in the Pay Corps – once made references in my absence to the desirability of getting rid of the public-school fascists polluting the place. That was me. The chairman, a pipe-smoking squadron leader from the equipment branch, although more understanding and altogether much nicer, also disapproved of my intransigent attitude.

On successive Saturday evenings, I was flattered to be the centre of several set-piece debates, upstairs in Alice's room. A particularly bright flying officer pilot, also a dedicated Marxist, had the main demolition task at these sessions. But armed with Koestler, Orwell and commonsense, I survived, at least according to my own lights. Alice didn't; the group she had founded had been hijacked and she was hardly the person to get it back; once on the left, unless you were far tougher than she was, it was almost impossible to fend off an assault from your friends and allies, the comrades. Still, as far as I was concerned, Alice West made Harrogate great fun.

To prevent people like me enjoying themselves too much, the authorities decided to send everybody on a series of outward-bound-type courses. As a result, I was included in a small group sent to Whitley Bay. We paraded on the sea front every day and filled out lungs with good sea air. Most days we changed into denim dungarees and skidded about the cliffs trying to climb them with ropes. We sprinted up and down the beach and ran out of breath. We got wet and very cold getting in and out of rubber dinghies in the sea just to acclimatize ourselves to ditching. We were fed in the old pier restaurant, now sadly bereft of all its old slot machines.

Back from Whitley Bay, I at last got my posting; not to an AFU but to a pre-AFU at Carlisle. As the pipeline of aircrew grew longer, the RAF was forced to invent new stages in the training process. A pre-AFU was virtually another holding camp but with training facilities attached. A certain Sergeant Brown and I went by train to Carlisle and installed ourselves. Next day, Saturday, we got a real posting effective the following Monday, to an AFU proper, at Halfpenny Green just outside Wolverhampton. This time, we were back on the ladder.

Halfpenny Green RAF Station had several distinctive features. First, it had a pub within the boundary. Second, its commanding officer, a group captain with fair hair and impressive bearing, was a martinet who screamed out orders and unpleasant observations wherever he happened to be on the station. It wasn't just a parade-ground phenomenon. In consequence the permanent staff, officers and NCOs alike, were very nervous. Brown and I were in ignorance of all this as we arrived at Wolverhampton station. We piled our kit into the waiting trucks and joined some thirty officers and NCOs, also recently arrived. The course was due to last until the end of September.

We were formed into small classes. Ours comprised

only twelve: six NCOs and six officers; two Canadians, four Australians, one New Zealander and the rest British; the senior ranking pupil was a Canadian flight lieutenant.

My troubles at Halfpenny Green began on my arrival. When our party got to the RAF station and was allotted its quarters, we went to a central point to collect our kit which had been brought on from the station. Brown and I had three kit-bags each: two for our worldly goods and a third for our flying kit. My third kit-bag wasn't in the pile. Time and again, I looked over the diminishing number of kit-bags. To no avail: it simply wasn't there. What could have happened to it? I'd put it on the truck along with everybody else's; I couldn't possibly have left it behind at Carlisle or Wolverhampton or on the train.

I thought it was bound to turn up; kit-bags were marked with name, rank and number, clearly applied by stencil. They weren't things which just disappeared. If the staff loading the truck at the station had left one behind, I was confident it would surface. Meanwhile, I would borrow somebody else's kit and report the incident.

This I did. Borrowing kit wasn't difficult as we didn't all fly at once. But the missing kit-bag still didn't turn up. Contrary to my expectations, the transport people said that they'd collected everything at the station. I began to worry: lost kit could only be replaced after a laborious procedure which involved being put on a charge for negligence. On some RAF stations such a charge was a formality. But not at Halfpenny Green with its overbearing group captain. Still, the permanent staff were very reassuring. The flight sergeant in charge of admin in the HQ block told me over a pint in the sergeants' mess that I just had to plead guilty, putting in a plea of mitigation saying I hadn't deliberately lost the kit, and all would be forgiven.

Meanwhile the course proceeded. Our small class was congenial. Despite being a mixture of officers and NCOs, we all went out to the pub together at least twice a week and had a good time; we also hit it off with our main instructor, a charming middle-aged flying officer navigator.

We gradually got used to flying around wartime England in our Oxfords. This was easy enough by day; but by night, when compared with the pellucid expanse of Canada, the British sky was almost opaque and usually congested with barrage balloons; it was also riddled with forbidden areas in which any stray aircraft was automatically shot at, and studded with operational airfields into whose circuits it was dangerous to wander, filled as they were with Lancasters or Halifaxes busily taking off, assembling or returning. We had to get to know this strange nocturnal landscape without becoming a nuisance. We did our best.

For this, I borrowed flying kit where I could. The end of the fourth week saw the completion of the procedures relating to the issue of a new set of kit, together with the setting of a date for hearing my charge. Then I happened to chat to an old flight sergeant who worked in the sergeants' mess stores. I told him my story as I was going to get my new kit from his section. I explained that, on advice, I was going to plead guilty and put in a plea of mitigation. 'You're a bloody fool if you do that,' was his reply. He finished his drink, wiped his mouth with the back of his hand, gave me a disdainful glance and left me feeling most uneasy. He clearly meant what he said. I thought of the mad group captain. Our instructor loathed him. So did most of the sane people on the station. But he had his supporters; these included quite a few NCOs on the permanent staff; they had to live with him and his regime, they were his creatures.

That evening I set about putting my case in order. It wasn't difficult to co-opt the support of Derek Brown, the sergeant who'd come with me from Carlisle. He would testify that I had put all three kit-bags on to the truck. As he was just another sergeant navigator trainee like myself, I approached the senior-ranking course pupil, Flight Lieutenant John Denning. He was a slight, neat man; quiet, but self-assured. When I explained my predicament, he said he was perfectly willing to say that he too had seen me at the station putting my three kit-bags on to the truck.

Next morning, I was on my charge. At half-past nine I arrived at the HQ block. I was the first of a number of cases. The flight sergeant who had given me the advice to plead guilty was there but the flight sergeant from the stores was nowhere to be seen. The routine went at a brisk pace that would have done credit to the Foreign Legion. In seconds, I was being marched in, bare-headed, in front of the ferocious commanding officer. Blue eyes glaring, he barked: 'Anything to say?' 'Yes sir,' I replied. 'I have two witnesses.' His eyebrows shot up and his long fingers drummed on the desk. 'Bring them in.'

The first to enter was Sergeant Brown. He saluted and stood rigidly to attention. The icy blue eyes turned on him and the fingers kept drumming. 'Well?' invited the commanding officer, and Sergeant Brown unflinchingly delivered his short and, from my point of view, satisfactory version of events. Once again silence except for drumming. 'Very well,' said the group captain, dismissing Brown. He made a gesture as though clearing his desk, an overture to pronouncing sentence.

At that point, I said, 'I have a second witness, sir.' This was a diabolical liberty, speaking up when not being spoken to during formal proceedings, but I was, after all, a sergeant. The group captain glared. Any second, and he was going to lose his temper. 'A second witness?' He had forgotten that I had said 'witnesses', plural. He looked hard at the flight sergeant admin conducting proceedings who said: 'I'll see, sir.' He saluted and stamped out of the room. A second or two later he reappeared with the Canadian flight lieutenant. For the first time, I realized that this was a knock-out blow. My witness out-ranked the NCOs on whom the prosecution relied. By producing the flight lieutenant, as long as he said the right thing, I would win hands down.

I needn't have worried about my witness's performance. He saluted, and the group captain said, 'Good morning, Denning.' The CO sounded almost civilized, although his greeting had come through gritted teeth. 'Good morning, sir,' replied the flight lieutenant; he then went on to give his evidence which, word for word, was the same as Sergeant Brown's. Silence. Drumming. 'Thank you,' said the group captain in a voice empty of gratitude. The flight lieutenant saluted and left. The group captain remained mute, drumming and breathing heavily. He glared and finally barked: 'Admonished – and if you had been guilty, Sergeant, I would not have had the slightest hesitation in giving you a severe reprimand.' In a trice, I was marched out and it was all over.

Outside, the flight sergeant admin and his cronies were crestfallen. The flight sergeant said to me, 'I'd no idea that you were going to have a commissioned officer witness.' He was expecting to see me severely admonished and sent on my way; in fact, I would probably have survived to stay on the course, but with that penalty on my record, I would never have got a commission. It might also have prevented me from getting a desirable posting. No Group, least of all Two Group, wanted aircrew with a past. Technically, the group captain had found me guilty but an admonishment was the lightest possible sentence and didn't go on the record. It was as near as the group captain ever got to a 'not guilty' verdict, a currency in which he never dealt.

Back at the class, our flying officer instructor jumped with joy. He whipped out his copy of King's Regulations and Air Council Instructions and told me how I could put in for a 'redress of grievance'. In his view, I was plainly 'not guilty' and an admonishment was wholly wrong. While he was right, I would have been mad to pursue the matter. The procedure for redressing grievances involved putting up the case to Two Group and the air vice-marshal. The mind boggled. Nonetheless I was a folk hero; a folk hero who kept well out of the group captain's way until the end of the course.

This we celebrated in mid-September with a massive thrash at the local pub. I really liked the class. Everyone in it had helped me through my difficulties, lending me flying kit, rejoicing in my success. By chance, we coincided with a harvest festival celebration. All the local produce had been brought to the pub to be auctioned off, half for charity. We had a wonderful time; what with the conviviality and unlimited supplies of the locally brewed beer, I slightly overreached myself. This resulted in my making the highest bids in the auction. Nothing held me back. I snapped up the biggest local wartime turnip grown. I gathered in the prize brace of onions, each the size of a baseball. To my aggressive bidding fell the top bunch of carrots and several of the finest jars of bottled fruit. My memory of the evening fades into a hazy blur of horticultural prizes.

Next morning, when we had to get the train to London, I woke up with a terrible head and several jars of bottled fruit – one under the pillow, another in the small of my back and two more down by my knees. As I awoke, I couldn't imagine how I had come by all this hot-house paraphernalia.

Our instructors waved us off as the truck took us through the main gate and on our way to Wolverhampton station. I'd taken great care to ensure that I had all three kit-bags with me. Sergeant Brown and I had our posting. In the last week in September, we were to report to RAF Swanton-Morley, part of Two Group, this station being the Group's headquarters and their OTU (Operational Training Unit). We'd been told we were very lucky as that part of Two Group flew Mosquitoes. As we only had a day or two before we had to report to Swanton-Morley, we only had a weekend's leave in London. Once again, there was not a seat to be had in the train. The six of us going to London tried to take over a reserved carriage but it was reserved for some mentally handicapped children. When they came in – all bobbing heads, laughter and disconcerting smiles – we retreated back to the corridor.

12 A Posting to Two Group

I spent two nights in London at the Overseas League which I'd joined mainly because of its marvellously cheap accommodation. I took Jane, the girl from the Post-War Society debate, out for dinner. We went to the ballet, then established at the New Theatre, and saw *Les Patineurs* and other short ballets. The liaison never recaptured its first Devonian rapture but she was charming and sympathetic all the same. On my second day, while lunching with her at an Italian place near the Middlesex Hospital where she worked as a physiotherapist, a doctor came and introduced himself. I could see he was going to propose to and marry her as she smiled at him in the way that girls do, once they've made their choice. I wouldn't have done at all because I was either going to snuff it in aircrew or survive, go back to Oxford and probably wait ten years before marrying.

I met up with the other five bound for Swanton-Morley at Liverpool Street Station. We put all our kit on to a porter's truck and then transferred it to the King's Lynn train. Swanton-Morley was in the depths of Norfolk; our instructions were to change at King's Lynn and take the train to Dereham. I lead the group into the local Trust House when we reached King's Lynn and we had an excellent lunch. We then caught the little local train to Dereham where we were met by the truck to take us to Swanton-Morley.

For us six new arrivals it was an important day: the end of our training period, but with another training session to go. The difference was that the Swanton-Morley course was run by Two Group, the operational organization in which we would go to war. Two Group was famous throughout the RAF. It had carried out many of the war's most daring daylight raids. It had flown Blenheims during the first year or so. Then it had switched to Beaufighters and latterly, starting in 1943, to *the* aircraft of the war, the highly innovative Mosquito.

The Mosquito was a cleanly, almost beautifully, designed fighter-bomber, powered by two Rolls-Royce Merlin engines. Its unique feature was its wooden skin. During the course of the war, fabric-clad aircraft had given way to metal-skinned aircraft – except for the Mosquito; while its main plane and fuselage structure were of metal, its skin was like plywood except with many more layers of separate ply stuck together with glue invented by a genius chemist, a recent *emigré* from Nazi Germany. The wooden construction meant that the aircraft could be manufactured by a completely different section of industry from that hitherto engaged in aircraft production: the Mosquito called on makers of cabinets, pianos and coffins.

By the time we got to Swanton-Morley, the Mosquito had become a legend. It had proliferated into a number of types, each with its specific use. There were photo-reconnaissance Mosquitoes, unarmed aircraft which cruised over Germany at heights then regarded as staggering. There were Mosquitoes in service with the US Army Air Force. Coastal Command had them for shipping strikes. Above all, Bomber Command had adopted the Mosquito. Air Vice-Marshal Bennett's Pathfinder Group used them for marking targets, conducting raids and, suitably adapted, as bomb-carrying aircraft in their own right. Gradually, the lifting ability of the twin Merlins was upgraded so that by 1944 Bomber Command Mosquitoes were carrying huge bombs to Berlin. It is now clear that Bomber Command would have taken a completely different turn if the Air Ministry had based itself entirely on unarmed aircraft such as Mosquitoes, swift enough to evade the German night fighters. As it was, Bomber Command opted for the four-engined bomber with its turrets and air gunners – and its vulnerability.

Two Group's aircraft were the Mosquito Six. These had flat windscreens, not the V-shaped windscreens of Bomber Command aircraft. They were armed with four .303 Browning machine guns in the upper part of the nose-cone and, more important, four thirty-millimetre cannon firing from the forepart of the aircraft's belly. To enable these to fire an explosive nine-inch projectile at a mind-spinning speed, the aircraft was fitted with an ingenious and extensive ammunition feed system. The cockpit layout had the pilot seated on the port side some six inches ahead of the navigator to starboard. The instrument panel stretched from one side of the aircraft to the other. The navigator's key instrument – a form of navigational radar named 'Gee' – was situated behind the pilot's seat so that, by turning round to the left, the navigator could operate the system and read the scope. The entrance door was a small panel on the starboard side level with the navigator's knees. The door was fitted with an extendable aluminium ladder which was let down to the ground some five or six feet below when the door was opened.

Swanton-Morley was not just the Two Group OTU. It was the HQ station of the Group and as such administered the wings and the squadrons; its airfield had also provided the springboard for various key operations. At the time, Two Group had become part of the Second Tactical Air Force, formed in 1943 as air support for the invasion forces about to be launched against Europe. Second TAF, as it was known, was meant to be mobile; in theory everything had to be capable of being picked up overnight, put on trucks and trundled off the next morning to a new site. The fighter wings of Second TAF had already left for the Continent following the successful D-Day landings and were now stationed in northern France. Following the outbreak from the beaches which (it was now September) had developed into an invasion of Germany, the heavier components of Second TAF were expected to follow soon, including Two Group's Mosquito wings. In the meantime, they flew from airfields such as Swanton-Morley and Thorny Island on the south coast. Most of Two Group's flying, for the Mosquito anyway, took the form of 'night interdiction': in other words bombing and strafing the enemy's communications by night. Some of the Two Group squadrons also interfered with German night-flying. Mosquitoes of these squadrons would join the circuit of Luftwaffe airfields and shoot German aircraft down as they came into land or just as they took off.

In addition to these night expeditions, there were occasional daylight operations. These had included spectacular pinpoint attacks on specific buildings. One of the most dramatic took place that September. The Maquis had informed the British that a large number of French Resistance fighters in a prison outside Amiens were about to be put to death. So a daylight raid was set up and the Mosquitoes came in at a very low altitude and breached the prison walls with five-hundred-pound bombs. Although some were killed in the raid, 'Operation Jericho' as it became known, enabled numerous Resistance fighters to escape. The leader of the Mosquitoes, Group Captain Pickard, and his navigator were the only aircrew casualty: they were shot down by a marauding German fighter. Subsequent raids, several from Swanton-Morley, included those on the two Gestapo headquarters in Denmark, at Aarhus and in Copenhagen.

The course started with our being formed into crews of pilot and navigator. We were all mixed up and left to it; the pilots proposed, the navigators accepted. The two non-commissioned pilots on the course were warrant officers, each with over one thousand five hundred flying hours notched up in Canada while training to be instructors. We navigators were very lucky: straight from training schools, we were all paired off with seasoned pilots who had done one or two tours of operations already or, like the two NCOs, had spent two or three years flying as instructors. This came about because the Air Ministry's statistical estimate, worked out a year or two previously, had allowed for too many pilot casualties. As a result, by 1944 there were far more pilots than navigators – who were in relatively short supply.

I was picked by one of the two non-commissioned warrant officer pilots, Reg Everson. As we were junior, all the navigators were non-commissioned apart from a flying officer and a flight lieutenant. The commissioned pilots varied from flying officer to squadron leader, several of them decorated at least once.

Pre-war, Reg had been in the railway police on the Southern Railway. He had graduated from nabbing non-farepayers to office-based detective work. He had volunteered for the RAF early in the war, gone across to Canada and thence to America to train as a pilot before the US had come into the war. He had been on the 'Arnold' scheme, and had much to say about 'Eat a square meal, Mister.' However, he had passed out successfully and gone to Canada as an instructor. I imagine he had been excellent in this role as he was patient, quiet and easy-going and he was a skilled, experienced pilot. Flying a Mosquito wasn't everybody's cup of tea. True, some pilots with only a few hundred hours flying time turned out to be extremely adept with Mosquitoes but they were the RAF category of 'above average'. Although it flew beautifully once in the air, the Mosquito was an unforgiving aircraft in less than competent hands. For the time, it was very high-powered and its two Merlin engines, mounted in its exceptionally light air frame, were separated by a fuselage no wider than the two crew members. In a cross wind, the aircraft would be tricky on take off.

In the early days at Swanton-Morley, we saw several pilots who developed swings on take off that grew worse and worse, necessitating a sudden throttling back and a taxiing round to start all over again. Indeed, some months later, Reg once misjudged a gusty cross wind;

after uncharacteristically making three attempts to take off, we had a rest and tried again an hour later.

I made friends with the navigator who crewed up with Reg's friend, the other warrant officer, and our two crews became a foursome, socially, for the rest of the course. His name was Derek and, like certain members of the Harrogate Discussion Group, he was a card-carrying Communist. He was an East End Jew, highly intelligent and most amusing. If we talked too much politics, our two pilots notionally knocked our heads together and we all had another round and reverted to darts.

Swanton-Morley was a happy and agreeable station. True, we were still training, but training conducted by an operational group was quite different, with all our instructors 'resting' between operational tours. Swanton-Morley was a pre-war RAF station and so, although we were billeted in Nissen huts because of its Topsy-like growth, the administrative buildings and the messes were permanent pre-war buildings in the old RAF style. The sergeants' mess was as large as the officers' mess: its ante-room was spacious; its bar, long and commodious. The food was first class, cooked and served by beaming, overweight WRAFs. There were regular ENSA concerts, including *Murder at the Red Barn,* complete with musical troop and dancing girls. After the show, the cast and all concerned invariably repaired to the sergeants' rather than the officers' mess. They knew where the fun was.

Our instruction mainly consisted of daylight map-reading exercises. We were forever practising the next raid on some Gestapo headquarters. Not for the first time was the preparation entirely out of kilter with what was to follow; during the five months Reg and I were on the squadron, we were only on one daylight raid; all the rest was night flying. But at Swanton-Morely we only did a handful of night-flying exercises and they were rarely appropriate for what was to come. All the same, daylight flying had its moments. During the Second World War, more pilots were court-martialled for unauthorized low flying than for any other misdemeanour. But here we were, with official blessing, flying around at one hundred feet. We were given targets like Didcot railway station and Blenheim Palace. Flying up the Great Western Railway line from Swindon and down the main London-bound platform in our Mosquito was a most agreeable experience. So too was practically flying into the french windows of Blenheim Palace, just clearing the building to skid across the roof. It was hugely satisfying to know that no one, but no one, could get us into trouble for dangerous flying.

Inevitably, some people flew into trouble. One crew managed to slice through the power lines connecting King's Lynn to the main grid. They returned to Swanton-Morley with a long piece of heavy electrical cable wrapped around the starboard engine and propeller. They were lucky to survive; their safe return said as much for the resistance of the aircraft as for the pilot's flying ability. Low flying entailed constant vigilance on the part of the pilot. As well as high-tension wires, there were factory chimneys, tall buildings, large looming trees and the eddies and gusts of turbulent air at low altitudes. It was also very tiring as the aircraft was continuously buffeted; as though in a giant sugar sifter, we were shaken up and down one second and side to side the next. After three hours flying at one hundred feet or so, to come up to one or two thousand feet was like entering a world of tranquillity where all was still.

Low flying also demanded much of the navigator. The painstaking, 'dead reckoning' navigation learned in Canada was farcically inappropriate: no one could possibly have maintained a plot whilst sitting in a Mosquito on a low-flying mission. The only navigation possible was simple map-reading. This required careful preparation with the expected course plotted on the map, together with notes of the expected time lapses between the start of the flight and key points on the route. With the aircraft doing two hundred knots, the navigator – with only a one- to two-mile vision, forwards and to the sides – could easily lose track unless he kept in constant touch with the position. A moment's absent-mindedness meant trouble. Total concentration was particularly vital when approaching a target if the procedure of preparing for the bomb run, opening the bomb doors and so forth, was to happen on time. And so we went on, roaring up and down England, prompting farmers to write letters of complaint but getting heartening waves from the workers in their fields.

We had only one major mishap at Swanton-Morley. The station was some twenty to thirty miles north of the Thetford battle area now used by the army for their increasingly realistic manoeuvres. By the time we were on our course, these exercises had reached a point where everyone used live .303 rounds and the aircraft dropped eleven-and-a-half-pound practice bombs to encourage them to keep their heads down, and strafed the troops with four .303 Brownings. Near the end of the course, we were involved in a full-scale exercise which required fourteen aircraft in consecutive pairs to strafe the battle area.

Being the junior crew on our course, we were paired with the senior crew, a squadron leader pilot and the flight lieutenant navigator with a DFC; this had been awarded at the end of his last tour on Spitfires flying out of Malta. We were on first at two o'clock in the afternoon. We flew down to the battle area in minutes. Our leading crew identified the 'Red Force' we were due to attack. We circled the area and began to go in; both flying very low towards the tanks manoeuvring on the ground. It was a clear day with excellent visibility, calm conditions and only moderate buffeting. There was one aircraft above us circling at about five thousand feet, an Oxford carrying the umpires regulating the exercise. As our number one, with the squadron leader and flight lieutenant, passed over the tanks, we assumed it had let fire with its four .303 machine guns; the aircraft then turned, banking steeply to starboard. The manoeuvre was wrong only because there simply wasn't enough height for it. The starboard wing tip touched the ground just behind one of the tanks and the aircraft began to cartwheel. While flying at two hundred knots, it had not seemed to us to be moving because our aircraft was travelling at the same speed. But once it touched the ground, the impact slowed it down and it careered towards us because we were still flying forwards at our original speed. In a second, we were passing the aircraft to port as it completed its cartwheel and began to disintegrate. We seemed to be flying through the debris, though in fact we missed it. Reg banked our aircraft, and we turned to starboard at about five hundred feet to see what happened. The tanks had come to a halt. There were men jumping out of them, there was some very ugly wreckage where the Mosquito should have been. We called up the tower at Swanton-Morley. Reg told them in matter-of-fact RAF language what had happened. We were recalled and the exercise suspended, although it started again forty-five minutes later. We realized before we landed that the crew must have 'bought it': this was confirmed when we got down.

Later that day, around half-past five when the exercise was over, Reg and I were called in to see the wing commander flying, the man in charge of flying on all RAF stations; he was a regular, a former Halton apprentice. It only took us two minutes to run through what had happened. 'Well,' he said, 'there's no mystery. It was a case of bad flying.' He smiled at us resignedly. 'Don't let it put you off.' We saluted. The interview was over. As we left, he called to me: 'Sergeant! You've only got your chevrons on one side.' It was true; for some reason it was an affectation of NCO aircrew to put their sergeant's stripes only on one side of their battle dress, the right-hand side. Another foible was wearing aircrew whistles hanging from our battledress lapels. These whistles were for advertising our presence if lost at sea in a dinghy having bailed out at night. But the wing commander flying had been at Halton in far off prewar days with strict discipline and correct dress. 'Put them on the other side as well one day, Sergeant.' The wing commander smiled. Two years later, he was killed in a flying accident at RAF Gutersloh in western Germany. His name was Paddy Maile. That evening we had a party with our army friends from the exercise, Pongoes we had called them, and we drank to the victims of the accident.

Swanton-Morley was a step nearer the war. There were numerous US bases in East Anglia with swarms of Liberators and Flying Fortresses coming and going on operations over Germany. Contact was unavoidable as the circuits of the various air bases were very close. From time to time, we socialized with the Americans who gave massive parties on their bases complete with big bands and lashings of food and drink. There were girls too, but they didn't have eyes for the likes of us.

As our course finished in the third week of December, I once again had Christmas on leave. Our postings came through a week before we left. Once again, Reg and I were in Paddy Maile's office. I still hadn't sewn on the stripes, but he didn't seem to notice this time.

'We're sending you to a Polish squadron,' he said. 'In France. You'll be joining them immediately after your leave on 28 December. You'll report back here the day before and fly out that morning. You'll like the Poles. Good luck.' He shook hands with us and we saluted.

What a rum deal, we thought. The Poles? We knew of course that there were numerous Polish squadrons in the RAF. One of the escorting squadrons in the Mosquito strike against the Gestapo headquarters in Copenhagen had been Polish, but we had no idea that there was a policy of filling up Polish squadrons with non-Poles. We certainly hadn't any particular qualifications for our new roles. I was no linguist, and Reg knew not a word of any foreign tongue. One consolation was that the other non-commissioned crew were going with us. 'Sergeant Ruddetsky' didn't sound bad.

My aunt had found a bolthole from which to take the occasional rest from her task at LMH, in a guest house in Blewbury, a small village near Didcot. I joined her there for Christmas. Festive cheer was limited but the place had a good atmosphere. In those days, there was no traffic except for the odd army lorry and so the villages of England were wonderfully peaceful. Meanwhile the news was disconcerting. The Germans had launched a full-scale attack on the Western front, the Ardennes offensive. To the weary British, it seemed that the war would never be over. There had been moments during 1944 when it had seemed as if the end for the Germans was at hand. The July plot to kill Hitler had looked promising; then there had been the phenomenal break-out from Normandy with our armies racing towards Germany on their various routes. But this had all dried up and instead of our delivering a quick knockout blow, the enemy had given us a nasty knock at Arnhem. Now he was up to the same tricks again. It wasn't all doom and despondency in Blewbury but optimism was strained. Furthermore, the weather had turned extremely cold.

I met Reg at Liverpool Street Station once again, and we returned to Swanton-Morley the day after Boxing Day. The next day, together with the other NCO crew, we flew in the Oxford across the Channel and over the bleak snow-clad industrial landscape of northern France to Cambrai, a relatively large air base holding the three squadrons of Mosquitoes which comprised 138 Wing, each situated separately several miles apart round the air base. At the side and on the main Cambrai–Douai road lay the administrative HQ of 138 Wing. Perimeter roads ran round the whole complex. Nearby, there were small French villages built of red brick. Each squadron had its 'nest', housing aircrew and administrative staff together with the briefing rooms. The 305 (Polish) Squadron nest was several hundred yards down the perimeter road from the main Cambrai–Douai road and about a half a mile from the nearest village which by coincidence had a number of Polish inhabitants. They had been imported from Poland during the First World War to help fill gaps in manpower in the local coalmines.

13 305 (Polish) Squadron

We were met by a fair-haired flight lieutenant wearing the ribbons of a DFC, a brightly coloured enamel Polish decoration and a Polish squadron badge. He and his navigator had just finished a tour and he was waiting for a posting. He handed us over to a Polish flight sergeant who showed us to our quarters.

The squadron's nest was a bungalow made up of several large rooms, passages, showers and ablutions and administrative offices. The officer aircrew were on one side while the NCOs were on the other, camped out in two rooms. All aircrew in Second TAF, once posted abroad, were equipped with a camping outfit complete with canvas bed. We were the last to use the 1944 version of the famous Irvine jacket, the wool-lined leather flying coat, first worn by aircrew at the start of the war. As there were nearly fifty aircrew in the squadron, half commissioned and half non-commissioned, our two rooms each held about a dozen; one room mainly Polish, the other mainly non-Polish.

Amongst the commissioned ranks, we had a motley bunch: a Canadian crew, an American crew who preferred to stay in the RAF, and two Norwegian crews. Reg and I were in the mainly Polish room. These Poles had been campaigning for a long time, some since 1939, while others had escaped from their mother country later on, reaching the RAF through the Middle East. They each had a tale to tell about their adventures. And most of them had strange ways. For instance, several of the pilots wore hair nets at night, a habit I learned not to laugh at. For these men were battle-hardened veterans, excellent pilots and aircrew. As far as the RAF was concerned, they were welcome to go to war in top hats and tails.

The only heating in the nest came from smoke-belching paraffin stoves. The Poles used these to heat billycans of red wine. As this wine had been specially bottled by the French for the German forces, it was distinctly non-vintage; still, it was tolerable when used to wash down giant helpings of rollmop herrings the squadron imported from England. While the ground crew and the administrative staff of 305 were entirely Polish, the aircrew Poles were becoming harder and harder to replace; hence our presence as stop gaps or honorary Poles.

There was some tension when we arrived. Indeed, most of the Poles were packed and ready to move. If you had fought a war for six years against a foe who frequently won the battles, you didn't have to be defeatist to look lively when danger loomed: you wanted to hang on to your kit and live to fight another day. So they were all set to move back from a 'bomb line' which only divided us from the Germans by forty-five minutes flying from Cambrai.

On our second night there, the squadron was very active. Some aircrew managed to fly three operations that night, virtually shuttling to and fro. But on the third day, it snowed continuously. After a day of inactivity, higher authority issued each of us with brooms and out we went on to the runway, muffled up in Irvine jackets, flying boots, scarves and gloves. As we desperately tried to clear the runway, the Walrus's lines from *Alice* ran through our heads: 'If seven maids with seven mops swept it for half a year . . .' But on we went, sweeping away in heavily falling snow. Meanwhile the Battle of the Bulge raged with our side tragically short of air cover.

Rumour had it that German parachutists, dressed not as nuns but as GIs, had been dropped in the area. For use on operations, aircrew had already been issued with huge service revolvers better suited to John Wayne; we were now ordered to wear these fearsome firearms whenever we moved around the station just in case we ran into an SS man masquerading as a GI. Inevitably some bright spark over-indulged in the mess and started shooting at the little red lights on top of the hangars. On the morning of 1 January, the news came through of a German attack on Melsbroeck. The story went that – with everybody hungover after New Year's Eve – the first wave of attacking German aircraft was given a 'green' to land. Instead of accepting the invitatin, they pulverized nearly one hundred of our aircraft. But the Luftwaffe lost even more; and unlike ours, their losses were not made up inside twenty-four hours with replacements flown out from home.

I had immediately decided that comfort was my top priority in the nest. Our camp beds had seemingly been designed for pre-war Indian Army colonels who had bearers to assemble, maintain and dismantle their sleeping arrangements. None of the aircrew, Polish or British, were capable of successfully assembling these intricate pieces of field furniture and our nights were usually interrupted by the beds falling to pieces. So I started looking for the components of a proper bed amongst the towering heaps of old rubbish in the area. I soon found an iron bed, not rich in brass finery, but a sturdy single bed, complete in three none-too-rusty pieces. I cleaned them up and carried them back to the nest, one by one. By late afternoon, they were in my corner position and, after about half an hour's panting effort, fully assembled. Once piled high with palliasses the result was a triumph, especially for someone like me who, like Corporal Nym, put a high premium on a proper bed when campaigning. My achievement attracted surprisingly little comment: two or three British aircrew thought I was mad, but the Poles just carried on heating up the Wehrmacht vino and consuming the rollmop herrings.

The snow abated, the runway cleared and flying

started again. Reg and I were soon airborne for the first time on a night-flying test. Every time an aircraft flew at night, it had to be tested beforehand by day. Cambrai had excellent facilities: it had a long concrete runway and was then the only Continental airfield to boast FIDO (Fog Intense Dispersal Operation). This device consisted of a piped flow of inflammable fuel either side of the runway which was laid beneath the surface of the ground under a grid so that, when the match was lit, a six-foot-high wall of flame burned with a tremendous roar down each side of the runway, generating heat intense enough to lift the fog several hundred feet into the air. But it was a fearsome thing to land on.

Later on, much to the annoyance of aircrew, Cambrai became one of the few airfields to be equipped with the new radar device for talking aircraft down. Returning from an operation over Germany, crews often found themselves flying on the instructions of radar operators in dire need of practice. Unsurprisingly aircrew chose to ignore the instructions and kept a weather eye out for themselves.

Reg and I were allowed one familiarization flight before we went on the battle order. This meant taking off from Cambrai and flying a triangular course at night over northern France just to demonstrate that we could function as a crew in the simplest terms. We navigated this successfully and were deemed fit to fly our first operational sortie a couple of nights later.

The task which Two Group, as part of Second TAF, had at the time was 'night interdiction'. This meant that aircraft from Two Group had to patrol the area behind the German lines throughout the hours of darkness. Virtually the whole of western Germany was carved up into areas of responsibility first by group, then by wing and finally by squadron. The squadron then fed an aircraft into its area of responsibility every half-hour or hour, depending on how far into Germany the patrol had to go and the flying time involved. As one aircraft came out after its patrol, another would enter. Thus the first aircraft would take off from Cambrai at say nine o'clock in the evening and the last aircraft would land back at six in the morning. While in the area, each aircraft was meant to look for any signs of movement, of road or rail transport or indeed anything else of interest, and bomb or strafe it accordingly. The operational height was one thousand five hundred feet. Higher than that, and the aircraft armaments ceased to be effective; lower, and there was danger of flying into the ground.

To start with, there were natural dangers in the form of weather and terrain. Even in central Germany there are some relatively hilly regions and there was a real risk of flying into the ground. To these dangers the Germans added their defences, mainly flak. Unnatural dangers took two forms: first the large fixed flak-barrages integrated with barrage balloons and search-lights surrounding built-up industrial areas such as the Ruhr; then the extremely accurate flak on pinpoint targets such as trains and airfields.

Once the immediate danger of the Ardennes offensive was over, the squadron's operational area moved into western Germany proper. This meant that to get to its patrol area, each crew somehow had to circumnavigate the Ruhr defences which lay like a wall across the path of any aircraft flying due east from the Rhine. Nightly pre-flight briefings kept us up to date on the shape of this barrage and its particular defences. These briefings included meteorological 'gen', news on flak and battlefield defences, details of the night's particular objectives and the armament and bomb configuration to be used, together with news and information from the army liaison officer. It was a formal performance, though not as elaborate as a major Bomber Command briefing.

Our navigation was based almost entirely on a radar device: Gee. Given the state of the German air defences, not knowing our whereabouts could have proved extremely expensive in terms of casualties. By the time we were using it, Gee had been in squadron service for almost two years. It was a system best described by analogy. Imagine a boy with three stones in his pocket standing by a placid lake. He throws one stone into the lake, twenty-five feet directly in front of him. The ripples flow out in perfect concentric circles. A second or two later, he throws another stone twenty feet out but to an angle ninety degrees to the left, more ripples, more concentric circles. A second or so later, he does the same thing with the third stone at an angle of ninety degrees to the right: again ripples, again concentric circles. By now, the pattern in the water is very complex. There are three sets of concentric ripples flowing outwards from the three points at which the stones fell into the water and these three patterns are cutting across one another. This series of patterns was created in the form of radar pulses by the Gee transmitters. The master station, the first stone, transmitted its first pulse in exactly the same manner as the ripples from the first stone. When the ripples reached where the second stone was dropped, which in real life was called the second slave station, it triggered a set of radar pulses and similarly when it reached the third station, another slave station, it triggered a third set of pulses. So in the air, instead of on the surface of the water, there were these three concentric circles of pulses going through the ether. The function of the Gee receiver in an aircraft was to measure the time difference between the receipt of the three signals. The time differential between the three signals was determined according to the position of the aircraft or receiving set relative to the three stations. If, for instance, the aircraft was almost on top of one of the slave stations, it would receive the signal from that station earlier in the cycle than if it was right over on the other side of the chart, a hundred miles or so away. Although infinitesimal, the time differences were perfectly sufficient for accurate measurement by the system. In summary, Gee was typical of the inventions that poured out of brilliant scientific brains during the course of the war.

Those of us who used the system were issued with maps overprinted with lines cutting across each other in a roughly parabolic shape. This meant that when we flew near the source of the signals, the lines crossed roughly at right angles but, when received from more distant stations, they cut very obtuse, very inconvenient angles, only fifteen to twenty degrees in difference. These lines were all numbered. In planning our trips, we would make up our itinerary along various Gee lines, switching from one to the other. In the aircraft, the receiving transmitter consisted of lots of knobs and a green cathode-ray tube about eight inches across. On the tube the operator got two scales corresponding to the two different colours of line on his chart. The set had two modes. One was fixed complete with a scale for measuring the signals. The other, which was the operational mode, showed the actual signals themselves. The operator fairly soon got used to the whole complicated procedure; fortunately it was a knack I rapidly acquired. Given that I had passed out near the bottom of my class at St John's, this was surprising; the demands made on the navigator by Coastal or Bomber Command – such as proper organization of dead-reckoning charts, sextants and so on – would, I'm sure, have been too much for me, but the Gee device in the little confined cabin of the Mosquito somehow suited me.

However it had two snags. First, the stations had only a restricted range. Once we'd got far away from the transmitting station, the lines went from parabolic to near-parallel. Second, the Germans had all the frequencies; since they also knew how the Gee worked, they could send out decoy signals which were sometimes all too convincing. To increase the confusion, they also filled the screen with 'grass'; masses of tiny hairy little lines that obscured the signals.

After a while, someone really used to the Gee could virtually fly the aircraft on his own. True, the pilot was still the driver, but the navigator, in setting up his co-ordinates, would direct the aircraft, ordering the pilot to turn, say, thirty degrees to starboard or fifty degrees to port, thus moving from one pre-selected Gee co-ordinate to another. Having reached the desired co-ordinate, he then set up the numbers for the next one and watched as the signals gradually converged on his pre-arranged point, always giving the pilot some ten seconds for the next turn. In this way the navigator, once past the bomb line, could zig-zag through the obstacles which, thanks to advance warning from Intelligence, he'd marked on his map in various colours: red for the flak areas, black for the balloons and so on. It was like a bending race at a gymkhana or going down a twisting path through a series of gates. Fortunately, the first and the last legs of the journey through these infested areas were relatively near the Gee transmitting stations, which moved forward with the Front Line. Luckily, defences were much thinner in areas far from the station, where the lines yielded a far less effective grid system.

14 On the Battle Order

Two days later, we were on the battle order – one of the eighteen aircraft fielded by the squadron on an operational night leaving up to six crews behind. We had to patrol an area just inside Germany, just the other side of the Ruhr. A piece of cake. Inevitably, we were both all fingers and thumbs. We paid great attention to the briefing. In the chair was the wing commander, a chubby, florid man in his late forties, which in our eyes made him an octogenarian. He had been flying since the First World War and was said to hold the record for a flight from Warsaw to Tokyo. It was he who took us through our orders for the night: where the squadron was to patrol; over what period; when the first aircraft would enter the patrol zone and when the last would leave. Then followed the Met report which, unless there was an absolutely filthy weather forecast, was of greater importance to the Bomber Command squadrons which, throughout any operation, desperately tried to allow for the actual wind as opposed to that forecast; all we cared about was whether we could see, whether the weather was bad enough to prevent take-off, or worse still, landing. Next, the army liaison captain seconded from the Polish Armoured Division told us about the latest developments along the front itself. Finally, the intelligence people reported on the sighting of German flak and other nasties.

Fortuitously, this first briefing also featured two officers in charge of the escape business. Both had been prisoners in the First World War, and both had escaped, one successfully and the other not. At this point in the war, we were strongly encouraged to evade capture when shot down. This was partly due to a rising incidence of successful escapes, and partly due to increasingly unsettled conditions in Germany. Anything could happen, so like Boy Scouts, we had to be prepared. Despite their language – a quaint mixture of Anthony Hope and John Buchan – they offered us an ingenious box of tricks which, in some ways, anticipated the esoteric equipment issued at the start of his adventures to James Bond by M. The simplest device was a pair of flying boots. These looked like ordinary RAF issue except for a little knife in a pocket inside the sheepskin lining which could be used to cut off the upper section and leave an apparently normal pair of shoes. There were yard-square silk handkerchiefs printed with brightly coloured maps of Germany; these were very popular as presents for girlfriends. One of the neatest devices was a pair of fly buttons. Once cut from the trousers, one, when placed face down, had a little bump in the middle; the other had a white dot painted on the rim of its underside. When placed on top of the first button, it swung free and the white dot turned to point to magnetic north. The two buttons formed a little compass.

I plotted out our own plan for patrolling the squadron area during our period of duty, and got everything else organized for the run in and out. I spent hours putting in all the data on my maps, complete with neat colouring and markings for the particularly dangerous spots. When I'd finished, one of the senior non-commissioned Polish crews came over and sat down with us. They were on their second tour. The Polish navigator looked at my effort and shook his head. 'You want to get past your first operation, eh?' A superfluous but disquieting comment. 'Look,' he went on, 'you go in . . . so.' A jab of his finger. 'You go twice round and you go out. See?' Another, more emphatic, jab of the finger.

Later on, I was to see what he meant. The statistics showed that in all operational activity, the greatest losses amongst aircrew occurred during their first three operations. The other great period of danger was near the end, but that was a long way ahead. At the start, most aircrew were a danger mainly to themselves rather than anyone else and that included the Germans. Successful wartime flying hinged largely on experience. Initially, the smallest things could go wrong in such a farcically embarrassing way that aircrew were unlikely to mention or report them. Once aircrew got wiser they could, given the talent and inclination, become moderately effective.

Our take-off time was ten-past one in the morning so we were to leave our nest for the flights at about ten-to for the five-minute ride in a three-tonner. After the briefing, we had supper in the sergeants' mess, bully beef and dehydrated chips washed down with lots of tea but no alcohol. Then we waited, with the rest of the non-Polish NCO aircrew, sitting in canvas chairs around two smokey Aladdin paraffin stoves, talking in a desultory way as one crew left and another returned. The night dragged on. It was blowing, rainy and cold but at least it wasn't snowing. And at least the Poles had unpacked, a morale-boosting gesture which followed the German retreat after the Battle of the Bulge. The bomb line had receded and operational trips were longer. Now the nasty fighting was in the Reichwald.

We collected our kit. Mine consisted of a parachute and a green canvas navigation bag in which I had all my maps, a torch, a spare handkerchief and some boiled sweets. Reg had only the pilot's parachute which he sat on. Mine was the chest kind with two hooks which snapped on to rings on the front straps of the harness. The truck was waiting outside. We identified our aircraft to the driver and climbed into the back. The truck ground its way from the nest and around the perimeter track to our aircraft. Its ladder was in place. So was the flight sergeant in charge of the maintenance crew and two other airmen. The auxiliary power unit and its motor were operating and plugged into the aircraft. Reg went round the aircraft checking the moving parts. At length he signed the requisite form on the flight sergeant's pad. We had taken formal delivery.

We climbed in, Reg first. Once he had settled himself into his bucket seat, I followed through the tiny door and crouched down in the restricted cockpit. I stowed my parachute to the right of where my feet went, unhooked the ladder and pulled it up, telescoping the sections; I then strapped it into the panel of the door. I leant out and pulled the door to, pulling down the locking mechanism. Now we were installed, Reg pressed the starter button for the port engine and the paddle-shaped propeller began to turn with a whirring noise. After three or four revolutions, the engine coughed. The propeller raced, then returned to the auxiliary power, whirring slowly. Just as we were getting worried, it caught properly. Reg pushed the throttle forward. The engine came alive and he was able to throttle back and leave it idling as he pushed the starter button for the starboard engine. This repeated the sequence. At length, both engines were idling. We were ready to go. Reg gave a thumbs up to the flight sergeant whom we could still see waiting to starboard. Reg switched on his RT and called the control tower to request permission to taxi from dispersal to take-off. It was given. He revved up both engines a little and at the same time took off the brakes. We edged forward. We were on our way.

I always admired the way Reg taxied the aircraft round the dispersals and the perimeter tracks with only a few dim indicators to see by. The base was under orders to minimize its visibility from the air since, in theory, it was vulnerable to enemy attack. The runway lights came on for only the shortest time. In the cockpit, Reg had done his checks before starting the engines. I was now checking the Gee box and the IFF (Identity: Friend or Foe), a device placed in the tail which emitted a signal identifying us as an Allied aircraft. I then organized the maps on the board perched on my lap under a tiny anglepoise light. I had to see, but without the brightness putting Reg off. By now we were at the end of the runway. Reg cleared each engine separately and ran them up in the process. Then we were ready for take-off and asking permission to proceed. We got it. Reg opened up the throttle on both engines and released the brakes. We were off down the runway. We were carrying four five-hundred-pound bombs; two in the bomb bay and one each on the wing mountings, equivalent in weight to carrying a dozen hefty people. The Mosquito could cope but it made for a ponderous take-off.

Reg had no trouble that night. By the time we were approaching one hundred knots, he had unglued the aircraft from the runway and we were airborne. He immediately retracted the undercarriage and, a minute later, as we turned to starboard and speeded up, he raised the flaps. I gave him the course to our first turning point just short of the bomb line in southern Holland. After nearly three years in the RAF, I was at last on active operations. My palms felt distinctly moist and I knew that, despite his matter-of-fact voice, Reg was every bit as nervous as I was.

What seemed to be rows of searchlights beaming along the ground were in fact lights marking the approaches to the bomb lines. I had them plotted on my maps and assumed that the land was lit up to reduce scope for surprises. It looked eerie. Then we turned to starboard. Our patrol area was well north of the Ruhr, and getting in and out didn't entail any particularly tricky manoeuvres. This was just as well because I had yet to handle my Gee with the necessary dexterity. As it was, I worked pretty hard, checking and rechecking what I was doing, with mounting concern that the signal I was meant to be following was almost indistinguishable from numerous others on the scope. I'd yet to acquire the knack of making the genuine blip stand out from amongst the 'ghosts'. Reg was a patient man: I had him turning this way and that as I corrected my errors but he didn't complain at all. He just corkscrewed around to the orders of his errant navigator. He treated me like one of his pupils in Canada a year or two back – with forbearance, relying on my ability to learn. It was fortunate he didn't harass me because, if he had, I would have taken much longer to learn. All I needed was practice and concentration.

For his part, Reg was never going to win the war in the air single-handed. He would always do a sound job, but we weren't the crew to blow up the Nazi's biggest ammunition dump. Still, we'd keep the Germans awake and manning their ack-ack weapons; every now and again, we'd score a near-miss near a railway station. Reg wasn't the pilot to go so low, when dropping bombs, as to embed pieces of the landscape in the underpart. He was too balanced, too careful and methodical to be a daredevil. As a result of flying hundreds of hours – teaching the good, the bad and the indifferent – he had generated an impressive capacity for self-preservation; in other words, one thousand five hundred hours flying as an instructor was not the ideal background for front-line operations.

The best target we could find that night in our patrol area consisted of some suspicious looking lights which might have been a convoy. We dropped our bombs and because at one point there seemed to be a flare-up of fire on the ground, we went round again; enormously daring, we gave the spot a punishing second and a half burst of our four cannon. This was the first time that we'd fired the main armament since we'd been on the range off the Norfolk coast. The noise and the sensation were like sitting on a footbridge while an express train pounded along below at ninety miles per hour. The first time we fired them, we thought they were going to tear the whole fuselage apart. Firing at night over enemy territory made such a noise that we felt sure we had drawn attention to ourselves for up to ten miles in every direction. But there was no response in the black night. So on we stooged following our simple pre-arranged route. Eventually our time was up and we flew towards the exit point of our patrol area with me working away at the Gee box as feverishly as ever.

On our return journey we had expected a sky blazing with flak and streams of tracer, dazzling with weaving searchlights. But nothing happened at all. Soon we were crossing the bomb line again, back into friendly territory. We were very relieved and rather puzzled. I suspect we hadn't fully allowed for being in a relatively quiet area. There was no great build-up of troops on the other side of the Rhine at this point and we hadn't been anywhere near the flak defences and the German night-fighter patrols. So no wonder we'd drawn a blank; only later were we to appreciate the difference between the easy and difficult trips. As we approached Cambrai, we called up the control tower and were told at which height to join the circuit. We requested permission to land. Reg flew calmly in on his approach, putting the aircraft down firmly as though emphasizing our return to Mother Earth. We came to a halt at the end of the runway and turned on to the perimeter track, taxiing towards our dispersal. When we got there, the ground crew was ready to help Reg park accurately. That done, he switched off first one and then the other engine. I opened the tiny little door by my feet and a hand grasped it and opened out the ladder for us. I climbed out facing into the aircraft, carefully stepping down the nine-inch rungs.

The three-tonner was waiting to take us back to the ops room. I couldn't wait to relieve myself. I walked towards the tail of the aircraft and breathed deeply. After two and a half hours in the air, it was a great relief in every sense. If you were caught short in mid-trip, the Mosquito ministered to your condition with a long flexible hose that ended in a funnel about three inches wide. Theoretically, it seemed the perfect answer but when I used it two months later on a long trip, it turned out to be blocked; I only realized this when I had a brimming vessel full of warm pee in my hand.

The three-tonner drove us off round the deserted perimeter to wing HQ on the other side of the air base for our de-briefing and, next door, our breakfast. It was nearly four in the morning. The simple de-briefing procedure was conducted by a wingless flying officer from Intelligence, assisted by a few airmen shuffling papers, yawning and smoking to keep awake. Each session started with the returning aviators being given a glass of issue rum, presumably acquired from the navy. It was very strong and very good and came in a wine glass with no base, presumably to prevent us from putting down the glass between sips. It struck me that the rum might have served us better before rather than after the operation; it was strange that nobody ever took up a bottle with them over Germany; perhaps they did.

We outlined our night's activity to the flying officer, who was most impressed that we had had a go at anything on our first trip. It was all written down to form part of the usual report to Two Group. We gathered from one of the airmen that one aircraft from Twenty-one Squadron was overdue, and that was that. Twenty-one Squadron, one of the two other on the base, drew a measure of its fame from its commanding officer, Wing Commander 'Laddie' Lucas, the noted golfer.

We walked down a passage to breakfast in an adjoining hut. A red-hot cast-iron stove in the centre cast a comforting glow round the little mess. And there, in a corner behind the counter, was a cook. As we came in we heard him frying a couple of eggs for us. The bacon and fried bread came from a stack, still warm but long since fried, kept with the pan of baked beans by the side of his fire. Tired though I was, it was one of the best breakfasts I had ever had.

When we got back to the nest at five o'clock the last crew were just about to leave for dispersal. The group around the paraffin stove had already gone. We fell into bed: I into my iron bedstead and Reg on to his issue camp bed. As we were due to fly a night-flying test later the same morning at eleven we weren't going to have anything like enough sleep beforehand – one of the key deprivations of operational life.

By morning, the weather had deteriorated: snow and showers of alternately sleet and rain were sweeping across Cambrai, and the cloud base was down to one hundred feet. Flying – and with it our night-flying test – had been cancelled. So we had lunch and went back to sleep. I dreamed Reg didn't manage to get the aircraft unglued from the runway in time and that we had gone on through a field and hit a tree with a tremendous bang. I woke up to find that one of the Poles had dropped a cup of coffee. That night we had our first real drinking session with some of them. Their songs were very Polish, and were sung with tremendous gusto and emphasis. They stamped their feet on the ground, raised their arms in great 'hoorays!' and rounded off every number with a rousing cheer. Some of these songs were original Polish Air Force material, others were imported from the Polish army, especially the cavalry which was famous for its singing. Performing the songs was vital to keeping their spirits up and preserving their sense of identity. They were, after all, patriotic survivors, in marked contrast to the overgrown schoolboys who comprised most of the non-Polish element in the squadron. On average, they were four or five years older than us, and most of them had been in the war since 1941 at least. We got on well, but there were problems.

For instance, the navigator in the other crew that had joined the squadron with us advertised his Communist sympathies, even going so far as to import copies of *L'Humanité*, the French Communist newspaper. The Polish aircrew were affronted and incredulous: only eight months ago, the Russians had let the Poles down badly by leaving their army to fend for itself in Warsaw. Moreover they knew about Katyn, and had no doubts about who was responsible for the massacre; altogether, they loathed the Russians as much as they did the Germans and were very sorry they couldn't fight both of them at once. The navigator was duly dissuaded from further brandishing copies of *L'Humanité*; he was also told by the leader of our international flight to keep out of trouble on pain of being posted. The affair blew over, but it showed just how strongly the Poles felt about certain matters.

When the weather had cleared a few nights later, we were back on the battle order for our second operation. It should have been a carbon copy of our first but this time everything went wrong.

15 Members of the Squadron

The squadron had been allotted a patrol area similar to that on our first operation, northern Holland verging on the German border. Our take-off time was ten-past three in the morning. Starting in the middle of the night, it wouldn't be easy to go to sleep beforehand and, assuming that all went well, we wouldn't be in bed until well after six in the morning. The briefing was a repetition of our first one, except for the weather which was worse: low cloud and storms. This time, the army wanted us to attack the ammunition trains bringing new supplies into the area. Every aircraft was to be fitted with flares on each wing tip. These turned the night sky to daylight brightness to reveal every ground movement; they also lit up the aircraft. We were to bomb with our two five-hundred-pound bombs and strafe with cannon.

This trip went wrong from the start. We couldn't get the starboard engine going. Reg nursed it, but it wouldn't catch. Eventually, there was a knocking on the door. It was a tall Polish flight sergeant, anxious to see what was wrong. He hoisted himself in, leant across Reg to the throttle and, pressing the starter, worked it backwards and forwards until the engine suddenly caught; with a burst of noise it was running and without a word he was gone. We felt humiliated, but without reason; after all, he'd started more Merlin engines than I'd had hot dinners. At last we were taxiing round the dispersal. It was a gusty night, as promised by the Met.

We lined up at the end of the runway, asked for permission to take-off, got it and were off. This time the gusts made Reg reluctant to open up the engines as quickly as on our first night. He avoided a swing which could easily have developed, what with the ground wind and with the extra-weight big flares on each of our wing tips, but as we approached the end of the runway we weren't going quite fast enough.

Then there was a surge of power. Reg had pushed the throttle through the 'gate', a gap in the throttle mechanism whereby the last inch was sealed off by two thin wires; these broke when the throttle was pushed to extract a final boost from the engines; the wires were there to prevent pilots from making unnecessary use of that last inch of thrust. Unless the pilot throttled back almost immediately, the engines were apt to over-heat and blow up. The aircraft took to the air at the moment we ran out of runway. For the first few moments, neither of us said very much. We headed off for our first turning point but on the way to the bomb line the weather changed dramatically. Flying at fifteen hundred feet, we emerged from cloud into a clear area and were almost blinded by light. We couldn't think what had happened. Were we in a cone created by several searchlights? We were about to try evasive action when we realized it was the light of the moon, a full moon! Within seconds, we were back into the clouds and at the base of an electrical storm. The turbulence was considerable. Then, just to try our nerves a little more, nature played another trick: a luminous green fire danced along the leading edge of the wing and alongside the cockpit. We learnt later that it was St Elmo's Fire, a type of electrical discharge – a member of the lightning family, but more playful.

By the time we passed over the bomb line into northern Holland, the weather had got even worse. It was, as they used to say, solid. We tried dropping down to one thousand feet and then to six hundred, at which level we started bucketing about. All we could do was go round our patrol area and bomb on Gee. There was no point in letting off flares in the solid cloud. I selected what should have been a railway junction according to the Gee co-ordinates, Reg opened the bomb-bay doors, I pressed the button and that was that. We made our way back.

Over Cambrai, the weather was equally foul and I thanked my lucky stars for Reg's skill. It seemed to me that we were skidding around far too close to the roofs of Cambrai. Then suddenly we saw the airfield lights to starboard at a slanting angle, and Reg had the under-carriage down and was swinging across to align himself with the airfield lights without so much as a circuit. Only a minute later and we were down, taxiing round the perimeter track. We came to rest, Reg switched off the engines and opened the bomb-bay doors so the ground crew could start their maintenance work the next day. There was a knock on the door and I opened it. A hand came up to fix the ladder for us. It was followed by a rather sullen face. What was wrong? What was wrong was that we had brought our bombs back with us. It was the final humiliation. Of course the ground crew would test the bomb gear thoroughly the next day to see if we had had a technical 'hang-up' with the complex wiring and trigger mechanism. It was much more likely though that I had failed to function properly. I had forgotten something in the drill and, when I had pressed the trigger to release the bombs, the circuit hadn't been complete. And sure enough, it was confirmed later that there was nothing wrong with the system.

They said on the squadron that everybody did it once, and told me to forget it. At the de-briefing, we hadn't known for sure what the problem was. But the intelligence officer knew well enough. He didn't bear down too hard on me but merely said: 'Take more care in future.' I was mortified. Reg was patient. It wasn't the end of the world so far as he was concerned. He confined himself to saying that obviously we should try not to repeat the error because, quite apart from letting the Germans off too lightly, we would incur official displeasure if we made a habit of bringing back our bombs. Nor did he really relish landing with them; if it could be avoided, it was better on the whole not to have them on board on the return journey. After that, with the warm feeling of the rum still with us, we went to have our egg and bacon.

Our third trip was uneventful. The weather was still bad so there was little to be seen. On our return, we were amazed to hear the new flight commander relating how he had managed to get below cloud over the Rhine and shoot up some barges. We marvelled. He was an earnest thin-faced individual full of goodwill and helpfulness but 'Press on' was his leitmotiv. He had an agreeable navigator, a portly, round-faced flight lieutenant. Both had DFCs from an operational tour together on Beaufighters. That night, one of the squadron's Polish crews failed to return. No more was heard of them.

After three trips, we felt we were emerging from the raw novice category; especially as we were eligible for our squadron badge. These were rare because they were actively discouraged by the authorities. But the Poles were different. They had had squadron badges in the pre-war Polish Air Force and they weren't going to give up the habit in the Polish squadrons of the RAF. 305 had a colourful squadron badge made of enamelled metal; in the centre was a field marshal's baton along with an elongated letter P standing for Marshal Pilsudski. On the side was what looked like the feathers of an Indian chief's head-dress, representing the insignia of the Polish cavalry. With the badge came a little card with your name beautifully written and a Polish inscription about the squadron and the Polish Air Force. Thenceforward we proudly wore our squadron badges exotically glowing below our wings. A further privilege was a trip to Douai; all part of our induction into regular squadron procedure. The entertainment on our base was limited to the drink in the mess and that could only be consumed after the squadron had been stood down. The cinema on the base had long since closed down.

So a few nights later, at about seven, Reg and I piled

into a three-tonner with the rest of the group and drove off to Douai. A draughty ride took us down an empty road past unlit houses. We stopped twice in Douai; at a brothel, and at a small café where our black-market eggs were turned into omelettes. Our visit to the brothel was more formal than functional; it simply enabled us to say that we had been there. At the last briefing, the CO had warned us to keep out of trouble: a fire-and-brimstone lecture prompted by a Norwegian crew that had contracted clap and gone sick. The CO was complaining about their unavailability, not their morals; he didn't want to lose any more crews this way.

The establishment was in a large building just off one of the town's main streets. Its large front door opened wide at our ring and seven or eight of us trooped into a marble-floored hall that could well have graced a bank. Across it were two ample ladies in late middle age, dressed in black; they sat at desks with ledgers on them. A GI and a girl concluded a conversation with the lady on the right and went up some stairs by the desks. Some tables and chairs surrounded a space on which a very tall girl danced with another GI; further couples lolled around on the chairs, watching, chatting and drinking. The place was delightfully warm after the winter weather outside. The girls' only concession to immodesty was bare legs, due probably to the shortage of stockings. They had good figures, but looked thin from rationing rather than choice – unsurprisingly, as there was no sign of anything to eat in any of the shops or cafés in Douai where people looked in a far worse way than in England. The bright lights were reflected in brass fittings around the bar which ran the length of the building, ending just short of the desks with the ladies. A bare-legged girl served us with a glass of white wine as thin as she was. Our 'treat' followed: a joyless strip-tease performed by a couple of women who had seen better days. We duly tipped them and turned down a menu of physical delights. With every stirring of lust totally demolished by the brothel, we went in search of the restaurant where our precious eggs would be turned into delicious omelettes. These were marvellous. Luckily, somebody had remembered to bring some bread as there was absolutely none to eat in the little restaurant.

Our operational flights continued at a rate of only two a week because of the poor weather. On our fourth trip we went deeper into Germany but saw nothing as the weather was again foul with a very low cloud base. That was the night that the eager flight commander failed to return. The veteran Poles in our room shook their heads. They had expected as much. He had doubtless been courageous, and had again got beneath the ceiling over the Rhine – but once more had proved, we surmised, once too often.

On the fifth trip, the aircraft succeeding us in the patrol area, manned by a flight sergeant crew who had done nearly twenty operations, got caught by flak on the way. They must have been very near us when it happened. We heard them call up and say they were returning to base. Later when we were well past the bomb line and were halfway home, we heard them again. With one of their engines put out of action and their hydraulics not working properly, they would have to do a belly landing. When we were back over Cambrai, we told the control tower that the aircraft behind us was in trouble and might need to make an emergency landing.

When we had landed ourselves and taxied well down the perimeter track, we heard them over the airfield. We waited to see them land, partly out of curiosity, partly out of camaraderie. We saw the fire truck draw up. Then, just after the landing lights had gone on, they came in to land. As the aircraft came in over the runway, its undercarriage was still retracted. It sank lower and lower and finally hit the ground. We heard the noise over the idling of our own two engines. The fuselage and two propellers screeched and tore at the tarmac. But the aircraft hardly deviated from a straight path. In the circumstances, the pilot had made an excellent landing.

On the night of our next operation, the youngest

sergeant pilot on the squadron, a Pole with the beardless face of a girl, bailed out on the way back. One of the best pilots on the squadron, he relished flying and loved his Mosquito. That night he had dropped his bombs slightly too low. They didn't have delayed fuses on them and he had been well below the minimum safety height of six hundred feet. As a result, a lot of brickwork entered the underside of the aircraft. On the way back his hydraulics failed and one engine packed up. Finally, the other engine began to overheat and with the prospect of it seizing up at any moment, he had told his navigator to bail out and had followed suit. They were in open ground in northern France. Their aircraft crashed into one field and they landed safely in another. They were back on the squadron by noon the following day. Zigi, as the pilot was nicknamed, was quite calm about the affair and was back on the battle order that night.

As a crew, Reg and I were improving. His flying, always competent, was settling down. He was getting used to the Mosquito and I was getting better at the Gee box.

16 February–March 1945

Life was claustrophobic on 305 at Cambrai because there was no escape from routine. Our day began late; just how late depended on when we'd returned from flying the night before. Breakfast in the sergeants' mess was meagre and if a crew had had eggs and bacon after the de-briefing the night before, they tended to skip it. Then around midday, we had the night-flying test. After our midday meal, we went back to the nest as there was nowhere else to go: no entertainment, no nice warm ante-room like the one at Swanton-Morley. There was no point in going to the little room in the red brick house in the village: it was cold, half a mile away and drinking was out of the question. So after an afternoon's sleep, we had high tea and then briefing. If the weather was bad, the squadron would be stood down but probably not before seven or eight in the evening.

Meanwhile, for those of us not yet inured to operational flying, it was hard to stop thinking about the risks we ran. I knew these thoughts were unworthy so I kept them to myself. Going by the last few months, the squadron lost a crew once every other operation. So far in our experience the average was slightly better. During our six ops, there had only been two losses, the Polish crew and the flight commander. Perhaps the dangers were lessening as the war swung into what we confidently anticipated was the final phase. The Ardennes offensive had failed. The Russians were advancing in the east. Surely once the weather improved, the

Allied armies in the west would make their final move and crush Germany in a vice.

Meanwhile we were cheered by the forthcoming distribution of three-day passes to Brussels, a city now established as a leave centre for the Twenty-first Army Group and its air support. The best hotels had been taken over and servicemen's clubs had been established in what had been leading restaurants. We were keen to go so we put our names in the hat and as luck would have it, our passes came out, dated for the following week. In the event we were doubly delighted as our fellow NCO crew – Reg's warrant-officer friend from Canada and my new chum, the Communist navigator – had also come out of the hat so we could make a foursome. We could hardly believe our luck. If we could avoid being shot down, we'd be between clean sheets in a week's time.

Both crews survived the next operation. It involved penetrating further into Germany than before, to areas where the parabolic lines on the Gee charts were at an angle of only twenty degrees or less. On the second of these deeper-penetration trips, our eighth op in all, we several times encountered light flak streaming up at us. It missed by quite a margin but was still too close for comfort. We were probably lower than I'd calculated. Our twin crew was less fortunate. It failed to return. Another crew, this time Polish, claimed their slot on the Brussels weekend so, in terms of chums, we were on our own.

Despite the gloom this cast over our break, we managed to enjoy ourselves. We flew up to Melsbroeck, an airfield a few miles outside Brussels which was being used by a variety of RAF squadrons as well as acting as the base for Two Group's HQ.

We were allotted a hotel in the city centre, not far from the Metropole. It was warm and welcoming. Reg and I shared a room with its own bathroom. The sheets were crisp and clean. It was fantastic to get away, especially to luxurious Brussels, then the only European capital of a combatant nation to seem untouched by war. The glittering shops down the rue Neuve displayed clothes apparently available without coupons. Even more extraordinary were the food shops which groaned with huge clusters of purple grapes, seemingly picked that very morning in some tropical paradise, oranges, lemons, grapefruit and melons . . . rich, glowing still-lifes that hadn't been seen in London for nearly six years. Unlike the French, the people looked plump and well-nourished. Although Belgium was still at war, the country was doing its best to forget it.

In this fairy-tale city we ate like kings. By chance, I discovered the most exceptional gastronomic treat. For lunch on our first full day, we went to a restaurant set aside for Allied troops and sat in its most formal part. This was my choice because ever since our dinners in Norwich on evenings off from Swanton-Morley, it was acknowledged that I took the lead in such matters. It was an off-duty extension of my navigational responsibilities to keep the pilot on the right gastronomic track. We chose Dover sole – available because the Belgian fishing fleet, having done its bit with E-boats or sweeping mines, had now reverted to its key priority: catching fish. I wanted a sweet white wine, a deliberate departure from the disgusting white wine at Cambrai, specially selected by the French for the Luftwaffe. So I asked for Château Yquem, one of the few wines I'd heard of; an unsophisticated choice, perhaps, but it complemented the fish superbly.

We went to the cinema. And we went dancing with British WRAFs or ATS working in the sprawling administrative machine now centred on Brussels. As they were heavily outnumbered by the men, they must have had a wonderful time; but although they were quite civil, it was rather less wonderful for us. We window-shopped; we ate magnificent meals; we had two long nights between crisp sheets; we luxuriated in hot baths. It was all over in a flash. On the third morning we awoke, packed our gear and went by three-tonner back to Melsbroeck where our Oxford pitched up with the next batch of lucky chaps. Soon we were flying over the desolate industrial landscape towards the coal tips north of Douai, towards our destination. It had been a wonderful few days but achingly short.

The next major incident was the 'daylight'. When we'd been at Swanton-Morley, we'd spent most of our time practising the low-level daylight flying used by the group's Mosquito squadrons for pinpoint attacks on particular buildings. Up to now, even after two months on the squadron, we hadn't been on a single daylight operation. Typically, when the authorities finally announced one, it wasn't the sort for which we'd trained. Instead we were to be part of a massive daylight operation over Germany involving eight thousand aircraft from all the Allied air forces, including France and Italy. There were to be high-level raids by Bomber Command and the US Eighth Air Force; medium-level raids by the medium-bomber force, and relatively low-level operations by the rest. It turned out we were to operate at a middling height, two thousand feet, on the way in but were to come back at ground level.

As this plan unfolded on the morning of the operation, at a briefing that started at the unheard-of hour of nine, the crews were pretty surprised; still if that was the plan, we had to go in and carry it out. The entire wing was to fly in formation, with 305 Squadron the last of the three. As the junior crew, Reg and I were to be the last aircraft in the last flight of the show. Some are born to lead and some, we mused, to follow.

Each squadron would field its eighteen aircraft together with reserve, a nineteenth man, in case somebody had engine trouble on the way up to the bomb line. Then the entire gaggle was to fly on into the Third Reich and only break up into its individual squadrons when two hundred miles into the heart of the country. At that point, the squadrons would disengage from the gaggle and in turn break up into pairs which would patrol for Huns on wheels or whatever targets took their fancy. Having dropped their bombs, the pairs would then return at tree-top height to obtain the protective covering missed on the way in at two thousand feet. That was the theory anyway. We then had various other briefings. The Met man predicted fine weather with a conviction reinforced by the blazing sun and bright blue sky outside. The intelligence briefing dwelt on a hammer blow of unprecedented magnitude, laid on at the direct request of the army, which was itself getting poised for some important manoeuvres; for security reasons, these were referred to only in vague terms, but we all knew they comprised the spring offensive and the leap across the Rhine; this would probably start in a month's time when the weather could be relied upon.

'Any questions?' asked our new CO. The rotund one with the Warsaw-to-Tokyo record had finished his tour and we were now confronted by a Polish squadron leader, a much younger, less jovial type, much more a product of the current conflict, tense, concerned, flying every possible mission. 'Yes,' answered a fair-haired officer called Flight Lieutenant Sitwell. 'Presumably, if we are attacked by German fighters, we break formation and go for them?' 'That's right,' replied the squadron leader. There wasn't really any more to say on that subject. Reg and I wondered whether the rest of the crews were as ignorant of fighter tactics as we were.

I also wondered whether others shared my doubts and worries. Our Mosquitoes looked beautiful and as medium-bombers, were sleek, manoeuvrable and far from slow. But they were not fighters. If we met some German fighters, we'd all do our best to get away but that was about it. Just as we were about to break up, the squadron leader asked another question: 'Which is the last crew?' Reg put up his hand. 'Well, your navigator'd better spend his time keeping a look-out.' Quite so. I had thought of doing that for our own safety, but I was now officially designated as the person to do it for the squadron and presumably for the whole wing. I prayed that I wouldn't get a speck of dust in either eye that day.

Two hours later we were queuing for take-off. As the last off, we banked round steeply to catch up our flight; then the flight had to catch up the one ahead and form the squadron which finally had to attach itself to the rest of the wing. It took us another fifteen minutes before the whole wing was assembled at two thousand feet. Eventually we were flying to the bomb line in glinting, bright sunshine. With such good visibility and at two thousand feet – for us a prodigious altitude – we could see for miles. Five minutes short of the bomb line our nineteenth aircraft, our spare crew, dropped out, falling away from under the squadron. We could see two other aircraft, one each from the other two squadrons, doing the same. There couldn't have been many crews in the formation who didn't envy their comfortable return to base and a quiet lunch.

Then as we passed over the bomb line and entered enemy air space, an aircraft in our flight began to have trouble. As it was only three up from us in the formation, we could see spray, presumably glycol, streaming out of its starboard engine. Within a minute, the prop came to a standstill and with only one engine, the aircraft inevitably began to lose its place. We saw it drop below us and then turn for home. When we got back, we found out that a stray bullet, probably from a rifle, had penetrated the engine and ruptured the cooling system. If so, the chap on the ground with his rifle had against all odds managed to disable one of His Majesty's aircraft with a single rifle bullet. It wouldn't have happened with an air-cooled engine.

We pressed on. I assumed a kneeling position on my seat, peering back to scan the blue sky for enemy aircraft. I saw nothing. Given that eight thousand aircraft were meant to be scouring Germany that day, the heavens were remarkably empty. 138 Wing flew slowly on towards the centre of Germany. With the sun now behind us, I kept looking round for enemy aircraft and only occasionally looked down. However, those few glances showed the ground to be asolutely still: farms, buildings, lanes, roads and neat fields seemed toy-like and uninhabited.

Eventually the wing arrived at its dispersal point and we saw the lead squadron turning to port and descending; the second squadron, Twenty-one Squadron, then did the same to starboard. We followed and shortly afterwards broke up into pairs. The rest of the aircraft, all fifty-four of them, rapidly disappeared and we were left to follow our single leader. At last, the moment had arrived for Warrant Officer Everson and his intrepid navigator to deliver their personal blow against Nazi tyranny. We flew along with our leader at six hundred feet with the unpeopled heartland of German agriculture now much closer, its detail in tighter focus. We later learned that by this stage of the war, the Germans were used to air attack and when aircraft were about they hid. Indeed in some areas nearer the front line, under near-continuous air surveillance, the normal work-day schedule was reversed, with all active life confined to night-time.

After a time we found a target: a railway line and a siding. It was better than nothing. We followed our leader at a decent interval, dropped our two bombs and saw smoke. Hoping we had hit the line, we dropped to one hundred feet and started flying westwards, over the fields, up and over the trees. We were careful to avoid all obstacles, alert to enemy appearances. But there was nothing; no scurrying figures, no horses frightened by our engines or any of the other sights so frequently encountered during our low-flying exercises over England. We flew on, mile after deserted mile. And I was now well and truly lost. We were too far east for the Gee box to give us a reliable fix. I tried my best, but the unchanging countryside had no features to help me. Presumably our leader knew where he was, and where he was going. We were flying due west which had to be correct in principle. But exactly where his course was taking us, I couldn't make out.

Then, as we flew over the outskirts of a small town, we ran into trouble. First, smoke started pouring from the port engine of our leader's aircraft. Then we saw the lines of tracer fire; sure sign that we were running into a belt of low-level flak defences manned, it seemed, by gunners who were good and ready for us. The smoke poured thicker and thicker from the engine ahead of us and it seemed likely that the other engine might also have been hit as the aircraft was now losing speed and altitude. We were flying so low there wasn't much airspace to spare. Reg was throwing our aircraft around. I told him to climb and head due north. As he did so, I saw our companion aircraft grind to a successful crash landing in a large field. We were on our own and completely lost.

After ten minutes' flying north we saw the sea. We'd been far further north than I had realized. We could just see the distinctive coastline around Bremen. I quickly switched Reg on to a course which would take us across the bomb line in southern Holland. Although the sky was empty, there was a layer of exploding ack-ack fire behind us. They'd got our height but not our speed. As we were already pulling away from the danger zone, I thought it better not to say anything to Reg. We kept at our height of two thousand five hundred feet, away from the intense and accurate low-level ack-ack fire. And as long as we kept out of the heavily built-up areas, we were not going to run foul of heavy ack-ack. Our calculations proved correct. We flew alone across the rest of Germany that afternoon without further trouble. The landscape continued as lifeless as ever. Eventually we crossed the bomb line, skirting wide and south of Antwerp as any aircraft flying across that strategic port during daylight was an easy target. We finally reached Cambrai half an hour after the return of the main group.

We hadn't achieved much. But at least we hadn't been shot down by the light flak. The pilot of our lead aircraft had had the bed opposite mine in the nest. He was a small chap who had laughed a lot and went to bed in a thick white cable-stitch sweater which reached his knees. I felt a pang of deprivation when the adjustment officer came round the next day for his kit. The adjustment officer was a young flying officer, an administrative type, invariably with a sergeant assistant. This team's duty was to sort out the belongings of aircrew who failed to return. They packed everything up, sorted out any mess bills and wrote up the crew's log books, complete with details of the operation from which they hadn't returned. The kit was then neatly labelled and sent off to a depot at Uxbridge. In the unlikely event that the aircrew was classified as killed in action, which would mean that they had been observed to have perished, the kit went to the next of kin. This was the fourth time I had seen the team doing its rather grisly job.

After the excitement of the daylight, we were back to normal; and after the exceptionally bright weather of the daylight operation, back to low cloud and driving rain. On one return trip, conditions were so bad that Cambrai closed down and we were diverted. All the NCO crews were secretly longing for a diversion to somewhere agreeable; preferably to Manston in Kent and, with luck, an unscheduled forty-eight hours on British soil, complete with sheets and good English beer. In the event, Reg and I achieved a good second-best in the form of Melsbroeck where bad weather smiled on us, keeping us grounded next day. We stayed at the NCO HQ and went into Brussels for the day, tanking up on Dover sole and Château Yquem. The next day the weather cleared a little and forced us to abandon the flesh-pots.

But there was more good news to come. The leave roster had been ticking over since the beginning of January and although we were relative newcomers, we were due for a fortnight's leave in the United Kingdom in ten days' time. I planned to spend the first week in Oxford with my aunt and the second in Harrogate with Alice and her friends. By the time the longed-for date arrived in mid-March, we had only done ten operations although it felt like more. This was because our operational flying had been reduced more than we realized, either through bad weather or being one of the five crews not on battle order. Moreover we had also had a case of engine trouble before take-off which, as we were last on the list, prevented our going on the operation.

And finally, I'd been ill for a few days with stomach pains which had recurred from time to time ever since Canada. That sort of illness was embarrassing as somebody might be tempted to think the sickness was just malingering. Eighteen months later, while on leave, I had to have what the surgeon at St George's in London called a 'stinking appendix' rapidly removed. What I had been sporadically suffering from was a grumbling appendix: the on-off overture that precedes the final explosion. After a few days off, I had returned to the fray still with the pain because I couldn't allow myself to go on sitting around in the sick quarters instead of being on the squadron.

On the blessed day, we flew off in the Dakota to Northolt, now no longer a fighter base but a Transport Command staging post for London. Far from leaving my troubles behind, I felt so ill on arrival that I couldn't go any further. A very sympathetic medical officer consigned me to Northolt sick quarters where I stayed in great comfort and slowly recovered. Because of this, I didn't go on leave until the beginning of the last week in March.

And now that I was on leave, I felt a bit flat. It wasn't that I missed the nest and its claustrophobic life; I was hugely relieved not to be at risk. The problem was that the only people who counted were my companions of the moment, the other non-Polish NCO aircrews; the squadron had become my centre of gravity. I liked seeing my aunt, but Oxford had become remote and for the time being, not very interesting. I was a poor guest at Alice's because I felt moody, tetchy and contentious. One day they took me to the Devonshire Arms near Bolton Abbey, one of those country hotels whose standards seemed mysteriously untouched by the war. When Alice's labrador chased sheep along a riverside path there, I pushed it into the river to save the sheep and to teach the dog a lesson. Alice duly roared with laughter but I doubt if she was really amused. I also stayed a couple of nights at the Overseas League in London and took Jane out to dinner at an expensive restaurant in Jermyn Street. The next day at lunch she reintroduced me to her doctor friend. As I suspected, they were about to get engaged. So that was that. Then I was back in the bus, Northolt-bound to join Reg and be flown by Dakota back to 138 Wing.

17 The Thirteenth Op

The squadron was very glad to see us back. My being sick for ten days had thrown the leave roster into a mess and delayed the departure of the next two crews. That aside, the squadron was far from happy. The Poles had been following every move in the battle of wits between the Polish government and the Allies. The problem was that the Russians were not prepared to recognize the government-in-exile in London once Polish territory was liberated. There had already been the tragedy during the previous summer when the Russians just sat and watched while the Polish army battered itself to near extinction against the Germans. Now as the Russian army swept through Poland and eastern Prussia and on into Germany itself, the Russians decided to set up their own puppet regime, the Lublin Committee. Our Poles expected this. But they were shocked when the Allies, especially the British, transferred their allegiance from what the Poles regarded as the constitutional Polish government in London to an upstart band of fellow-travellers in Lublin.

The Poles on the squadron were deeply incensed; they felt bitterly wronged, horribly betrayed. The British people were slow to understand the Polish case. They knew the Poles didn't really believe the western Allies capable of stopping the Russians from having their own way. If anyone knew the power of Russian force and coercion, surely the Poles did. But that did not mean the British government had to legitimize the

Russian move. The Poles felt the British should have behaved honourably and rejected the Russian 'diktat' outright. In retrospect, the London Poles and the Poles of the RAF, including 305 Polish Squadron, were victims of fashion. In 1938, the British establishment had adopted appeasement so wholeheartedly that disagreement was tantamount to disloyalty. By 1945, the establishment view had swung the other way. *The Times* leaders, so keen on Mr Chamberlain in 1938, now fawned over the Russians. The Poles who had joined us in the fight for freedom were about to be ditched and 305 Squadron knew it. Yet they were still flying and fighting. Our Mosquito still proudly sported, alongside its RAF roundels, the Polish national insignia. Despite the recognition of the Lublin Committee, these Mosquitoes still fired Polish cannon shells at the Germans and would do so to the end.

During our time away, the squadron had been active: it had lost two more crews, bringing the total to six since we joined, and it was now penetrating into Germany more deeply than ever. It was hard to tell which armies we were supporting: the British and American, or the Russian. If anything, we were helping the Russians, as our patrol areas now lay behind their lines, well beyond the range of the Gee. On our front, the big news was the brilliantly successful crossing of the Rhine. As a result the Allies were now well on to German soil both north and south of the Ruhr.

On our first night back we were on battle order. Although the weather had improved, we still didn't see very much during our three-hour trip. That night a recently joined British crew failed to return, bringing the score to seven. Next night we were on again: again in good weather, again in a patrol area far to the east. This time we saw lights which might have been transport. We strafed them with our cannon. We were more confident now and perhaps slightly more effective as a weapon of war. That night, a Polish officer crew was the eighth casualty. We were on again the next night. At the briefing, the squadron leader CO, understandably more tight-lipped than ever, gave us a personal briefing. He wanted no more casualties and told us to fly carefully. 'By all means attack, but do so with prudence; one crew a night is far too many.' Reg and I chatted about it afterwards as we waited for take off at half-past one on yet another long trip. It was good of the CO to be concerned, but what could he do? The powers-that-be wouldn't take the situation seriously until we started losing aircraft at the rate of two or more a night.

So once again Reg got his parachute. And once again I collected my navigation bag and the maps which our ever-lengthening trips had made more numerous and complex than ever. We took creature comforts on the operation. I carried a small flask of coffee for the return journey and, instead of sweets, we both took plenty of biscuits. We each carried a big service revolver tucked into a holster attached to a webbing belt. And in case we fell into the hands of our Russian allies, we took brightly printed cards with a Union Jack on one side and the legend '*Yar an Anglichani*' in Cyrillic on the other.

We took off on time without incident. It was our thirteenth operation. We were headed for a patrol area in the Berlin-Magdeburg region. It was to last just under four hours and was to take us to the point where the Gee lines ran almost parallel. To augment our fuel supply, we had wing tanks which we used first and then jettisoned. We saw a few lights in our area but nothing very exciting. It was a dull trip. We headed back after three-quarters of an hour in the patrol area. We had gone out and were to return on a course that went below the Ruhr; for us a southerly route which took us into the US rather than the British war zone.

Towards four in the morning, as we headed back over the hilly country south of the Ruhr, we couldn't tell on which side of the bomb line we were flying. Our intelligence briefing had done its best to update us on the fast-moving scene at the front. The German armies were beginning to break up. The thrust of the British in the north and the Americans in the south had penetrated into Germany by well over a hundred miles on each side. They would soon reach a point at which they would join hands to form a pocket behind the Ruhr; its formation came about because the Allies wished to avoid having to fight through the heavily built-up industrial areas. It was expected to be complete within the next twenty-four hours.

The Allies' natural line of advance lay in the open country on either side where their armour could deploy. Once past the Ruhr, the pocket could be reduced at leisure. By the time we were skirting the lower side of the pocket-to-be, we were relaxing. Thirteen didn't threaten to be an unlucky number for us after all. I poured the coffee and fished around for the biscuits but was interrupted by a low rumble. We couldn't make out what it was; we might even have imagined it. Reg checked the engines. Nothing. He and I scanned the sky. Nothing. Was it a stray bit of flak behind us that we hadn't seen? Possibly. We went back to our tasks. I checked our position from the Gee box and we were bang on course. A second or so later it happened.

There was a roar as though from a cannonade. Our starboard engine exploded, flooding our cockpit with light. A bonfire raged in the middle of the stricken engine. The propeller was windmilling. The wheel and one oleo leg of the undercarriage were fully extended under the starboard engine. We had been mortally hit.

I don't know how long it was, probably only a fraction of a second, but, during that fraction, I experienced for the only time in my life a wave of complete panic and terror; it washed over me, taking with it every ounce of my self-control. For this micro-second I was just a creature; technically alive but quite incapable of rational thought or movement. It was a terrifying sensation like falling down a well with sheer sides and no bottom; it induced total despair. I came out of the spell as quickly as I'd gone into it. Reg, competent to the last, was handling the aircraft as smoothly as ever although, instead of the airworthy Mosquito with two Merlin engines of two seconds ago, he was now flying a crippled aircraft on its port engine with the starboard landing gear dragging through the sky. Reg was fully engaged. So I pushed a large red button to activate the Graviner fire-extinguisher system built into the engines. In vain: the bonfire burned as furiously as ever. So I turned to the pair of buttons which feathered the airscrews and firmly pressed home the starboard one. It worked: the starboard prop immediately stopped milling round. At least the engine wouldn't totally disintegrate because the blade ran out of control. Reg then spoke the only words which were to pass between us during this incident: 'Bail out, Tony.'

We were losing height; we hadn't much height to lose before we hit the ground. I unfastened the harness holding me into my seat, knelt down on the cockpit floor, picked up my chest parachute and clipped it on to the buckles on my parachute harness. I then pulled the red lever housed inside the cockpit door frame. This not only opened the door, it unhitched the hinges. The suction of the slipstream immediately pulled out the door and it flew into the void. I pushed my navigation bag out of the gaping hole. The coffee was sloshing around in it and I didn't want Reg to slither in the liquid or catch his foot in the bag itself. I then knelt on the lip of the hatch just long enough to get a brilliant picture of light and fire. The roaring bonfire sent vast coiling ropes of burning fuel a hundred yards back behind the engine. At the same time, burning fuel was pouring down the oleo leg of the undercarriage. Once on the wheel, now revolving in the airstream, the fuel blazed and roared like a Catherine wheel. It was an awe-inspiring sight. I fell forwards.

Next, I found myself swinging lazily beneath the canopy of my parachute. I had no recollection of anything between my slow fall forwards into space and feeling comfortable and secure, suspended from the parachute. As I looked into the night, I saw our aircraft at several hundred yards range: a comet with a tail in the night sky. As I watched, transfixed, the incandescent Mosquito described a slow gentle arc. Then as it drew further and further away, the angle of descent increased. Finally, it turned sharply downwards. Two seconds later, it exploded on the ground. As I drifted slowly down, it seemed to me that the aircraft had travelled quite a distance, possibly a mile or more. But had Reg escaped? The design of the cockpit made it harder for a pilot to get out of a Mosquito than a navigator. I also had the benefit of a chest-pack parachute, which enabled me to turn in my seat and do my stuff with the Gee box and so forth. The pilot sat, like all pilots, on his chute. This arrangement meant that the navigator had to go first; next the pilot had to get his left leg round the control column and get his bottom, complete with chute, from the bucket seat. Thus encumbered, he then had to pull himself across the cockpit and out of the little aperture at the side. And while he did all this, he also had to keep control of the aircraft itself.

In Reg's case, I reckoned that he had had a maximum of ten seconds from the moment that I had left the aircraft until it had impacted on the ground. Not long to do all that, especially with the aircraft in its unstable state. With the starboard engine feathered and, worse still, with half the undercarriage down on the starboard side, the aircraft's inclination was to roll over. Was Reg smashed to pieces in that bonfire? He probably wouldn't have burnt to death because everything had happened so quickly. Anyhow, the engines in a Mosquito were too far apart for a fire in one of them to have spread to the main fuselage. But if he hadn't got his leg round the control column or hadn't managed to get to the door in time, there would be nothing left of him by now. Or so I gloomily thought as I hung in the dark and windy sky.

Judging from the flight path of the stricken aircraft, we'd probably had more height than I'd thought. Fifteen hundred feet perhaps, possibly even two thousand feet. I never saw the ground at all until it shot up to meet me and my feet touched the top of something dark and soft: a pine forest. Next, I was being swept through it at about fifteen knots with trees rushing past me, brushing my body, almost whipping me. It was strange: inside a second, I had lost the sky and was plunged into the midst of this heaving foliage, descending into the upper branches while the wind still tugged at the canopy of my parachute. Suddenly I came to a halt. My chute had become entangled in the tree-tops. I hung there, swaying slightly but caught absolutely fast; it was only a minute since I'd been pouring coffee in the Mosquito. I pondered my predicament. I might well be quite a long way from the ground. I remembered stories about people who had parachuted down safely only to break an ankle or, worse still, a leg because they had been too quick to undo their harness. I resisted this temptation and instead began deliberately to sway from side to side.

Slowly I worked up a pendulum motion. I still didn't manage to touch anything. I was well and truly hung up in this barbaric forest of soaring German firs. I swayed to a stop, caught my breath, and began swaying again, this time determined to keep it up until I swung far enough to catch one of the trees. I swayed and swayed until I developed a rhythm like that of a manic pendulum in a grandfather clock. My hands were outstretched on either side. At last I felt a tree on my right. I kept going. Here at last, was my escape route. Eventually, with a huge swing, I managed to catch hold of the tree on my right. I gave myself time. I got my legs round it as well as my arms, my hands just met round the trunk. Once settled, I took a deep breath and squeezed the release of my parachute harness. It fell away with a snap and I was left like a monkey clasping the tree. Slowly I began to let myself down. It was a long way down; mercifully, being night, it was too dark to see how far. I slithered down bit by bit until the trunk grew smoother and I slid almost uncontrollably down the last stretch. I hit the ground hard and rolled, perfectly safe, on to a deep bed of pine needles.

My first thought was to have a cigarette. Like most aircrew, I smoked. I then found that I was missing many things – such as the two tins of cigarettes always tucked into my battledress shirt and my webbing belt complete with service revolver. The jolt of my parachute opening and catching my falling body had shaken off anything even slightly detachable. Even my spare maps had gone. The service revolver didn't matter as I wouldn't have been tempted to shoot my way out of the Ruhr pocket. But my cigarettes were a real loss. God, how I wanted one.

Although I knew roughly where I was, I didn't know whether I was on our side or theirs. Clearly, I hadn't landed anywhere busy. Everything was silent apart from the stirring of the wind through the tops of the pine forest. It wasn't raining, and it wasn't too cold. The date was 9 April so spring had started. Very faintly in the distance I could hear a dog barking. I was warmly but incorrectly dressed with, under my battledress blouse, a white cablestitch sweater with the Blundell's trimmings round the neck. Sporting and convenient for flying (138 Wing tolerated informality) but hardly the gear to be captured in – if that was to be my lot. However, there was one thing I could do. Cut off the tops of my aircrew boots with the clever little knife slotted into the sheepskin lining. I pulled it out, opened its single blade and then carefully cut along the line where the upper part joined the shoe. Except for looking rather fat, the remaining shoes looked perfectly ordinary and unlikely to arouse suspicion. Unfortunately the rest of my outfit would hardly pass as normal in daytime Germany.

I decided to stay where I was until first light. When this appeared on the horizon, I got my bearings – or at least I thought I did – and set off in what I took to be a southerly direction. This way, if I was the wrong side of the bomb line, I would at least be walking towards the advancing US troops. I was soon out of the pine forest and moving cautiously down a field. I found myself on a small and seemingly deserted road. I walked along it and came to a crossroads. The road was white, probably the colour of the chalky ground itself, with gullies on both sides. In the half-light, I saw several uneven hummocks in the gullies. To my intense surprise, one of these suddenly rose a few feet from me and spoke a few words of German. The figure wore a forage cap and the greatcoat of a uniform. Six further hummocks stirred into life. I had walked into and woken up a group of sleeping German soldiers. Yet more now arose from the other side of the lane.

18 The Other Side of the Hill

I was fortunate in the weather. It was unexpectedly mild for the second week in April. The night had been almost warm and the mist in the valley was wispy and fitful. Altogether, I was surprisingly comfortable in my eccentric outfit. The Luftwaffe ground troops were almost amiable as they took me to a local HQ. Once there, I was left with a junior officer in the front room of a farm house along with two NCOs amidst a miscellany of signals equipment. As I had no German and the lieutenant no English, we communicated in very broken French. In reply to his questions, I gave my name, rank and number and said I'd been shot down by a German night-fighter. He accepted what I said in a bored way and waved me to a chair. This was my first leisurely view of the other side. These were representatives of the army which had almost brought off a world coup, single-handed. I initially registered that they smelt different from anyone on our side; not strongly, just strange. This was hardly surprising as the soap I'd washed in, my clothes, everything about me, came from other sources. Their country had been sealed off from mine for over six years. So it and everyone in it was bound to emit a strange bouquet: a slightly sour, sickly, fusty smell, redolent of wet blankets; the odour of the ersatz, of shortages, of living too long in the same uniform.

The improvised office was busy. A typewriter clattered away, heads were down, telephones rang and messages were written on pads. From time to time, NCOs came and went. From the doorway, I could just see a funny looking truck rather like an old Bedford fifteen hundredweight. At length, the officer turned to the older NCO and gave him a string of instructions, ending up by pointing at me. He was getting rid of me. I was clearly unwanted baggage to be passed down the line as quickly as possible – as a German prisoner would have been in the hands of the RAF. The NCO got up and motioned to me to follow him. A tough wiry man, he was armed with nothing more than a pistol in a leather holster on his belt. The officer said the sergeant would accompany me to HQ. He hardly looked up; he wasn't hostile; none of them were, just uninterested. We went outside and passed the truck. It *was* a Bedford fifteen hundredweight. The sergeant saw me glancing at it and drily commented: 'Dunkirk.' It said much for British workmanship that after nearly six years service in the German army it was still running. It also bore testimony to the Germans' skill at make-do and mend. This was further exemplified by three patched-up wagons drawn by horses. The last working horse I'd seen was in Devon.

The sergeant and I set off along the road through hilly countryside. We were in an area of villages just south of the Ruhr. The houses looked fairly modern so we were probably close to suburbs. There was no traffic and little conversation. My sergeant was pensive and withdrawn. He only volunteered that he'd been in the German army since 1938, a year before the war started; and that he'd been in a number of places. He looked a real veteran, the sort of German soldier who could be relied on to go on for ever. There wasn't the faintest sound of war but I was still almost certain that I'd landed near the bomb line; at a guess, five to ten miles north. I was amongst the scratch forces specifically assembled to hold the southern flank of the pocket. I forecast that the Germans would be squeezed out of the Ruhr inside a month.

I estimated that we walked for two to three miles. It

was a good thing my modified footwear was comfortable as I was going to cover a fair distance on my two feet over the next few days. We arrived at a hamlet. It was busier: along with the usual horse-drawn wagons, with scruffy German soldiers, there were two German-made army trucks, a small, very old vehicle complete with wood burner, stack of wood and gas tank, and a newish jeep, probably picked up in the Ardennes – all camouflaged and very carefully parked under trees. We entered a building. I was told to wait in the hall while the sergeant got rid of me. I could hear his explanation. Mission accomplished, he came out, waved goodbye and went. He was immediately followed by a much younger man with two small stripes on his arm. 'Come with me,' he said in English. 'We must wait now.' So we sat on a bench in a field behind the local HQ.

'You play chess?' my escort asked. There was nothing I wanted to do less. 'Yes, a little,' I answered, without enthusiasm. 'Good,' he said producing a wallet from his breast pocket. When opened, this turned out to be a chess set made of thin cardboard, every piece in place; every square with a little slot in it. I'd never seen anything like it. Our game started at about noon. My tummy registered a rumbling protest at the lack of bacon and egg. Out came his knights. As he took the first of my pieces, he said: 'I must take your watch.' 'Yes, of course.' It was an American-made Waltham. I wondered whether I should have strapped it round my ankle but decided that probably it wouldn't have been any use as I was bound to be searched eventually. As my escort seemed pretty harmless, I decided on a counter ploy. So bringing out my bishop I said, 'I really would like a cigarette.' In fact, like any other smoker in an emergency, I fervently craved one. He brought out a packet and took out two, one for himself and one for me. 'Now give me your watch.' 'What about another cigarette?' I replied. There was a pause. 'Give me your watch, and I will give you a packet.' He produced a packet of ten, German army issue. As I was bound to lose the watch, I hadn't done badly. Cigarettes in this particular context were like gold dust. I gave him the watch and pocketed the packet. The cigarette was quite like a Balkan Sobranie but lightly packed and with foreign bodies which, as I smoked, flared up.

The chess game dragged on. I wanted to shut my eyes and sleep, but prisoners can't be choosers. Appearances had to be kept up. I managed to spin out the game for some thirty moves before he soundly beat me. It was another example of the German master race asserting its intellectual superiority. One game was enough for my warder, thank God. He pulled out a newspaper, and started reading. I wondered whether they were still being published every day. Eventually it was time to move on. He looked at his watch. Mine was now safely in his tunic pocket. Apparently we were due somewhere soon. After another long walk, we fetched up amongst a further group of soldiers. It turned out that my chess-player was to accompany me in a truck. We piled into the back of one driven by a wood-burning appliance. It crawled down the empty road at a snail's pace under a sky mercifully free of aircraft.

After only a few miles, we stopped in a pretty little valley, this time in front of an older house. The corporal took me inside, through a front room full of signalling equipment, along a corridor strung with wires and upstairs to a bedroom at the front. He clattered off downstairs. I looked round at the furniture covered with white lace-trimmed cloths. On the chest of drawers there was a photograph of a sternly handsome young man in Luftwaffe uniform, presumably the son of the house. At the bottom of the photograph there was a date, 20 September 1940; almost certainly, he was a victim of the Battle of Britain. A blonde middle-aged woman came in with a large plate of potatoes. She put it down on a table, smiled and left me to get on with it. A spoon was stuck in the mound. I was very hungry and pitched in straightaway. It was quite delicious: light, fluffy potatoes laced with sauerkraut. It was much the best thing that had happened so far that day.

An hour later, the corporal and I were off again; this

time once more on foot. During a two-hour walk, we met only one soldier, nobody else. Then we arrived at another little house with more soldiers about this time. My corporal handed me over to another corporal. He waved and went. After a wait, I was taken indoors into an office where a German officer sat behind a desk. He spoke perfect English. 'So how is "merry England" these days?' He must have seen me puzzling over this extraordinarily inappropriate expression because he then said, 'I worked in London for several years. In the German State Railway office in the Haymarket, you know.' He smiled knowingly, like one Londoner talking to another.

'How interesting,' I said rather lamely.

'I liked England very much,' he said before switching to a more business-like tack. 'Let's see what you've got in your pockets. Turn them out, please.' I began to do so. He chattered away in the meantime. Had I heard all the propaganda about concentration camps? I nodded. 'Yes, well, what a lot of propaganda! Such silly stories!' And a good deal more along those lines. He contended that the Germans and the English were really good friends; friends who would soon be fighting the Bolsheviks together ... I realized that he was building a reinsurance policy; pretty desperately too, considering he was only talking to a flight sergeant. He was very interested in my little message for our Russian comrades, and said that his colonel would like to see that. He was surprised at my packet of German army-issue cigarettes and said that it was very unlike German soldiers to be so generous. I didn't tell him about the corporal and the watch. He made a few notes. 'For my files,' he said. But I didn't really believe him, it was too late for files. I imagined the whole show would be on the move again if not tonight, certainly tomorrow night. 'You'll be meeting two American prisoners we've got here. Don't make a lot of noise when you greet them. You'll have plenty of time to talk later.' He probably meant to be friendly. The war might be very nearly over, but there were some very irascible Germans still around, including perhaps his colonel. His parting shot was: 'I look forward to seeing merry England again.' I said nothing and he waved me out of the room.

The two American GIs were not in the mould of Patton's warrior race. They were civilians only recently thrust into uniform. One was dark, overweight and gravel-voiced. The other was tall, about my age, with a slightly high-pitched voice. They were both uneasy. Being put into the army had been bad enough, to have been shipped across to Europe and into the fighting was worse still. To have been pitched into the middle of Germany and on the wrong side was a sheer nightmare. Two days ago, they'd got separated from their unit in a mêlée just to the south of where we were. The Krauts, as they called them, had well and truly pinned them down in the crossfire and they had surrendered. Wisely, probably, or they would have been dead by now.

When I talked to them (quietly, following the captain's warning) it didn't seem that anything dreadful had happened to them since. They'd been treated much as I had: pushed under armed guard from one place to another, but no one had paid much attention to them. Meeting them made me feel more at home, more confident, probably through being European. To them the whole environment was completely strange; that's why they were as jumpy as burglars caught in the act.

We were assigned a guard, a young man as tall as the tall American. He was a correct but amiable infantryman, complete with rifle. It appeared he had orders to take us somewhere. We marched off. While we were visible from HQ, he made us march rather than walk. But once away from the small hamlet, we shambled along as we wanted. We walked up the little valley for about six miles. It was dusk. We came across troops. We were now on the edge of a forest like the one I'd descended into fifteen hours earlier. In the woods, we saw thirty or forty vehicles, including some very American-looking half-tracks. A driver, seemingly dressed in black pyjamas, was manoeuvring one of them round the trees. Our rifleman was looking for somebody in authority. Eventually the half-track driver came over and talked with him.

We slept that night in the back of a small truck with just enough straw to soften the boards underneath. We were each given a blanket. The encampment was busy through the small hours; busy enough to keep me fitfully awake. Vehicles were coming and going. So were horses. Night was busier than day hereabouts.

When we woke in the early morning, the place was much quieter. There were only a few soldiers. Our guard, as good-humoured as ever, led us off to get some breakfast. Under one of the trees was an ancient cooking range on wheels. It was shaped like one of those devices for boiling clothes in, and was heated underneath by a wood fire; it had a large pipestove chimney about five feet tall. All it produced was brown coffee substitute made, the tall American told me, of acorns. It tasted like it too, but at least it was hot. Otherwise our breakfast comprised two slices of pitch-black bread smeared with a greasy, white substance unrelated to butter or even margarine; it looked and tasted like a by-product of IG Farben Industries. With this was a sausage seemingly knitted from the intestines of the devil himself: knock it, and it would immediately disintegrate into its original constituents. Boarding school inured you to this sort of food – indeed, the sausage was similar to the brawn at my first prep school – so I wolfed it down, not having eaten since the wonderful potato mix the previous day. However, to avoid looking at the sausage, I carefully wrapped it up in the black bread. The two Americans couldn't get their portions down at any price.

Realizing perhaps that our delicate Anglo-Saxon digestions might need help with Wehrmacht sustenance, our escort took us to the black pyjama'd half-track driver of the evening before. He was still fiddling with the vehicle. 'US Army half-track,' observed the tall American. The soldier in black chatted away to our escort and then produced from the cab what looked like a methylated spirits bottle but with clear liquid inside. He took off the top and took a good swig, passing it to our escort who did the same. It was then passed to us. It tasted like raw spirit. It was probably Steinhager, the German gin which, taken neat, is enough to take anybody's breath away. It was a generous and very welcome gesture but I felt that, on top of the sausage, all I needed was to light a cigarette and I'd have gone up in flames.

We waved goodbye to the soldier in black and began another day's march. When we reached some farm buildings two hours later, our escort suddenly pressed us against the wall. We realized why when he pointed up to the sky. Circling round several thousand feet up were American fighters on the lookout for something to attack. They saw nothing and went on their way. An hour later we came across the first signs of their handiwork. Broken wreckage in a ditch stretched for about a hundred yards. There were several vehicles and beyond in the field, several dead horses. One had been inexpertly raided for horse meat. Two had distended bellies, a feature of dead horses with which I was to become familiar. In several places cannon shell had gouged inch-deep channels in the road surface. No wonder vehicles moved at night.

By mid-afternoon we had arrived at another makeshift HQ. It was similar to those I'd seen yesterday but rather more elaborate. A good deal of telephone wire was strung out between the buildings and improvised signposts pointed to various units. We entered a house guarded by two sentries. A door opened and our escort ushered us in with a quick, muttered goodbye. As he did so, he smiled. This was a mistake. For inside the room was an officer like a caricature German: a frog-like man with deep jowls, bald head and large ears. The metal insignia hanging by a chain round his neck indicated that he was a military police officer. He roared with rage at our poor escort who stood petrified, close to rigor mortis. The only evidence that he was still alive stemmed from a deep red blush over his face, neck and quite possibly the rest of his body. The appalling

Germanic tirade rolled on. It stopped with a sudden flourish which could have been a sentence of death. Our escort did an about-turn which would have done credit to the Brigade of Guards and shot out of the door, banging it behind him.

For a moment there was silence. Then the frog-like officer advanced slowly towards us, smacking his lips as though preparing to expectorate. Both the Americans still wore their US army webbing equipment. Standing in front of them, he plucked and pulled at these pouches; when they came away, he threw them with contempt on the ground. He glowered at us. I found him deeply terrifying. Up till now all the Germans I'd met had been very different from anyone else I'd ever encountered, but at least human. Here at last we had a sample of what all the fuss had been about: a barely human specimen who was very nasty and quite likely to bite, still breathing heavily and vibrating with anger at the fraternizing behaviour of our escort. He urgently wanted to emphasize that this was totally irregular: any sane German, he implied, hated us and held us in the deepest contempt. He might have been deciding whether to have us shot or boiled in oil.

At length he turned and went back to his desk where he picked up a field telephone and started talking in very guttural German, conducting himself vigorously with his free arm. There was a knock on the door and it opened almost simultaneously to admit a younger German officer, also with the metal plaque of the military police. As he was talking urgently across the desk, he suddenly noticed us, stopped and made a remark to the frog-like officer, who grunted. The newcomer shouted. A sentry came in and escorted us out; he took us away, if only temporarily, from what threatened to be torture and execution. We went through the back of the building across a yard into a barn. There we were amazed to find at least twenty-five American servicemen sitting around on chairs and on the floor. The guard shut the door behind us and joined the group of German soldiers outside.

19 Prisoner on the Move

Most of this group were from the Eighty-second Airborne Division. There were two officers, one captain, a lieutenant and several NCOs; the rest were privates. They were part of a unit which had got ahead of itself and had been cut off. One was slightly wounded with tiny fragments of shrapnel mainly in his back. They were good natured and only mildly curious about us. They had been prisoners for three days. Of the rest, there was a tank crew led by a second lieutenant who had had to jump out of a Sherman when it had brewed up and a tiny American pilot who, when artillery-spotting in an Auster, had himself been spotted and shot down.

And there was one Englishman, Jim, a slim, narrow-faced nineteen-year-old from Preston, also a survivor of a tank that had brewed up. His unit of Churchills had been attached to an American group on the southern flank. When his tank was hit by an eighty-eight-millimetre shell, it was the third time he had been shot up in that way and, he told me, it was only because of his experience that he had got out this time. He had then rapidly crawled back down one of the ruts left by the tank tracks, thus avoiding a hail of machine-gun fire. He explained that his paybook described him as a wireless operator. Had he been an operator of flame-throwing equipment, he'd have been shot there and then; indeed he was the only member of his crew to survive. Jim's immense experience of tank warfare was hardly reflected in his very limited views of life in general. Nonetheless it was a pleasure to have an Englishman as a companion.

That evening the group got fed from another *Mother Courage*-style field kitchen. It was soup or stew or gruel, again with very black bread. I gave one of my five remaining cigarettes to Jim and one to the American couple to share between them. Even then, compared to most of the group, I was still rich in cigarettes.

There were no blankets so we bedded down using straw to soften the floor of the barn. I noticed that the prisoners looked pretty scruffy, and I realized that I must look the same myself. None of us had washed or shaved for several days, and we must, collectively, have smelt; but not, I hoped, as much as the Germans.

The night went peacefully. After a breakfast of acorn coffee and a slice of black bread, we were left in the barn all day. The talk was desultory, everybody was nervous. We didn't think the peaceful interlude could last, but it did. In the afternoon, we got soup from the *Mother Courage* field kitchen and another piece of bread. Much more of this diet and some of the overweight American soldiers would be looking quite slim. In the early evening we were told that we'd soon be on our way again. As the light faded, a noise outside heralded the arrival in the barn of another group of American prisoners; twelve infantrymen and three American air-crew. Two were from a neighbouring base in northern France, St Quentin, from where they'd been flying twin-engined bombers on daylight raids.

The third was the dirtiest man I'd ever seen. He was a second pilot, aged twenty, from a Flying Fortress which had been shot down three weeks ago on a daylight mission over Berlin. He had evaded capture when he bailed out and had hidden during the day, walking westwards by night. He had carried on for over a fortnight, living off raw root vegetables in the fields. Once, he had been growled at by an Alsatian guard dog in a farmyard. He decided that the dog was going to attack him, so he took pre-emptive action by lunging at it suddenly, football tackle-style, grasping it round the neck and throttling it to death. He had finally been caught when preparing to swim the Rhine. His capture may well have saved his life. He looked extraordinary because the rain had run down his dirt-encrusted face and made little channels so that his face had a map-like overlay masking his features. When he smiled, his white teeth contrasted dramatically with his dark, grimy skin. Jim, the spotter pilot and myself joined forces with the three airmen to form a sub-group amongst all the infantrymen.

The barn doors soon opened again and several German soldiers ordered us out of the barn and formed us up into a column. This was done in a leisurely manner and without too much shouting. There were over forty of us straggling along the roadside in twos and threes; moving westwards; with two guards at the front and two more in the middle and at the back.

As it grew dark, we could see winking lights and flashes to the south and behind us in the east. We also heard the grumble of guns. It was the front. We felt – indeed we were – cooped up in the pocket. Now it was night there was plenty of traffic, most of it horse-drawn vehicles and the odd truck going in our direction. As we passed through a small town we saw the railway on our left up an embankment. A blacked-out train steamed and clattered past going in the opposite direction, and I wondered where on earth anybody could be going within this encircled remnant of the Third Reich. On the other hand, it demonstrated that until the Germans were actually overrun, soldier by soldier and yard by yard, they would go on functioning whatever the circumstances. They were survivors. Doubtless the soldiers around us had been in pockets before, had time and again been surrounded and cut off and separated from the main body; they had just learnt to be phlegmatic. To us prisoners, the scene was bizarre and dramatic; as the flashes closed in on us, rich in promise of imminent violence, we knew this war was about to end. The pocket would be pinched out within a day or so and the rest of

Hitler's Germany would be squeezed between the Allies and the Russians and extinguished within the next few weeks. We all knew that; all except the Germans who, even if they knew it in their heart of hearts, kept it out of their faces; perhaps they were so inured to trouble, they simply didn't realize that this was the last time. I was reminded of this years later when I heard stories of the last twenty-four hours on board the *Bismarck*. The bakery had gone on baking bread well after the ship had been mortally wounded, right into the morning of the day the ship sank. Perhaps it was this capacity to carry on regardless that had enabled the Germans to survive for so long.

We struggled on through the night. Fortunately we were all young and had been very well fed up to the time of our capture, so we were fairly fit for what was becoming an ordeal. Nobody dropped out or made much fuss. We stopped every two hours for a ten-minute rest. We straggled into a village at dawn and were directed to a large café, empty apart from tables and bentwood chairs which scraped on the tiled floor. We immediately collapsed on to them in a variety of exhausted poses. There wasn't any food or drink. Although the wall mirrors there advertised various German beers, it seemed that the last glass had been drawn many months ago. Our escorts stayed at the door. We rested there for an hour; then we were on the move again, but not for long. Half a mile down the long village street we turned off to a barn attached to a house and relieved ourselves behind it. We soon discovered that we were in the middle of a sizeable encampment. It was our final destination.

We got one meal that day, soup and black bread again. A German army doctor came to look at our slightly wounded infantryman from the Eighty-second Airborne. Then a civilian surreptitiously opened the door between the house and the barn and tossed several packs of cigarettes into our midst. There were two each. In those days, there weren't many non-smokers.

Later in the day we heard the odd shell exploding

nearby or whining overhead. Slowly but inexorably, the front line was rolling towards us. Our nervous tension increased. The spotter plane pilot particularly disliked the situation. Artillery was his business and he could estimate each whine and crump in terms of its potential danger. Nothing fell on us and the routine wore on. The kind civilian from the house looked in again and produced still more cigarettes. Whenever the door of the barn opened, we could see that the number of German soldiers outside had increased. Evening came. We settled down in the straw unfed; the capacity of the master race to feed us seemed finally to have run out. All of us, prisoners and guards, were waiting for the end. During the night there were odd bangs every ten minutes or so; enough to keep a nervous man awake but not enough to terrify him. The group was largely silent. I could see the occasional cigarette glowing in the dark. That was all.

Next morning, events took us by surprise. As we filed out to relieve ourselves and get some fresh air, we saw that there were even more German troops in the immediate vicinity. There were now droves of them, surprisingly without rifles; these were now neatly piled up in the middle of the road. Even if it wasn't going to be formal, it was going to be a neat surrender. As we looked, the first American troops began coming down the road, sauntering, almost loitering. They were casual yet effective. They held their rifles in the crook of their arms. The Germans busied themselves with forming into their equivalent of platoons and companies; disciplined to the last, they were going to march into captivity in the order in which they had marched as conquerors. It was a bloodless handover. Our party of former prisoners were very relieved at so peaceful a release.

The American soldiers walked past us; they were concentrating on their advance and had no time to stop and speak. Clearly we were not the first group of prisoners they had come across. Somebody started to lead us down a path at right angles to the road running across the fields. We were going one way and the American infantry, spread out across the fields, were coming towards us. Only by badges of rank and helmet did a stocky lieutenant dressed in British battledress confirm that he was a US infantry lieutenant.

After our group had gone two miles, over the brow of a hill and down the other side, we reached a point where an American lieutenant told us to stop because some transport would be along in due course. 'In due course' were the operative words. We were supernumeraries, nobody's responsibility. Just off the lane, there was a flat field in which were parked three newly painted, very effective-looking eighty-eight millimetre guns; they all pointed south, from whence the US troops had come. It looked as though the eighty-eights had hardly been used before they'd been overrun. There were the remains of a half-dug emplacement. The personal belongings of the gun crews still lay where they had been dropped a few hours earlier.

While we were examining this material, a couple of shells came screaming overhead and exploded on the other side of the lane. Doubtless these came from some eighty-eights further back which hadn't yet surrendered. We all stood where we were, waiting for more. But nothing happened. Those two missiles were the last to be sent our way by the retreating Germans. Although the noise had been extremely frightening, we knew that the Germans were ready to surrender, and that all the US infantry had to do was press on and everything in front of them would yield.

No transport arrived for us though. What did arrive was a truck which peeled off from a convoy and came towards us. It proved to be full of K rations and tins of beverages, mainly Coca Cola. The K ration was the lowest common denominator of American service rations: a small box with a varied snack and a small supply of lavatory paper. It came from that far distant land which had invaded Europe from across the Atlantic, bringing unimagined plenty. Apart from containing thousands of calories the quality of these rations was infinitely superior to anything of local origin; needless to say, we all had a very good lunch indeed.

Two trucks came for us and we piled in. We were the right side of the bomb line now where everybody could do what they wanted during daylight hours. Power and plenty were flaunted under the warm April sun. We made off to yet another barn. There was some groaning at this. But where else could the authorities send us? To all kinds of units in different places but only 'in due course'. Meanwhile the army was much too busy moving on, and before anybody could do anything about us, the rear echelons had to catch up. At least there were no guards at the new barn. Furthermore we were soon issued with two blankets each: thick, warm, unworn American blankets, not the thin semi-ragged central European variety. Later on, in the early evening, a chow-wagon turned up, a truck with a built-in mobile field kitchen; it produced stew, white bread and coffee in luxurious contrast to the thin gruel and black bread of the past few days. Although we were disappointed not to have been magically catapulted home, we began to accept this step-by-step reconnection with Allied living standards as it allowed us to savour each separate stage at our leisure.

20 By Police Car to the Rhine

Vehicles ranging from massive trucks to nimble jeeps drove past our barn. And as the battle of the advancing army filled the quiet countryside, we marvelled at the foresight, discipline and organization of this immense American monster. Compared with the world we had just come from on the other side of the hill, the contrast was extraordinary. The sights and sounds of the Americans amazed me: even after eighteen months in Canada and the US during training and continuous mixing afterwards with Americans in the UK. It must have been the impact of the undiluted American presence; and if it made this impact on me, the locals must have felt not just culture shock but surprise mixed with the envy that results from seeing people from what is virtually another world. It reminded me of a scene from the pre-war film *The Shape of Things to Come* when a radiant Raymond Massey steps from a space capsule into a world broken by cosmic strife, to walk amongst its inhabitants: just as the latter could hardly credit the dramatically arrived symbol of power and might, so did the locals stare, amazed and confounded at the Americans.

We were in grave danger of setting fire to ourselves, or rather to our barn which was dry and full of straw, because we were all busily smoking our heads off as dozens of two-hundred packs of Camel, Chesterfield and Lucky Strike had been distributed. After two minor conflagrations, the captain from the Eighty-second

Airborne had two buckets of water brought in ready to throw over the next fire. He accompanied this useful action with a personal lecture on not burning ourselves to death now that, for the time being anyway, we had avoided the dangers of war.

The next day, halfway through the morning, we were off again in two trucks, each man carrying his precious blankets. This time we went north to a suburb of Gelsenkirchen, a town in the southern Ruhr. We stopped in the main street and were shown into a large five-floored warehouse with plenty of room to spread ourselves. One floor had been used as the dispatch point for the local laundry. Numerous neat parcels of clothing still awaited laundering. In another room, further parcels of clean laundry awaited collection. Many of the citizens of Gelsenkirchen would have to wait forever for their deliveries as we didn't hesitate to forage for clean underwear.

On another floor there were countless French clocks so tightly crammed together it was almost impossible to walk across the large room without treading on them. It looked as though a German collector, working perhaps for a Nazi bigwig, had scoured France, lifting clocks off every mantelpiece.

I decided to try and clear up one of the smaller rooms in case we were going to stay for several days. I press-ganged young Jim and he helped me shift a store of office desks out of the room and into the long passage outside. I had found two iron bedsteads on the top floor and we brought them down to our new quarters. In another corner of the building we came across bolts of cloth, presumably the stock of a local black marketeer. I took a bolt of fabric, a light green stripe on dark green, and turned it into bedspreads and a rough tablecloth. It all looked rather effective.

With Jim and an American, I explored the cellars. Our research proved that we were in some black-market Valhalla as we found a cache of food clearly arrested in transit. There was almost enough to start a shop: several hundred eggs, ten pounds of butter, no meat but masses of vegetables. That evening, we organized a four-minute boil-up for everybody. The eggs and the fresh butter reinforced the K rations. As some people wanted two minute-eggs and others six-minute eggs, there was some confusion and several complaints but, by and large, it went well.

I was to discover that the American youth was gripped by enthusiasm for the internal combustion engine. Put a car at his disposal and he was in paradise. The wily Germans had already spotted this in the first couple of days of occupation. Three German saloon cars appeared in the courtyard of the warehouse, all in quite good repair. In these, the GIs took turns to joy-ride round the suburbs of Gelsenkirchen. Interminably over the next two days, they cadged petrol off the corporal in charge of the local US transport depot two hundred yards down the road. The obliging Germans provided a pioneering example of fraternization as well as the cars, by hanging around, joking and chatting with the GIs – unlike the rest of the German populace, which remained stern and stony-faced and avoided all contact with us.

On the third day, a truck arrived for the first of our group, leaving about thirty of us behind: the Eighty-second Airborne contingent and the assorted aircrew, plus Jim and myself. Life slipped into a routine. We had a guard roster and I was on it. I did my duty one evening along with one of the Eighty-second chaps. To carry out my task, I was given an unfamiliar US firearm. I didn't ask how to operate it for fear of demonstrating my complete ignorance of such matters. I seldom met a nicer group of Americans than those from the Eighty-second. They were friendly, open and completely devoid of that slight tendency toward boastfulness which sometimes characterizes the American warrior. These men were warriors all right, the very best, with the modesty typical of the true product.

The next morning we woke to find that they had all been picked up in the night by their unit. So that left the two airmen from St Quentin, the pilot who had walked across Germany, Jim and myself. The spotter pilot had gone with the Eighty-second chaps. What's more, the three civilian vehicles had disappeared too. Each night, the owners had garaged them taking the distributor heads with them and reappeared in the morning with the vehicles and the distributor heads. This morning they didn't reappear. So we were truly abandoned and without any mode of transport. There was nothing for it but to make our own way back. Nobody was going to come and collect us; so far as officialdom was concerned we had ceased to exist. I worried most about Jim.

Fortuitously, shortly after breakfast, I met a British officer in battledress in the street, the first of his kind I'd seen since our release. He belonged to some Indian Army regiment, and was desperately looking for Indian Army personnel released from prisoner-of-war camps. He wasn't remotely concerned about me but I somehow managed to arouse his interest in Jim, to such an extent that he finally agreed to take him back in his jeep later that day. He would report to his local HQ and it would send Jim back to the nearest British army unit. So we said goodbye to Jim, swearing to meet up again in the UK, which of course we never did.

There were now four of us. Leaving behind the pilot to look after our few oddments and blankets, I went with the two Americans from St Quentin to hunt for some transport. We walked down the road and scoured the side streets in the hope that a car might have been left behind. Some hope.

We came to a garage set back from the road, built against the side of a house. There was nobody about. We didn't wait to find anybody but opened the door of the garage – to discover a small Mercedes saloon painted with German camouflage markings. It had probably been requisitioned by the police as it had blackout hoods over the main headlights and a small siren fitted above the bumper. It was perfect apart from having only three wheels; to deputize for the fourth, a large wood block nestled under the axle. We shut the garage door and went in heated search of a wheel.

Further on, the road dipped slightly into a valley where there was a factory building. We went down to it and pushed our way through the factory gates. Again, there was nobody about. As I took my first step on to the factory floor, I trod on some tiny ball-bearings which, as far as I could see, covered the floor. We were clearly in a small ball-bearings factory. All three of us glided around the floor; it was almost like ice-skating without skates. Suddenly there was a cry from one of my companions. 'Look,' he shouted, 'down there!' And he pointed to a corner where three or four spare car wheels were neatly stacked.

One of my companions knew even more about cars than most Americans. In fact, he was an expert as he had worked in a garage in the days when you needed to know a good deal about the mechanics of the vehicles. He chose one of the wheels and we went back with our prize. The miracle was that it fitted. Whoever had taken the fourth wheel off the Mercedes had neatly put back the bolts by a thread or two, all ready for the missing wheel. We quickly took off the bolts and our expert hoisted the wheel on to the axle. It slotted in perfectly, a true marriage. On went the bolts. Two of us lifted while our expert kicked away the blocks below the axle. Soon the car was resting on four wheels.

Next we had to get the engine started. Our expert knew how to activate engines without recourse to ignition keys. After fiddling around under the bonnet for ten minutes, he got the engine turning but it didn't fire. So we went back down the lane to look for petrol; we were pretty sure we'd find some around the factory as it had obviously been abandoned in a hurry. Sure enough we found some jerry cans, several of which were full. We carted one back. Our expert repeated his starting routine with the engine and this time it fired. Our friend jumped in, let in the clutch and slowly the car moved forward. But the locking mechanism on the steering column was firmly in place and the car could only describe a small arc of a few feet. This was solved simply and swiftly. The expert latched on to an axe lying by some chopped wood at the back of the shed, and hacked at the lock until it fell away. The steering wheel turned perfectly. We were in business. All four wheels present and correct; petrol in the tank; starting mechanism working, albeit in an improvised manner, and steering unlocked. Slowly, the expert drove the vehicle out on to the street. The few people who were around took no notice of us.

First we drove down to the factory to exchange the empty jerry can for a full one. I then found some white paint and a brush to paint an emblem on the roof of the car. We then drove back to pick up our fourth member, the pilot. He looked at our magnificent prize, sitting on the edge of the pavement, and was gratifyingly amazed. It was pure Third Reich, resplendent in German army camouflage, complete with police siren mounted on the off-side wing. No wonder nobody looked at us. We were an embarrassment, a living anachronism – even though the war in these parts had only ended a few days ago. A new leaf had been turned. Now nobody was a Nazi or had ever been a Nazi, so this glaring demonstration of their immediate past must have been a source of great embarrassment.

We thought it by far the most powerful and impressive vehicle we'd ever seen, let alone owned. While we packed everything, helping ourselves to a pile of K rations and Coca Cola cans, I set about painting a white star inside a circle, post-D-Day the insignia of the Allies. It looked quite good so long as you didn't examine the star's shape too closely. The point was that a marauding aircraft, seeing a German police car speeding along under its gun sights, could well take a pot shot at it even though it might be on the Allied side of the bomb line. With luck, this white D-Day star, so recognizable from the air, would guarantee us safe passage. That, anyway, was my theory.

Soon we were ready to proceed. But where? The others felt it was up to me as the navigator. 'You're the expert,' they chorused. I pointed westwards into the sun; towards the Rhine. Once across it, we would be in friendly territory. As we drove out of the town, the road forked slightly north and south. I chose south as we didn't want to drive into the Ruhr. The countryside was beautiful; the weather was perfect, and the road, through narrow, was good. The car ran smoothly. We were so pleased with ourselves we could have hugged each other.

There were obstacles though. One long, straight stretch of road had been shaded by an avenue of mature trees on each side. In its retreat, the Wehrmacht had attached a standard explosive device to every tree. When exploded, this device neatly folded the tree across the road at about chest height. As the invading troops had come north, a couple of tanks had driven up the road and pushed all the trees aside; leaving just enough room for one vehicle to go down the middle. There was no traffic coming the other way so down the middle we went.

Then we came to our first major bridge. Or rather its remains as it had been blown up, leaving us to cross a medium-sized river of clear, fast-flowing water. Again the tanks had cleared a kind of pathway, passable for heavy vehicles but possibly not for us. We slid and bumped down the track which lay along the embankment of the road. This was no problem; unlike the river itself. A stone-made ford of a kind had been partially pulverized by tank tracks. We edged gently forward into about a foot of water. Then the stones got bigger and the depth greater. We stalled in mid-stream. Not promising.

On the far bank, a small crowd had assembled. They were clearly DPs (Displaced Persons): men in dark suits with flat caps; women with shawls over their heads. We got out of the car and into the clear ice-cold water. We walked to the far bank and the small group. The men smiled and spoke in a language we didn't recognize, probably Russian. We gesticulated and pointed at the car in the river. The men spoke to the women. The latter, about twenty of them, dutifully went down to the river's edge and walked into the water to the car. They then picked it up and walked out of the river. They put it down where we stood. Although there were twenty of them, with considerable collective lifting power, it still looked a feat worthy of Charles Atlas. They made the car look feather-light. We produced one of our many cartons of two hundred cigarettes and gave it to the men. Great expostulations and laughter followed. The women had done the work and we paid the men. It was expected. We switched on the engine and the reliable Mercedes started immediately. We were once more on our way.

Fortunately we came across no more bridges for a while. As we approached the suburbs of Cologne, the countryside got more built up. There were signs of air-raid damage everywhere. As a result our road ran a peculiar course. It took us up on to a section of autobahn for a few miles. Then we came to the broken span of another bridge. It had sheared off on our side and dropped to the level of the road below, which the bridge had once spanned. The broken section sloped up, complete with railings and street lights all still intact, to the other side. It was as though somebody had come along with a knife and cut the bridge off with a neat surgical stroke. A track took us down the embankment and thence on to the road running at right angles which we would have spanned had the bridge been intact. This then followed a tortuous route past two factories bereft of roofs and windows. It was the only way through. We'd got to a point where the streets were filled with rubble up to the first-floor windows of the gutted houses. The ruins seemed uninhabited and still in the warm April sunshine.

The devastation was far more total than any in London; it was the end result of not just one raid but raid after raid after raid. Saturation bombing had driven the locals to abandon huge segments of their city. We found out later that until the end of the previous February the Germans had managed to clean up after each night's activities, returning the city to some semblance of working order for the next day. It was only the last month that had finally overwhelmed the city's capacity to survive. We were now seeing it some ten days after the raids finally ended. It was impossible to imagine how the place could be brought back to life again.

We went on along our track very slowly because it was all too easy to turn off the proper route and get caught in a bombed *cul-de-sac*. At one such turning we stopped to deliberate. There was another car there with three British soldiers: one draped over the front bumper, one in the driving seat and another behind. We went over to them. Unlike us, these men were hardened veterans. They had been captured by the Germans in the desert. Their battledress was neat but paper-thin from years of wear. At first glance their faces looked tanned, but this tan was not the result of sunshine, but of exposure and hunger spread over years. They smiled as we met them, but laughter didn't come easily. They too were driving home, having obtained their vehicle by good fortune. They didn't go into details. We decided to link up together, at least for the next stage of our journey. We drove off in a convoy of two.

We threaded our way through the remains of Cologne and came out on the southern boundary of the city. Once on the open road again, we looked for a place of refreshment as we were all parched. We had noticed how the dust in the bombed city was beginning to stir due to busy traffic, all US Army. The desert rats led the way and waved us down when they reached a café. It was clean and bare. When a middle-aged woman came to serve us, our companions were correct but curt and their German sounded fluent to us. The woman was tight-lipped and hostile but would have got the same response from the desert rats if she'd been friendly. They weren't keen on fraternization. The tea – my first cup since leaving Cambrai over a week ago – was marvellous. The three Americans dutifully drank it but I guessed they were longing for coffee. We finished, left a few marks and departed. Our two cars were held up shortly afterwards by a fleet of tanks coming towards us.

We pulled on to the right-hand verge in front of a turning to the left which the lead tank took when it reached it. Swivelling on its tracks and churning up the road, it turned across at right angles and took the easterly route. The tanks were a commanding sight with their long gun barrels pointing straight ahead. Each one was directed by a crew member sitting in the open turret. About twenty-five of them lumbered past us, followed by a convoy of trucks. Whether these armoured vehicles would ever get to grips with the Germans before the fight was over was doubtful. It was half an hour before we could resume our journey south.

21 The Road Home

We headed for Bonn, towards the only bridge across the Rhine – in the US sector anyway. There were no bridges left at Cologne. After another hour or so we reached Bonn which was then just a provincial town. The road took us straight to our destination, the General Hodges Pontoon Bridge. It led off a sizeable square dotted with parked vehicles. We joined them and got out as we guessed that we'd have to get a pass to cross. In the event, there were other formalities as well.

A cigar-smoking major in the US infantry was in charge. Standing on the steps of an office building, he gave rapid-fire orders left, right and centre. Privates with messages got immediate answers and immediately disappeared. There was a lot of gesticulating and shouting. The major's deep, gravelly voice travelled well. I got the impression that he thoroughly enjoyed being at the eye of the storm; relished every minute of controlling access to the sector's only bridge across the Rhine. From the west came the rear echelons, complete with the reinforcements necessary to sustain a US army forging steadily eastwards. It all had to cross the bridge. Going westwards, our way, there was an amazing assortment of vehicles and people like ourselves. They weren't all allowed to pass. The sudden shrinking of the Ruhr pocket was precipitating the release of hundreds of thousands, even millions of DPs: foreign labourers and POWs who'd been working in the German munitions industry and miscellaneous groups that were, like ourselves, each making their own way home from a collapsing Third Reich. We found the barrier at Bonn unexpectedly lax because the regulating powers which follow an advancing army had yet to arrive. Had we been four SS colonels disguised as Allied soldiers, we could have escaped with little or no difficulty and then driven on through France and into Spain; quite a few probably did just that.

Eventually we caught the major's eye. 'Carry right on,' he barked helpfully. 'No, you don't need a pass. Fill up with gas over there,' pointing with his cigar. 'And boys, report to the medical unit just over there,' another jab, 'and good luck!' That was it. We got our petrol and went on to the medical unit, one of the most basic any of us had come across in our service careers. It consisted of four medics in white coats with hand pumps filled with a white substance. When they pressed the pump down, the nozzle extruded a cloud of DDT. First the nozzle went down the neck of our clothing and several vigorous pumping motions followed. The same treatment was applied to the end of the sleeves, round the wrists, and then up the trouser legs until a white cloud was storming around inside our clothing. We were being disinfected, like everyone else who moved across the General Hodges Pontoon Bridge. The Allies used DDT widely over the following weeks. It was judged afterwards to be one of the period's great medical triumphs: while dreadful typhus epidemics broke out during the First World War, particularly in the Balkans, there were none after the collapse of Germany in 1945, despite the millions of people moving around at the time.

Our two-car convoy then joined the motorcade queuing to cross the pontoon bridge. After an hour our turn came. We were in front of the desert rats and behind a smart low-slung saloon of indeterminate make pulling a trailer with a tarpaulin neatly roped over its contents. Fussing around them was an RAF squadron leader with pilot's wings but no medals. His uniform was trim but exhausted and his cap badge seriously faded. Seated in the front passenger seat was a young lady who was, as far as I could see, neatly turned out; certainly no sort of DP. The squadron leader waved at us in a vague way and said 'hallo' in a friendly but firmly distancing tone. He wasn't approachable. Nor, in a way, were the desert rats. Our shared difficulties in finding our way through the bombed suburbs of Cologne had prompted them to tell something of themselves but not much; without that common experience, they wouldn't have unbuttoned at all.

Looking at the line of vehicles ahead, it struck me that there was altogether very little *bonhomie*. People were keeping themselves to themselves and getting out of Germany just as rapidly and independently as they could. They weren't keen to share their experiences or their joy at their new-found freedom. We four airmen were a noisy exception that attracted several disapproving glances. But we weren't really part of their world even though we were travelling in the same stream; we'd only briefly tasted Nazi Germany, they were returning from goodness-knows-what experiences. The squadron leader seemed to be a paradigm of the Englishman who quietly but firmly imposes order on disorder. I'd no idea how on earth he'd come by this vehicle and trailer, let alone this lady. I liked to think myself a good organizer but compared to his performances, my efforts paled into insignificance.

My American companions were oblivious to all this. They were similar, under the skin, to our recent companions, the men from the Eighty-second Airborne. Like almost all Americans in north-west Europe, they were only there for the duration; for twelve months at the most. They had arrived in the ETO (European Theatre of Operations) just before D-Day. This included the second pilot from the Flying Fortress. They all had been on operations and as soon as peace broke out a few weeks' hence they would be amongst the first to get home. To them Europe was a blurred vision – a Theatre of Operations, in the phrase of the day. The fact that it was also a place where people lived, where the war had started, where civilization had sprung from, didn't impinge on them. They weren't interested and even if they'd known, they wouldn't have cared. The talk as we drove along in the Mercedes police car was all about their families, jobs, cars – and accidents they had been in. The two aircrew from St Quentin had done most of the driving. I could hardly drive and, strangely, the Flying Fortress pilot couldn't drive at all; by the time he was old enough to learn, petrol rationing had come in.

At last the queue began to move. We edged forward between the squadron leader and the desert rats. The pontoon bridge was a robust affair with two highways, one for each direction. Heavy vehicles rumbled along on the other side and the bridge was clearly capable of bearing tanks. The pontoons heaved gently – about a foot or so up and down – as vehicles negotiated the bridge. As we drove slowly across, a panoramic view of the Rhine unfolded before us.

Once on the west bank, we were in a far more ordered world. Military sign-posts pointed to this or that unit and every square foot of ground was bespoke. We had come from a vacuum: a Germany where millions still milled around as occupation zones had yet to be established; a limbo where there was no law, authority or government. In retrospect it was surprising that we hadn't come across more violence over there. There were rumours of marauding gangs, of Russian POWs on the loose, but we'd seen nothing. The Germans we'd come across were quietly going about their business, sweeping the pavement in front of their houses in the areas which hadn't been bombed. I remember a quintessential German woman, young but matronly, with plaited hair, in a red dress with a patterned bodice in the local style, sweeping a yard on a farm. She struck me as the epitome of how a woman should look in Hitler's Germany. But she had also looked quite serene and composed. There was no fear in her face nor in those of any Germans I'd seen. Sullen yes, but fearful no.

Before we headed for the Belgian border, we said

goodbye to the desert rats. They'd had enough for the day. In measured response to their new freedom, they were pacing themselves carefully. They needed rest and were off to the laager for the night. In my mind's eye, I saw tanks forgathering in the desert and char brewing up on a camp fire. We shook hands, smiled at each other and that was that. We were too excited, too young, too full of energy to hang about. We wanted to be on our way.

In the evening we drove over the Belgian border and came to a major garrison town full of American troops. We passed a mess hall. This was too much for the Americans. We had to stop and get something to eat. We parked our German police car and walked in. We were served without comment: ham, eggs and good American coffee. It was our first meal that day and we were famished. An officer wandered over and sat down with us. 'Deserters?' he asked in a friendly manner. Initially I thought this was an extraordinary thing to say. But I soon realized that – now that we were travelling through the rear echelons – we must look suspiciously unkempt; to the trim, clean people in the ordered world we could only be one thing: deserters. We tried to explain, gently, that we'd all been shot down in various ways and were now, after several incidents, on our own way back. 'But how did you get across the Rhine?' the officer asked. 'Not by swimming,' we said, but he didn't respond: humour wasn't in order.

We drained our coffee. It was time to move on. If we stayed here, somebody would fetch the MPs and we'd have to explain ourselves to all kinds of busybodies. We thanked the officer and returned to the Mercedes. We turned off the main street into a side street, just in case somebody was following us. It was odd. Here we were back amongst friends yet we felt insecure. Ideally, we wanted to make our own way back to St Quentin and Cambrai. Meanwhile, the fact that we had no currency, no papers, a stolen foreign car and looked like nothing on earth was going to be something of a handicap.

We spent the night in the car in a side street of

Namur. Next morning we were stiff but content. We later dropped off the Flying Fortress pilot at a small USAAF depot in the city centre. They'd see that he got back to his base in Suffolk. Then we were on our way again.

Our next stop was Cambrai where my homecoming proved to be a mixture of joy and disappointment. We drove down the Douai-Cambrai road, turned to the right and homed in on the nest. A few hundred yards short of the building, we passed a flight sergeant navigator, Tom, who was crewed with a Canadian flight lieutenant; they'd both arrived on the squadron some six weeks ago. I waved at him. He stared, open-mouthed, but recognized me and raced back to the nest. We drew to a halt outside. It was about half-past eleven in the morning. There was nobody about. Obviously the squadron had been on an operation the night before. I got out and went in to the room which contained most of the British NCO crews. There they were, the ones that I knew, lying about on their beds or still in bed listening to the radio. The surprise on their faces was well worth seeing. The point was that no crew which had gone missing had ever, until then, reappeared. In the unlikely event of survival, they were POWs. Otherwise they were dead. We were the first to get back. So the surprise was genuine; they simply couldn't believe it. Then of course there was the fun of introducing them to my two new American friends and showing them the car. That really took the biscuit. We had got used to it, but to them the sight of the Mercedes with its bizarre camouflage police markings parked outside the squadron building was utterly fantastic.

I felt as though I had returned from the dead. And as far as they were concerned, I had, for I was told that Reg Everson, my pilot, had got back five days earlier and reported me as dead. For that was what the Germans had told him. They said that my body had been found in the woods, and that I was *kaput*. He had no reason to doubt it and had returned to tell the tale. Although he had landed only two miles from where I came down, he had fared very differently. He had been captured by German soldiers who had in turn themselves been captured next day by the advancing Americans. So he had been returned through their rear echelons to Cambrai nearly a week before my return. The authorities at 138 Wing had written me off and had recrewed Reg with a recently arrived navigator who for some reason was lacking a pilot. They had then sent the pair off on leave.

While some of the chaps whisked the Americans off to the mess for a drink and some lunch, I was taken to the CO. He seemed very pleased and very surprised to see me. He offered me a cigarette. And I was in such rocky shape that I helped myself to three of them. I checked myself too late and he smiled and told me to keep them. Even though I had only been in Germany a few days, I had got used to cigarettes being by far the most valuable commodity in circulation. While some of my aircrew friends jumped into the Mercedes for a joy-ride, I was conveyed by jeep to the station HQ. Here I was taken to see the station 'brass': the group captain, the wing commander flying and the 305 Squadron intelligence officer, an Oxford-educated Pole who spoke perfect English and sported a handle-bar moustache. Gratifyingly, they showed considerable interest in my recent history. 'We were getting very worried about you,' said the intelligence officer with the handle-bar moustache; his concern sounded genuine although to him I can only have been just one more member of a missing crew.

Then things began to go wrong. As I came out of station HQ, I was shattered to see 'our' Mercedes – front wheels in the air and an RAF redcap standing on the rear bumper – being towed away by an RAF pick-up truck. It moved slowly towards the RAF police vehicle parked behind the building. I asked what the hell was going on and was waved towards the RAF police hut beside HQ. As I entered my heart sank. For there were the two Americans with several American MPs in their ridiculous white snowdrop helmets and two RAF police together with an American intelligence captain and his aide. I later found out that on their joy-ride my friends had had a burst tyre. Our faithful Mercedes, having brought us back through thick and thin, had finally succumbed to a mere blowout. All things considered, it was extraordinary that we hadn't had one before. But it was sod's law that it had happened now – not on the perimeter track where it wouldn't have mattered – but while our chaps, dressed in pyjamas and flying jackets, had been belting along the Douai-Cambrai road. There they were fair game for the RAF police who had picked them up with great relish. The MPs could do nothing about the motley crowd in the car; putting them in jug was out of the question as the crews would be on ops that night. But the MPs had at least had the satisfaction of swiping the car. The Americans had then come over to HQ to reclaim it. By then the American authorities had been contacted and my two friends were caught in the net of their intelligence people.

I felt thoroughly depressed as I could hardly refuse to be involved in the interrogation. The de-briefing angered all three of us. It was conducted by the American captain and a British flight lieutenant, both intelligence officers, and their assorted NCOs. The US captain was particularly supercilious and given to innuendo. He shook his head with disapproval at our story of crossing the Rhine by car. He could hardly believe that we'd got away with it. Where were the security checks? Where indeed? His cross-questioning brought home to us that we were now up to our necks in an administrative area: an area always rife with pompous irritating people. They had hardly impinged on us before because we were protected by the 'front line' status of the airfields; operational needs usually guaranteed immunity from the intrusions and attentions of intelligence personnel. But this time our own people were apparently powerless to protect us. The two Americans were driven off by the American contingent and I never saw them again. Our faithful Mercedes police car also disappeared and that was that. I was rescued by a request from the wing intelligence people to make myself available for de-briefing. Depressed beyond words, I left the MPs' hut and went over to the HQ building.

The de-briefing was extremely interesting. The most important piece of information required of me was my estimate of the time and place at which we had been shot down. I knew the time all right and I thought I knew the place, within ten miles anyway. When I gave these, heads nodded, new cigarettes were lit and significant looks were cast at the maps spread out on the table. I had all along assumed that we'd been shot down by a German night fighter, probably a JU88; victims of misfortune as, at that late stage of the war, the Germans were flying from only a few of their airfields.

But I was wrong. A US night fighter had put in a combat report claiming it had shot down a German JU88. This had been within too few minutes and too few miles of my estimates for it to be mere coincidence. It was us they had shot down. The aircraft was a twin-boomed US night fighter, the P51, usually called the 'Black Widow'.

We later learned that this incident generated much interest not only on the wing but in the Group generally. Air Vice Marshal Sir Basil Embry was far from happy at having one of his aircraft shot down by a supposedly friendly fighter. And I understand that he gave the Americans hell. That said, the Allies frequently scored 'own goals' during the war, particularly in the closing stages when the field was seriously crowded. Amongst many such incidents were the tragic shooting down of Allied aircraft carrying troops at the time of the Sicily landings and Bomber Command bombing our own lines near Caen in France. So we were far from unique. On the other hand, the incident betrayed excess of zeal – exuberance even – on the part of our American allies. We had been headed due west and apart from the Ruhr pocket, where no German aircraft were operating anyway, we had left the main front line hundreds of miles behind when this P51 had decided to knock us out of the sky with its sudden strike. To think we could have been a German aircraft stooging quietly along at an altitude of about one thousand feet required a great deal of imagination; a commodity in which these bright young lads, fresh over from the US, were clearly rich. We could only thank our lucky stars that the aim of the pilot was a fraction off so that his four-cannons-worth of shell bored into our starboard engine rather than the main body of the aircraft – a hair's breadth difference which saved our lives.

The next day I was off on leave again; this time for fourteen days' 'survivor's leave'. The squadron couldn't use me as Reg had gone a week earlier and I was spare. The squadron was busy flying some extended missions. Because the bomb line had by now run right across western Germany, operations were concentrated north of Hamburg and up to the Danish border, taking in Sylt, the target for the earliest raids of the war. We'd been shot down the night after the CO had given his little morale-boosting lecture about careful flying and cutting down casualties. He must have thought us perverse to have gone missing straight after his strictures. We'd been the ninth crew to go missing since our arrival at the end of December. While we'd been away losses had abated and only two aircraft had failed to return, which meant that, during our time, a total of ten had disappeared; over half the battle order of eighteen; just under half the total of aircraft and crews on the squadron. Our return notched up a 'prodigal son' notoriety.

Our unprecedented reappearance, albeit piece-meal, confirmed that, even if the question of life after death was still unanswered, life after being posted missing was possible. Our kit had been collected and annotated by the adjustment officer and we would have to go back to Uxbridge to reclaim it. Everyone on the wing soon knew our story, especially the final flourish of my return in the Mercedes; it was a great source of encouragement to them all. The episode also gave the fire-eating Air Marshal Embry another issue with which to berate

Higher Authority.

The squadron admin office caused a telegram to be sent to my aunt. By then she had of course also received the telegram so dreaded by next of kin during the war: the one that said a loved one had gone missing. Sadly, the second type of telegram was sent very rarely. I collected my things and boarded the daily Dakota now on a milk-run that included Cambrai before returning to Croydon.

22 VE Day

I first called on Reg Everson who lived quite near Croydon aerodrome. As I got on to the trolley bus that evening, I registered for the first time that it was 24 April and therefore, my twenty-first birthday. I soon found Reg's – or rather his parents' – home, a neat, semi-detached house. It was a quiet reunion. Reg's parents put a bottle of whisky on the table and in one hour we had two drinks each; that was all. We each told our stories in turn. Compared with my adventures on the ground Reg's were rather dull. The Germans had picked him up very quickly and advancing Americans had almost immediately released him. He had then been fed back through administrative areas which functioned far more efficiently than those I'd passed through, and thence to Cambrai.

But I was most anxious to hear what had happened in the few seconds after I had jumped. Reg told me that as I bailed out of the small door on the starboard side, the aircraft was already hopelessly unstable with a dead engine and one wheel sticking out in the landing position. Reg tried to get his left leg round the steering column and at the same time, to lift his parachute out from under him. He had succeeded and was just descending into the crouch position when the aircraft started to roll over on to the dead engine. This was extremely dangerous because in seconds the aircraft would go into a spiral and pin him to the floor – and thereby prevent him from throwing himself through the small aperture. His only option was to push his way back into the aircraft, knowing that at any second it could well smash to the ground.

He violently wrenched the steering column to port in a desperate attempt to right the aircraft. He succeeded. With one hand still holding the column to the last split second, he got as far as he could across the cockpit and then released the column and threw himself out of the aircraft almost simultaneously. There was no time to count before pulling the ripcord of the parachute. Quite the reverse. Reg saved his life by pulling it the very second he was caught in the free air outside the aircraft. His parachute opened perfectly, took his weight – and the next second he hit the ground. He was probably two hundred feet up, no more, when he left the aircraft. In terms of time he was dealing in tenths of a second. I marvelled at his skill and good fortune.

Reg and his parents bade me farewell with a familiar wartime sentiment, 'The best we can do is let you get on with your journey.' By nine o'clock I was headed for Oxford. I had to see my aunt, indeed wanted to do so, but in a way, I also wanted to stay with the squadron. Hearing Reg's story caused me continually to relive my own adventures; and that made me feel as though I ought to have been travelling back to the psychological security of Cambrai. It was a very strange sensation.

A trolley bus and a Southern Railway train saw me into London where I spent the night at a YMCA next to Victoria Station. I now had a flight sergeant's gold crown above my sergeant's stripes which made me a little too senior for the YMCA but there it was; I had no hope of getting a train to Oxford that late at night.

Next day, when I arrived at Oxford, I went straight to the Eastgate where I was going to stay. As I was dropping my kit, I saw one of my trainee doctor friends who shouted merrily to me, 'Still fighting the war from the Eastgate, I see.' I then walked to LMH to collect my aunt and take her out to dinner. She looked frailer than ever. My disappearing act had shaken her badly. It had brought back all sorts of unbearably vivid memories of the First World War.

For her, as for all relatives of service people, a telegram was assumed to be a portent of doom. Knowing this the RAF had been very considerate. Straight after the first telegram came the enquiry, 'Are you in any immediate need? If so, contact us now and we'll sort everything out.' In the event she wasn't, but she greatly appreciated the gesture. The CO at Cambrai had written a thoughtful, touching letter. So had the padre whom I'd never met and who couldn't have known me from Adam. Right up to the end of her life my aunt was never to forget the RAF's good manners at this very difficult time.

As we walked across the Parks I told her my story. Once the excitement of watching her reactions was over, I was bored stiff with my leave. I simply couldn't wait to return to the squadron. But VE Day supervened. We had won in Europe. The Germans had surrendered. 305 (Polish) Squadron had flown over Europe for the last time. The Far East question was another matter, but just then it was far from everybody's mind. Oxford celebrated in great style. A huge bonfire in the middle of Carfax burnt the rubber tiles off the surface of the road. I met several people younger than me from school who were up on short courses or at the university in the normal way; we duly celebrated and it was all enjoyable enough, but I still yearned to be back at Cambrai.

At last my leave came to end and I could return to the squadron, to share with my friends the sweetness of the war being over. This time when I climbed into the DC3 at Croydon, I had an extra kit-bag and two more suitcases. I had been to the centre at Uxbridge to collect my kit which, like all kit belonging to missing aircrew, had been sent there automatically. By coincidence I had arrived there on almost the last day of the war in Europe, at the end of what must at times have seemed like an endless process of accumulation. I found it, with some help, down a wide corridor of near-infinite length with a floor almost entirely taken up by small piles of kit. The place was silent, waiting for thousands of missing airmen to reclaim their belongings. I reflected that most of the owners would never come to that morgue-like lost-property office.

I got my stuff on to the DC3. Only three other passengers sat in the bucket seats ranged lengthwise against the sides of the aircraft. We smoked and chatted as we flew across northern France in the bright sunlight. At Cambrai, the aircraft parked on the apron in front of the control tower while I got out. The others were going on to Melsbroeck, outside Brussels. I got a fifteen-hundredweight to take me around the perimeter track to the 305 Squadron nest. It was late afternoon so hardly anyone was around. I went into the nest and found my bed intact and waiting for me. Last time, when I'd got back from Germany, it was missing. I wasn't expected to reappear and they'd thrown it out. But I'd found it on a rubbish tip and had promptly returned it to its proper place. Not for me the wretched little camp beds so oddly tolerated by everyone else.

As nobody was around, I wandered into the briefing room at the rear of the building. I was curious to see how the big wall map of Germany had been left. Little had changed since I'd sat in the room on the evening of 9 April. Gone was the dark area around and over the Ruhr, the shading which indicated the huge flak fortress with which the Germans had tried to keep us out of their homeland. The last few defended areas were around Hamburg and Sylt. The tracks of the last operation which had taken the squadron up to that area where still on the map.

I left the briefing room and walked around outside. The squadron's aircraft were parked in the usual places around the dispersals. Like everywhere else that afternoon the place was deserted.

Then a three-tonner drove down the perimeter and turned off to the building. From inside came yells of 'Welcome back!' from the aircrew, fresh back from bathing in a nearby canal. To celebrate our reunion, we went to the little *estaminet* which now doubled as the sergeants' mess bar. I can see them now, all smiling and laughing. It was a time for laughter. The war was over and the peace which was to worry us so much had yet to happen. We had survived, the weather was lovely and there were no pressures on us. For the past four or five years, we'd been on a moving staircase and now it had suddenly stopped, leaving us in the group in which we'd met each other and made friends. We were out of the reach of the busybodies of Training Command and we had everything we needed. Above all, there'd be no flying that night.

Throughout the station, togetherness and good cheer prevailed. That weekend all ranks joined in a station party, an occasion that must have been the high water-mark of equality, of the RAF comradeship that dissolved all barriers of rank; thereafter the pendulum was to swing the other way. As it was a fine evening the chefs cooked in the open air. Tables groaned under food and limitless beer and wine. The group captain wanted to hear my story so I ended up with his party along with two WAAFs who'd just arrived, the first women to be attached to the wing. I felt very flattered.

The only serious matter was the war with Japan. We knew that the Allies had made great progress but the conflict was still far from won. The key question was: would we be needed? Our minds boggled over the Mosquito's suitability for carrier-borne operations; it was hard enough to get it off the ground with a nasty cross wind so how were we to unglue it from the pitching deck of a carrier? Let alone get it back again. For all this unnerving chatter, nothing actually happened. Nobody came round asking for volunteers – which was just as well as there mightn't have been too many of them.

However, contemplation of these events brought home to our little group of NCO aircrew the need to apply for the commissions that were clearly ours for the asking. So we all trooped into the squadron admin office and got the appropriate papers from the sergeant. They were sent to Group and, within the surprisingly short space of two weeks, we were on our way to Brussels. We were to be interviewed by the redoubtable and celebrated Two Group AOC Sir Basil Embry. He was an airman's airman, idolized by all the aircrew of Two Group. He had often flown on operations, usually as a supernumerary navigator, almost up to the end. He had some famous RAF people amongst his staff up at Group. His last exploit, we were delighted to learn, was a victory party in Brussels; this ended with the commandeering of a yellow Brussels tram which the AOC and his staff had then driven down one of the capital's busiest streets.

Our party of eight flew up in an Oxford and stayed at an excellent hotel which had been taken over by the services. After a boisterous evening, we presented ourselves at Group HQ, a fine building near the Palace. The AOC's PA was a very pretty WAAF officer. She was also very poised and cool so chatting-up and badinage were clearly not in order.

We had been briefed that when we were asked what we wanted to do when the war was over, there was only one answer, 'Stay in the RAF, sir.' I was second in. I saluted and the bushy-eyebrowed figure with rows of medal ribbons, smiled and gestured that I should sit. His opening remark was: 'I don't like the Americans shooting at my aircrew.' I wasn't meant to say anything so he continued, 'What d'you want to do when the war's over?' I looked him straight in the eye, 'Stay in the RAF, sir.' 'Good, it's a fine life. I shall recommend you.' The interview was over. I rose and saluted. He was already looking at his papers for the next candidate. I about-turned and left the room.

I'd heard on the grapevine that the AOC had taken a personal interest in our being shot down by an American night fighter, and that he looked on the error as extremely unairmanlike, as culpably unprofessional. It reminded me of Wing Commander Paddy Maile's laconic comment to Reg and myself after the accident over the Thetford battle area, 'Bad flying.'

Meanwhile life at Cambrai drifted on. We flew on

sightseeing trips over Germany and once down to Paris. As we circled the Eiffel Tower, out of the clear blue sky came three P47 American Mustangs which promptly formed a tight circle on our starboard wing and flew round with us. Our immediate neighbour's wing tip was only a few feet away from ours. They waved gleefully but Reg was very glad to see them go; he didn't at all approve of larking around in the sky. We also managed a few trips to the UK, using Blackbush as our terminus. These were useful because, following the example of our Polish friends, we had started going in for trade. As entrepreneurs, the Poles were far ahead of us. They were used to surviving on their wits and extreme shortages of cigarettes, bicycle tyres and other items provided immense scope for their innate commercial flare.

At the time, duty-free cigarettes could be sent overseas to members of His Majesty's Armed Forces by their friends and relations in the UK. Our Poles had innumerable friends and relations who frequently sent cigarettes to their compatriots in quantities which the authorities had never envisaged when making provision for these particular comforts. Bicycle tyres, however, had to be directly imported – usually by stuffing them into kit-bags which were then crammed into the bomb-bays of the aircraft. I was always amazed at just how large a load a Mosquito could absorb.

Apart from this, and bathing in the static water tank or the canal, there wasn't much to do. There was still no food, at least in our part of France, so there was no dining out. One weekend, wearying of the wing, I looked around for a little action. Realizing that the following Saturday was 14 July – the first Bastille Day since VE Day – Ken, another navigator, and myself decided to make off to Paris. We had no problems in getting a pass and on Friday midday we positioned ourselves on the main road out of Cambrai towards Paris to wait for a friendly Allied vehicle.

We were lucky. A staff car soon drew up alongside us. It was a British major from some army unit on a 'swan' which 'urgently required' him to be in Paris that evening. As the Americans had liberated Paris, it was essentially an American city in the way that Brussels was British. Their munificent leave facilities were generously open to other Allied soldiers who managed to make their way legitimately to the leave hotels. Once dropped by the kindly major, we went to the Grande Hotel where NCOs could stay without charge. The hotel was in full peacetime swing except that there were no civilian guests, just NCOs. As Ken and I took possession of a magnificent double room we reflected that you had to be in the military to have access to material comforts and luxuries; if we'd been civilians, we'd have been in a subservient position with little to eat or drink and our only hope would have been to provide goods and services to the ruling caste, to the military. This disgraceful but, for us, delightful state of affairs was to last another three years or so.

On Bastille Day we spent the morning on a conducted tour of major sights from Napoleon's Tomb to the Eiffel Tower. Everyone on the bus was American apart from Ken and myself, so we took every opportunity of correcting the guide's historical commentary, frequently capping her remarks with: 'But it was Wellington who won the battle of Waterloo,' and other handy footnotes designed to redress an over-Gallic interpretation of the past. In the afternoon we went to Versailles where they celebrated by switching on the fountains for the first time since 1939. It was a great moment: a moving symbol and a superb spectacle. Parisians who'd crowded into the great park for the occasion, loved every minute of it, as well they might.

The evening was given over to revelry. We went to good places and naughty places. We hobnobbed with the smart and the not-so-smart and ended up by being adopted as the mascots for the night by a crowd of students. Although I was fit and had a young man's massive capacity for alcohol, I had the worst hangover of my life the next morning. A huge American-style lunch at the hotel restored some sort of physical order and we then slowly made our way back to Cambrai by train.

23 In Limbo

Meanwhile there was sadness in the squadron. We were breaking up. Our Polish aircrew contingent had already gone. The international background to their departure was strange. At the end of the war, the Poles confronted the British government with a serious problem. Britain had gone to war to defend the integrity of Poland. The First World War had demonstrated that to win on land against Germany, it was vital to establish two fronts, one in the east and one in the west. So when the Germans obliged the Allies by attacking Russia, a prerequisite of victory at last slotted into place. The price was subjugation to Russian ambitions on her frontiers. The Poles who loathed both Germans and Russians equally had been ill-used by both simultaneously, and were therefore in an impossible position. So were their allies, especially the British.

Worse was to come. The Russians did nothing to support the Warsaw rising so the Germans promptly put it down. And the Russians, their hands already bloodstained by the Katyn massacre, equally promptly took Warsaw. The London Poles tried appeasement, but the Russians would have none of it and set up their own puppet government – the so-called Lublin Committee. When the war ended the British abandoned the Polish government in exile and, in so doing, stripped the Polish armed forces of all legal status. That said, the British government did at least accept responsibility for the serving Poles. They set up the Polish Resettlement

Corps, a transitional organization to which all serving Poles in the west were gradually transferred and from which they were, in due course, demobilized. In this way 305 (Polish) Squadron was gradually disbanded. One by one, our aircraft lost their Polish markings. It was only a matter of time before the rest of us non-Poles from the squadron were posted elsewhere, to the sister squadrons and wings of the group. It was a sad ending.

VJ Day came and went. The war was over in both theatres. Reg and I were posted to Twenty-one Squadron, now under the aegis of Wing Commander Paddy Maile. In the first week of September, we flew up to Melsbroeck where the squadron was to be stationed for the next month or so. A week after our arrival our commissions started to come through. We had a final party as flight sergeants and behaved extremely badly. Considering myself the Charles Atlas of alcoholic imbibers, I accepted a challenge in the local *estaminet* that I couldn't finish, in one slug, a fifth of a bottle of Prunella, a peculiarly disgusting liqueur. This I duly did, with a pint of Belgian beer as a chaser. Shortly afterwards, I felt it was time for bed. So I said farewell to the heavy-drinking throng and once outside, decided to go the direct way back to my billet. The normal, slightly indirect way was about a mile along the suburban roads. But no, I had a perverse drunken urge to go as the crow flew or, in this particular case, staggered. This involved climbing over several garden walls, walking through a certain amount of glass and careering through a garden shed. Fortunately no buildings stood in my path, otherwise I would have tried to crash through them which might well have led to trouble.

So at last I reached commissioned rank. NCO aircrew had arguably been the most popular rank and activity in the UK during the war. We were the people's choice; true, exploits by the likes of Bader and Cheshire had put the RAF on the map, but there were also numerous heroes amongst NCO aircrew. I felt very privileged to have served with them, albeit in a junior capacity.

Reg and I had one last flight together, he as a warrant

officer, I as his flight sergeant navigator. We were to whisk a wingless wing commander in the equipment branch of Group, up to some place in Germany. I got the maps and, from the briefing officer, details of the airfield where we were to land our Oxford. It was on some just-completed airstrip but we were assured that we'd find it all right. And so we did but, there again, we didn't.

Flying across the Rhine, Reg asked me whether I wanted to take over. I warmed to this civil gesture and we duly changed places, with the aircraft pitching about a little as we did so. The wing commander, no spoilsport he, grinned and waved and we grinned and waved back. The weather then promptly blew up into a thunderstorm. I tried to keep her straight and level in the buffeting air pockets but after ten minutes Reg wanted to take her back. Quite so. More pitching, this time more pronounced, as we switched back. We waved to the wing commander. He waved with markedly less enthusiasm. Picking up the maps, I asked Reg where we were. 'Ah well,' he said, 'I don't quite know. Tricky job, navigation.' I agreed and set about trying to locate our position.

Outside it was getting gloomier by the moment. We could hardly see the ground. We flew on, roughly in the right direction but quite lost and with no option but to land on the next airfield, any old airfield, and find out where the hell we were. The skies began to clear, and the weather improved but we were still lost. Suddenly, out of the corner of my eye I saw some parked aircraft. I pointed them out to Reg and he immediately turned towards them. We were going to be all right. But what should I say to the wingless wonder in the back? I was reminded of a scene in that priceless Will Hay film, *Oh, Mr Porter!* An engine suddenly runs out of a railway station, seemingly of its own accord, and the fat boy and the old man, Graham Moffatt and Moore Marriott, run after it. Will Hay, the station-master, suddenly realizes that some explanation is due to the travellers waiting on the platform. 'Just having some runaway engine practice,' he says smiling, glasses glinting, 'just in case an engine really *does* run away one day, you know.' Following suit, I explained that we wanted to ask control whether our airstrip really was ready. 'Quite so,' said the wing commander, now white-faced and longing to feel the ground – any ground – under his feet again.

It turned out to be RAF Celle, then just a strip with a dozen Spitfires. We took off again and made for our destination. We reached the right spot and circled around. The strip looked very small but there it was on our map, clearly marked by the briefing officer. There was no mistake, we were flying around it. Perhaps we should have been a little more sceptical; briefing officers had been known to get this kind of thing wrong. But down we came. Too late, Reg realized that it couldn't possibly have been the right strip or, if it was, Brussels had over-optimistic ideas as to its condition. In the event, about two dozen soldiers witnessed Reg pancaking the Oxford with great skill on three hundred yards of strip. He very nearly managed it, but we overran the end and finished up in a field of tall wheat. At the last second, he tried to swing the aircraft round on the starboard wheel but it sank into the soft ground and, although he gunned the engine, it wouldn't budge. We were in the alien corn all right.

The soldiers ran up. We'd landed on ground destined to be the field marshal's personal strip. Meanwhile the wing commander had gone chalk white as though he'd seen his own ghost. For a chap without a flying career, he'd certainly logged up some experience. An officer appeared and when I showed him my map, he agreed that this was where we'd been told to land. 'Bloody fools,' he said, 'it'll be another three weeks before we have the strip extended to the right length.'

So we abandoned the Oxford amongst the wheat with its protective ring of soldiers. In a few days' time, somebody would have the pleasure of flying it off that postage stamp, but not us. It was just the kind of challenge that several of our more senior pilots would relish. Meanwhile we got some transport over to the HQ for which the wing commander was bound. He was very decent about his eventful little trip and joined us that evening for a thrash laid on for our benefit by the local RSM.

Life as an officer was much the same as life as an NCO. We stayed in exactly the same billets. We had no batmen so we had to fend for ourselves as before. Our mess was smaller, the food was the same and the bar rather bigger. The chief difference was the great quantity of Australians – the outcome, we thought, of all the aircrew automatically being granted commissions. Our easy-going life was only interrupted once – by a flypast in aid of what we were never to discover. Whoever was in charge made a complete cock up of it because, when the time for the flypast was due, nothing on the ground was ready. So the whole gaggle of squadrons in formation on that afternoon had to go stooging on, round and round, one thousand feet above Brussels, with the Australian language on the R/T getting more colourful by the second.

It was high time, I decided, for another navigator's initiative. I put in for 'local leave'. I discovered that service personnel within Twenty-one Group could get leave to visit relations, no matter how distant as long as they lived in the liberated territories. I domiciled a fictitious relative at 7 rue République in Grasse in the South of France. I then persuaded another navigator, John Negus, to come with me. We got our two-week passes and travel permits. We also stuffed our kitbags with tinned food such as bully beef, a useful currency at the time. Thus equipped we took a train to Paris where we put up at a hotel assigned to officers, and made our HQ in the officers' club next door to the British Embassy. Wandering round Paris that beautiful autumn, we felt on top of the world. Which was where we were: everywhere we went there were pretty girls, smiling people and free drinks.

We went over to the Gare de Lyon to find out about travel to the south. At that time rail travel in France was relatively comfortable, first-class carriages being in far better nick than their British equivalent. But the system itself had taken a hammering. The route to the south was particularly slow because the retreating Germans had been strafed all the way up the Rhone valley, and wherever it ran with the road, the railway was shattered. One of those sterling characters unique to the British army was firmly in charge at the station: a burly sergeant who harangued the locals in fluent Franglais which they seemed to understand well enough. He allocated us first-class seats on the next train going south. In just a day or two, he could have got us sleepers but we didn't want to wait that long. He seemed to think we were letting the side down by slumming it in a first-class compartment instead of having a sleeper, but he wished us well all the same.

We left at ten in the morning and didn't reach the Mediterranean until early the following morning. When we stopped at a little station, everyone got out to take the air. It was wonderfully fresh and scented. The train ambled along the coast, creaking over damaged viaducts shored up by wooden scaffolding. We had plenty of time to gaze at the colours of the sea – indigo, Prussian blue, sapphire – glinting, inviting, ever-changing.

By the time we reached Cannes it was evening. John and I had no idea of what we were going to do, but that didn't worry us. However, we were surprised to hear an American voice over the loudspeaker as the train waited in the station, puffing at the front. 'All officers de-train here,' the announcement said several times. So we got off and followed some American officers walking out of the station. 'In here, please,' shouted an American NCO, and we climbed into the rear of a truck and sat alongside the rest. The truck moved off into the night. When it stopped, one of the NCOs from the cab came round to the back and said, 'The two British officers, please.' Wondering what was afoot, we complied. 'Over there, please,' said the NCO, pointing at a door with a beckoningly lit window. Once we were walking towards it, he climbed into the cab, and the truck swung off down the road. We went into the lobby of a small hotel. A man behind the desk said, 'How long will you be staying?' This was no time to look surprised so I said, 'About two weeks.' 'Thank you, sir. Please sign here. Here are your keys. The bar is on the left, and dinner is at eight o'clock.'

We subsequently discovered that we were delivered to that hotel because the RAF had taken it over as a leave centre for its forces in north-west Europe. Called the Hôtel Montana, it lay behind the Carlton, only two blocks from the sea. Its existence appeared to be known only to the higher echelons of the service, but if junior officers found their way to the Montana, they were tolerated – as we were to find out for ourselves. The rest of the place was rife with group captains and air commodores, apart from the top floor which was occupied by Major General De Guingand, Montgomery's chief of staff, and his family.

The next day, the resident administrative officer, Flight Lieutenant Johnny Jones, showed us the ropes. He was well qualified to do so as he had his feet firmly under the table in Cannes. One well-wisher had lent him and the hotel a light-blue Hudson, a pretty pre-war convertible with a small RAF roundel on the right-hand front mudguard. Another had loaned an open speedboat with a rakish, rather fascist appearance. The casino offered officers entry and dinner for two for a nominal sum. John and I went round the bars and nightclubs, and soon found some shady characters to whom we sold our iron rations. Flight Lieutenant Jones kept us entertained. He drove John and me in the Hudson to Juan Les Pins to call on a charming family that kept a souvenir shop and consisted of an elderly couple and their two daughters. The couple – a delightful English lady and her Czech husband – had both had a very difficult war. They had stayed on in France and taken refuge up in the hills, away from the far from friendly local French. They had sent their two daughters home to England in 1940. One of them, Margaret, was a dark very attractive girl. I saw why we'd come. I bought an ashtray in a vague attempt to make my mark and was later thrilled to learn that Johnny Jones had invited her to some sort of guest night next evening. It turned out to be a formal affair, complete with place names. Sensing an opportunity, I darted out of the bar well before dinner to check the placement. As I suspected, Margaret was firmly sandwiched between a brace of group captains. I swiftly rearranged the seating, substituting myself for one of them – one of those adjustments which early in life I'd come to regard as pushy but vital.

I spent most of the evening dancing with Margaret; she was vivacious and full of laughter. The fortnight in Cannes was packed with pleasure: taking the boat out for picnics, joy-riding in the Hudson, evenings at the Casino, it was one long party. All this took place in a virtually empty town. The Americans had landed on the coast the year before, allocating Nice to enlisted men and Cannes to officers. As a result, Nice was overcrowded and Cannes half-empty. There were no civilian holiday-makers and when I strayed into the Carlton one evening, it was practically deserted. We were the hard core of the Casino's clientele. Our Hudson was one of only three convertibles visible in the town; and our fascist motorboat was the only large speedboat I saw in use. The harbour was a shambles from demolitions and, as far as the local girls were concerned, we were the only chaps in town. Selfishly speaking, I have never been in a situation where the sexes were better balanced. I also felt very strange being one of the few people with resources. It was like a dream.

24 RAF Gutersloh

By the end of September, we were due to move from Melsbroeck to Germany; to Gutersloh, an airfield near a medium-sized market town some twenty kilometres south of Bielefeld, an area which lay north-west from the Ruhr in pleasant, rolling countryside. I'd twice flown up to Gutersloh so I knew what to expect. It was a pre-war Luftwaffe station, built in the mid-thirties, with a mass of solid administrative blocks and living quarters, all very neatly laid out.

138 Wing had been disbanded altogether so we were now part of 140 Wing which had had an advance party up at Gutersloh since early May. Using some three-tonners and various other vehicles, it had scoured the local countryside and, in the first week of May, had retrieved most of the furniture and fixtures looted from the officers' and sergeants' messes. The trucks went further afield: to Bavaria to get porcelain; to the Ruhr for cutlery and kitchen utensils, and so on. By October, the windows of the administration blocks were reglazed; the offices had been re-equipped and the workshops refitted so the place was altogether ready to receive the squadrons. That said, we bade a sad farewell to Melsbroeck. We'd all hugely enjoyed the fleshpots of Brussels and each had put on several pounds, in every way making the most of our life of luxury in post-war Belgium; such a contrast to the austerity of post-war Britain. It was the last time that 140 Wing heaved itself on to four wheels. It was a great struggle for the MT

officers and staff but they somehow managed; and the RAF caravanserai then wove its laborious way north while we flew comfortably by Mosquito, a journey of about ninety minutes.

Compared to Melsbroeck, Gutersloh was ghastly: a dreary, middle-sized, middle-class town in the middle of occupied Germany with practically no entertainment to offer. Fraternization, meaning the development of normal relations at a human level with the local German population, was at the time forbidden. But the airmen quite rightly took no notice of this ridiculous rule. Within weeks, they had established local footholds; and within months, these had blossomed into full-scale human relations. From there on, matters never looked back. But it was harder for the officers. They had no network for making local contacts; a subversive activity far better suited to NCOs. While many of the officers had themselves, like me, been NCOs, they found that, once commissioned, such skills started to fade fast.

The station was organized in three layers: the Germans, the airmen and the officers. Between them lay wide gulfs: there was an abyss between the Germans and the rest, and a yawning crevasse between the airmen and the officers. All told, there were some one thousand five hundred officers and men at Gutersloh that autumn. From then on it didn't vary much, the steady drain from demobilization being filled up by inward postings and the arrival of regulars. There were at least as many Germans, probably rather more. They did menial tasks such as cleaning, maintenance and repairs to buildings. They all lived off the base and arrived by truck or train early in the morning, departing at various times. They were a grey, woebegone lot, mostly carrying continental briefcases with imitation leather pouches sewn on the outside. They looked like the losers they were: pinched, cold and shabby, the women with no make up.

But despite all looking the same, to us anyway, their previous rank and status survived, somehow transcending their state of privation. In charge of them all was

Herr Flottmann, an upright middle-aged man with thin, grey hair, steel spectacles and an altogether commanding mien. He spoke excellent English and was important enough to have a room in the HQ block, the Von Richtoven Haus, only three doors down from that of the group captain himself. He was an extremely effective leader who enjoyed a good deal of power. It came as no surprise to some of us when, about nine months later, he was suddenly bundled off having been unmasked as a former SS colonel. By then he had moved next door to the group captain from whence he was moved straight to the local gaol. And that was the last we heard of him.

The airmen lived in the big barrack blocks to one side of the administrative buildings. That first winter of peace and the winter that followed weren't much fun for NCOs. With hardly any parades, the airmen usually wore a motley mix of uniform and other garments chosen for warmth. Big sweaters and scarfs were much in evidence; so were army-issue leather jerkins. On the whole, they looked much more like followers of Mother Courage than members of the RAF. In contrast to the Germans, they did at least have plenty to eat and drink. Apart from beer in the NAAFI and tea in the Sally-Ann (the Salvation Army), there was plenty of Steinhager (German gin). But there was precious little official entertainment; a factor which swiftly motivated the airmen to get their feet under the local table. As ever with other ranks, language was no barrier.

Only officers had a civilized existence, and that was painfully self-contained. Down a short road from the main gate was the mess, a large handsome pre-war building. The ante-room was spacious and comfortable and predictably Teutonic. The dining room was vast with a gallery down one side and an eighteen-foot ceiling. The bar and the other rooms were hardly smaller, and the whole place was rife with mod-cons, German-style. For instance, the basement featured a *bierkeller* equipped with a special loo-cum-vomitorium for the use of Luftwaffe aircrew between missions. A standard fitting in pre-war stations, this was like a giant dentist's spittoon, three foot across and one foot deep, beautifully plumbed with filaments of shining steel.

The mess also boasted a tower. This contained the commanding officer's drinking room, an eagle's eyrie in which only his closest cronies were permitted to drink themselves into a stupor. When this place was being fitted out, the then commanding officer evinced the *Schadenfreude* so typical of his nation. One of his stories ended with the punchline, 'And if I tell a lie, by Gott, may the ceiling fall on us.' Strategically placed in the floor, just to the right of his low wooden chair, was a trap door four inches square; to pull this up, you thrust your finger into a small hole; under it was a little handle. When the handle was pulled, a wooden beam running across the ceiling creaked down at least eighteen inches, seemingly dropping a wooden chandelier, for all the world as though the ceiling was indeed collapsing on those below. The engineering of the arrangement was breathtakingly ingenious. It was easy to imagine the young officers dutifully exploding with merriment the umpteenth time as their commanding officer yet again played this trick on them. I assumed that any officer who failed to laugh was sent straight to the Eastern Front.

The officers' accommodation consisted of eight two-storey buildings in front of the mess, around a private road. They were beautifully equipped to the usual German standards, which were very far from standard in Britain. There was marble in the bathrooms and amongst much else, steel fittings which snugly slotted round the windows and doors. We were very comfortable and thanks to the ubiquitous central heating, very warm. We also had plenty to eat and drink; although the food was predictably appalling.

For all that, we were very very bored – presumably like all occupying forces until the barrier between them and the occupied country evaporates. This didn't happen for at least a year. Meanwhile we went through the motions of training. From time to time we attended flights, which meant sitting around for half an hour and then falling out. There wasn't much training because nobody was at all enthusiastic about it; and anyway, flying was rationed since wartime plenty had made way for peacetime penury. Reg Everson had forsaken flying to become an excellent second-in-command on the engineering side at Gutersloh; which made me a spare navigator, there for any pilot who needed one. For much of the time, no one took up the option. This suited me as my zest for flying had gone. It now struck me as a dangerous and pre-eminently dispensable luxury. Accidents occurred at a distressing rate: Wing Commander Paddy Maile had been killed; likewise several other people. All in all, flying Mosquitoes was the wrong activity for anyone with any sense of self-preservation. So I flew whenever I was allocated to a pilot but looked around for other things to do in the meantime. And during that first winter when Germans from the Ruhr used to comb the fields for something to eat, I found myself three occupations.

First, I started a magazine on the station. I was following a long tradition in the services. Newspapers were produced in the trenches during the First World War and they reappeared in the Second World War. I aimed to issue a monthly magazine rather than a newspaper which would have involved a news-gathering network and was altogether far too much like hard work. So I put up a notice in the NAAFI asking for volunteers and attracted two corporals and two airmen. One was from the photographic section with all the resources of that important department. The second was a rapid, versatile artist, virtually a cartoonist. The third, an ex-printer in Fleet Street, had all the necessary technical skills, while the fourth fancied himself as a writer so he was appointed staff writer.

We rang up the Two Group welfare people to see whether they could help launch us, but they were at once sceptical and patronizing so we wrote them off as a dead loss. We costed it out and came to the conclusion that we needed a circulation of at least five hundred for each of our monthly issues; a tall order given that the station complement was only one thousand five hundred. In the event, our circulation rose to well over one thousand. Recruiting contributors wasn't easy as 140 Wing was low on creative talent. But we picked up one or two gems. Flight Lieutenant Robin Skynner did a superb take-off of the *Daily Express* Beachcomber column, and our one staff writer wrote under three *noms de plume*. I also contributed the odd article. There were plenty of drawings and photographs, and an excellent printer in Gutersloh could do practically anything for us as long as we provided zinc plate and fuel. Getting the zinc furnished a cast-iron excuse for a weekend in Brussels; fuel was more difficult, but we succeeded somehow.

Our first issue was for Christmas 1945. I asked our group captain, Group Captain Bateson DSO DFC, for a personal message which I then had the temerity to rewrite; to his eternal credit, he let me go ahead. Gratifyingly, the magazine was a great success from the word go.

My second job was to become education officer. This came about because the magazine demonstrated that I could both read and write and, as our real education officer had been demobilized, I was his obvious successor. The job was a doddle. All I had to do was ensure that the German language classes continued. I had one nasty moment when a totally illiterate airman was sent to me. Quite what I was meant to do with him, nobody explained, but it was somehow implicit that I could give him a crash course in literacy like giving him a concentrated course of jabs in the medical centre. So I solved the problem by getting him posted.

A useful aspect of my new role was that details of all the educational or outward-bound-type courses available to the Group came to me first. In February there appeared on my desk a file labelled 'Skiing Course – Winterburg'; this announced that the army division in the mountains some one hundred and fifty miles due south of us was starting a series of two-week skiing courses. The instructors would be ex-Wehrmacht ski instructors. Our Group was allocated six vacancies for the course starting in two weeks' time. I immediately banged in a request for three candidates with myself heading the list. And after a week, confirmation came through that all three of us were to go on the course.

By today's standards, Winterburg would be regarded as pretty tame. Still, although it wasn't very high, it had plenty of snow and the accommodation was excellent as the army had commandeered as ex-SS leave centre. It was a luxurious set-up, liberally staffed by Germans who waited at table and the bar, also cleaning every inch of the accommodation at least twice a day. We were divided into three classes of a dozen each. Our particular instructor was a wizened veteran of a Wehrmacht mountain division. On skis, he assumed a hunch-back posture; force of habit, we guessed, from years of carrying a light machine-gun. He'd skiied before the war, so his repertoire embraced ancient formal manoeuvres, such as the telemark. There were no lifts in Winterburg in those days so we all became pretty fit during our two weeks.

My third occupation was to become mess officer. I complained about the food so much that one evening I was inevitably overheard by the group captain himself. Word was soon passed to the station adjutant – 'Rudd for mess officer' – and I was unanimously elected at the next mess meeting. This was no more a full-time occupation than any of the other mess appointments. But with one hundred and forty officers at Gutersloh, it was much the most serious of my three jobs. Apart from being mess treasurer, from which I'd been warned off at the Oxford University Air Squadron, there was nothing so onerous as being responsible for food. That was so at all times in the RAF but in Germany, as we came up to the first anniversary of peace, it was especially the case because food and drink were our two major diversions.

There were two reasons why the food was so awful: the ingredients and the cooks. During the first week of my appointment, I went on the early morning trip to collect our basic rations from the RASC depot near Hamburg. The vegetables were rotten, the meat substandard and fresh ingredients very scarce. To take the edge off this fearsome regimen, there were innumerable cases of 'Burma' and 'Flag' sauces, strong evil-smelling liquids, dark brown and very thick, the poor man's answer to HP. However, there were numerous cases of Californian dried fruit, of biscuits and bully beef, unpopular comestibles which were ours for the taking.

My course was clear: I had to go on the black market. My conscience was also clear: I would only swop food for food, not cigarettes or anything more sophisticated. My currency for barter would be the two sauces, Californian dried fruit, and biscuits. Nobody could have entered the markets more richly endowed. I had exactly what the Westphalian farmers wanted. And they had what we wanted: geese, chickens, hams and fresh produce of all kinds. I enlisted the station signals officer, Flight Lieutenant Morgan, to help me; this he did by volunteering himself and a signals van for weekend forays into the countryside. Farmers are the same throughout the world. Come war, desolation and even defeat, they remain islands of well-being, insulated from hunger and shortage by their unfailing capacity to produce. Even after the privations of that first winter of peace, smoked hams still hung in quantity from the rafters.

That virtually took care of the produce. The second problem was the cooking. The two RAF cooks in the mess were called Dai and Taff. They were tiny Welsh miners whose skills had not been significantly enhanced by a short RAF cookery course. From their point of view, cooking was better than mining; from ours, the faster they returned to mining the better. Their only aid was the *RAF School of Cookery Handbook*, by far the thinnest, bleakest and most unappetizing cookery book I've ever seen. Hence the poor digestion and pale pinched faces of the one hundred and forty officers who ate at that mess. So we got Dai and Taff posted down to the airmen's mess – poor airmen – and recruited a cooking staff from the mass of German auxiliary workers already at our disposal. Several had been in catering pre-war before becoming, in one case, a Stuka pilot and, in another, the navigator captain of an ME 110. They were good and willing; and we soon set about restructuring the menus.

Not altogether to everybody's satisfaction. As I introduced fresh salads, coleslaw and, when possible, fresh fruit salad, some of my customers turned out to have palates better suited to the fare of Dai and Taff. But everybody enjoyed treats such as fresh goose and chicken. My achievement peaked at Christmas 1946. I'd found out early in September that the turkey ration was little more than two ounces per head. I assumed that we would get two huge frozen Argentinian birds between the whole mess and so we did. I made (for me) a unique effort at acquiring rations on the hoof, and in early October corralled a dozen small turkeys. We put them in a clearing at the back of the mess and fed them left-overs, bearing in mind that most of the left-overs disappeared off the station to feed the families of our German workers. The only trouble was that on Saturday evenings when the drinking got boisterous, the turkeys found their way into the mess where they were put to running races up and down the ante-room. Remonstrating with the merry-makers on such occasions was difficult, but it had to be done as they were running pounds off my birds.

25 The Last Summer

As the war receded, 140 Wing changed. Wives started to arrive and married officers to leave the mess for married quarters outside the base. The prevailing atmosphere became more domestic, more sedentary, with bachelors like me falling into a self-contained category. A new group captain turned up, Group Captain Favell, who had distinguished himself on the staff. He was very agreeable and competent but quite different from, and ten years older than his predecessor, the twenty-six-year-old Bateson. Administrative ability took over from flying as the touchstone of performance. And no wonder as demobilization was now taking its toll in earnest. Each month, large groups of experienced airmen, NCOs and officers, left for civilian life. Those of us who were younger and had had shorter wars, were left behind for their own fast-approaching day of release.

In my case it was February 1947, five years after I had walked into the Air Ministry and joined up. Those who stayed on, regulars and signers-on for short periods, tried to maintain their enthusiasm for all the old tasks, but they had an uphill job. Most aircrew had done everything for real and didn't want to practice it just for fun. There were one or two assignments. The Nuremburg trials involved the wing in providing a courier service. Aircrew – including myself and a spare pilot – were sent off for a two-week training course at Sylt. We dropped some live bombs into the sea and fired our cannon on the range. Reassuringly everything still worked. More important, delicious food was ferried down from Denmark and Sylt itself was not without charm. I never saw more Luftwaffe aircraft than the vast collection of them that had been parked on the airfield there since May 1945. There were night-fighters with extraordinary radar antennae shaped like Christmas trees, and one or two enormous transports with bus-size fuselages.

We became aware of various contradictions in the Allies' policies towards Germany. It was obvious to us that the Allies would soon be relying on German help. We were in a potentially rich country, and there was no point in grinding our collective heel on the Germans. The initial attempt to prevent contamination by keeping everybody at arm's length from the former enemy had long since broken down. The fraternization which started with the other ranks, had inevitably spread throughout all personnel by the summer. Not that all the Germans wanted to fraternize with us. There were some chilly encounters in Gutersloh when RAF personnel first ventured into the shops. But the mood was gradually relaxing. We went to the opera in Bielefeld. In June there was an open day in the hills ten miles north of Gutersloh; a kind of fair to which the local Germans were invited. A famous German glider pilot with a distinguished Luftwaffe career put on a spectacular gliding display for the assembled crowd.

After that winter I longed to get away. So I applied for and got three weeks' leave in June. I made arrangements to return to England and see my aunt as on previous leaves. But, at the last minute, I decided instead to make for the South of France again. My chums agreed it was the right move, so next day I caught a flight as navigator as far as the old 138 station at Cambrai. It seemed almost deserted when we landed there. I gave my pilot a very basic lesson in navigation to get him back to Gutersloh and off he taxied in the Mosquito. A jeep came from the control tower to pick me up. The French Air Force was about to move in and take over. I got a lift to the railway station and arrived that evening in Paris where I put up at the officers' club. I rang up Margaret who was by then running the Hôtel Montana, in fact if not in name. She was very nice to me but the outlook was bad all the same. Officers were only allowed to visit if they had been granted an allocation. 'And how d'you get one of those, Margaret?' I said rather testily over the indistinct, crackly line to Cannes. 'It's not my fault, Tony,' came the answer, 'you should have applied to your own group HQ. There's nothing much I can do although I'd like to see you.' And that was that.

I returned morosely to the officers' club for a drink. And as so often happens, a seemingly insoluble problem was cracked at the bar. I was bombarded with all sorts of advice. But much more to the point, there was somebody there whose group HQ was in Paris. 'Never mind,' he said, 'we've got plenty of allocations. We'll give you one tomorrow and ring the Montana. Come round to our HQ before lunch tomorrow, and we'll fix it up.' So after a convivial evening, I repaired next day to their HQ in the avenue Foch. The chap was as good as his word. That evening I was back at the Gare de Lyon waiting for the train, my allocation safely in my pocket.

The journey was twelve hours shorter than that of the previous autumn so I was in Cannes by the afternoon. Pretty Margaret was there to reward me with a smile and a kiss. 'Really,' she said, 'trying to get here without an allocation . . . whatever next?' But her severity was all pretence; in fact, she was very impressed by my initiative.

The Côte d'Azur was even emptier than the previous autumn; the Americans had mostly gone, and nobody had come in their place. This was typical of the ETO as a whole; the Yanks had largely gone home. Meanwhile there was the Hôtel Montana in lonely but splendid isolation at the disposal of a handful of people like myself.

Cannes was charming that early summer. It was the South of France of Hitchcock's *Rebecca* or a Leslie

Howard film like *Intermezzo*: no crowds, no traffic jams, practically no tourists. Only two of the main hotels, the Carlton and the Majestic, were functioning. The harbour had been badly damaged, presumably during the 1944 landing, and had yet to be repaired. The only place of formal entertainment was the Casino in its old building, just along from the harbour. In its backwater, behind the Carlton, the Hôtel Montana had settled down since my previous visit. The food was better, the French chef having reasserted his authority in the kitchen. And Margaret now regulated the comings and goings of all the service personnel. One aspect was unchanged: most of the hotel's visitors were at least of group captain rank, often higher. I had travelled down on the train with an Australian flight lieutenant and his girlfriend, a WAAF officer. They were clearly well connected and, shortly after their arrival, they were asked out to dinner with the Duke of Windsor who had once again taken up residence in the area. It was all a far cry from the gloom of Germany and the austerity of the United Kingdom.

It became even more removed from harsh reality one evening when Margaret and I went to the Casino. Standing out from the crowd there at a formal dinner dance was a tall, comfortably built man, bald with a thinnish moustache, who continually smiled at his partner – as well he might for she was stunningly beautiful and dressed in a formal ball gown which billowed from her narrow waist. Her dark hair was entwined round her head, ballerina-style. The smooth Australian – he and his girlfriend were sharing our table – identified them as Faiza, one of King Farouk's sisters, and her Turkish husband. The WAAF girlfriend, who was stationed in Paris, claimed to know her slightly. And so she did. Because a few minutes later, a note came over from Faiza's table, inviting her and her Australian escort to join them. Making their excuses, they did so. And Margaret and I went on dancing. Half an hour later a note came over summoning us. We looked at the table and caught the eye of Faiza's husband who waved.

It was a charming gesture. They hadn't wanted us to feel left out, so we were to make up the party. That was when we stepped on to the magic carpet for two solid weeks.

Faiza was staying at the Carlton for a month. There were four of them. Ali, her husband, had brought along a friend called Ugues, a handsome fellow of six foot four, a muscular twenty-five-year-old who was the elder son of a land-owning family in Madagascar, then a French colony. His Parisian girlfriend was, by normal standards, very pretty but she had the misfortune to be alongside Faiza whose staggering beauty would have eclipsed practically anyone.

Everybody danced with everyone else. When it was my turn to dance with Faiza, I thanked my lucky stars that after four years of treading on the feet of countless girls, I was at least adept enough to stay off her toes. She smiled and made light conversation – 'Are you down here long?' . . . 'This is my favourite time to be in the South of France . . .' Anyone would have thought that she came there every year which, given recent history, was an impossibility. It was all part of the dream world.

Just after midnight, there was a move to extend the evening into the night club below. Faiza excused herself and said that she would come back a little later. So we went downstairs, switching from champagne to whisky-and-sodas with the change to the less formal venue. A quarter of an hour later Faiza reappeared. She had changed. Instead of the formal ball gown and tightly entwined hair, she was now in a long green and black dress which clung to her excellent figure and her black hair flowed down to her shoulders. We drank and danced into the early hours before strolling back along the Croisette to the Carlton and, for us, the Montana.

It might have stopped there except that next afternoon I went shopping for some shorts and a playshirt along the Croisette. I went into a sportswear shop for both sexes and in there, buying half the stock of girls' swimsuits, was Faiza. She welcomed me like a long-lost friend and asked me back to have a drink. It was about six in the evening so we walked back to the Carlton and she hailed her husband from the garden. They had a room at the end of the second floor on the corner. He came out on to the balcony and waved to us to come on up.

Later that evening, Margaret and I dined with them in the hotel. We made plans to hire a fishing boat next day and have a picnic on the Isle de Lerins. The smooth Australian hired a boat, complete with crew of owner-captain and boy, and I procured a picnic – gastronomically French-English – from the kitchen of the Montana. Ugues came too, although without his girlfriend.

It was a great day. Ali delighted in little things. There were some English biscuits embossed with the word Uttoxeter; and Ali claimed that the more he consumed the word Uttoxeter, the more English he felt. Meanwhile, we left a crate of Provençal *vin rosé* to cool in the sea. Faiza sedulously avoided getting sunburnt while Margaret tried to get as brown as she possibly could. After a long lazy lunch we looked round the monastery and walked about the island; we ended up at a little café where I was introduced to my first *pastis*, a drink I've greatly enjoyed ever since. It is an index of my *naïveté* that when I first heard the word *pastis*, I though it referred to the local form of high tea. When I admitted this, I provoked much merriment.

To repay our hospitality, plans were immediately made for a very special dinner. This provided my introduction to the gastronomy of the very rich: a phenomenon far removed from the much vaunted three-star meal beloved of heavy eaters and big spenders. The very rich prefer simple food. We went to a quiet, almost rustic restaurant, with the *patron* and his wife in attendance. We started with caviare from vast round tins opened in our presence; next we had tiny lobsters, not *langoustes*; then chicken grilled in herbs. As for the wines, they were a revelation – to me, anyway.

During dinner Ali related some of his adventures. He had wished to marry Faiza during the war but he had been in Turkey. So the British had sent a destroyer to take him to Cairo where he had married her. They now spent only a small part of the year in Egypt and otherwise camped out – one month in the Carlton, three winter months in Madrid and so on. There was little talk of politics, they far preferred to gossip and speculate about their circle of friends. I think their hospitality stemmed from boredom: there weren't many people around and they liked company. Their manners were exquisite. When Ali and I were in the bar at the Carlton, waiting for the 'girls' as he called them, he warmly shook the barman's hand. 'Bonsoir, Prince,' the barman said, smiling with pleasure. Ali greeted everyone else with great courtesy too, and they always replied in kind.

So the days rolled by. We had a trip to St Tropez in a 1939 Buick sedan which they'd hired for the month complete with chauffeur. On the evening of the dinner with the Duke of Windsor, Ugues and I were given *carte blanche*. We began with dinner at the Carlton and then progressed by the chauffeur-driven sedan through all the bars and nightclubs of the town. At five in the morning, Ugues took a very striking-looking tart back to the Carlton while I returned on my own to the Montana.

Every day Ali received a surprising quantity of begging letters. One evening, while waiting for Faiza, he read some of them out to me. They were mainly from elderly ladies seeking to advance the careers of their younger sons. The ladies were all titled: the duchess of this or that place, usually with a long unwieldy Teutonic name, from some part of the Russian-occupied half of the continent. They were members of great families cut adrift by the war. They had survived gas chambers, transportation and the rolling forward of the front line; and they were now in a world in which it was impossible for them to gain any sort of foothold. So every other day, Ali would settle down to write replies on Carlton Hotel writing paper, regretting that, for the time being anyway, there was nothing he could do for the sons of these charming old ladies. I felt somehow suspended: a fly, not so much on the wall but in the air, watching events in a world quite foreign to my old world – that to which I'd shortly return.

At last it was my turn to play the host. The smooth Australian and his girl had gone back to Paris a few days earlier so it was up to me to lay on the festivities. Opting for dinner at the Montana, I briefed the proprietor and the chef, both of whom already appreciated the importance of the occasion and the status of my guests.

The evening started well. Margaret was in tremendous form and looked her best. Ali and Faiza loved having drinks in the bar which, over the past year, had become festooned with RAF bric-à-brac and mementoes of parties. Then we sat down to dinner. To my horror, I found that the proprietor and the chef had, with typical French arrogance, produced exactly the sort of fussily elaborate meal I'd sought to avoid. We started with a velvet-smooth fish soup and Faiza hated soup. Next we had a dish which initially defied analysis: something fishy in white-wine sauce on rice. Faiza emitted a sudden short scream, then laughed. 'It's *poulpe*,' she exclaimed in triumph. With a sinking heart, I realized that the chef, eager to demonstrate his mastery of the local dishes, had served us octopus as our fish course. Luckily, there was plenty of excellent white wine. From then on the dinner, now established as an unqualified disaster, became a highly enjoyable farce for everyone except myself. And soon even I shrugged off despair and joined in the fun. I was acclaimed the anti-hero of the evening, the perpetrator of the most devilishly clever trick of the month: a dinner so appalling it reduced everyone to helpless hysteria.

The third course was well up – or rather down – to standard: slices of Charollais beef so underdone as to leave little pools of blood on the plate, and Faiza hated blood. The meal was rounded off with a massive *bombe surprise*, a combination of hot and cold that rattled even the firmest of teeth fillings; to douse the impact of fire and ice, we drank lashings of the champagne served with it. It was a fitting end to a holiday that had everything: Margaret, a still unspoilt Riviera, constant entertainment and a social education. Ever since then, whenever I've been in France, I've always tried to shake hands with as many barmen as possible.

Having overstayed my leave by several days, I reluctantly boarded an austerity version of the Blue Train and went back to Paris. While I could get away with a few overdue days by pleading travel trouble in war-ravaged Europe, I hadn't time to experience such difficulties in reality. I vaguely knew that there was a milk run from Paris up to one of the German airfields near the BAOR (British Army of the Rhine) HQ. On the off-chance of getting a lift, I tried the Grand Hotel as a likely haunt of aircrew. And sure enough, I found two aircrew who were flying up in the morning. 'Put your name on the manifest,' they said, 'be downstairs in an hour and we'll be happy to take you.' At three that afternoon, I got a lift from a staff car outside Bielefeld all the way back to Gutersloh.

The last six months at Gutersloh began to drag. We few survivors of 305 did our best to keep amused. We drew Norton motorbikes from the MT (motor transport) section and had an aptly named crash course on how to ride them. They gave us some mobility and also contributed to several parties which ended up with the mess variant of the TT races.

As an example of an operational unit in good working order, the station was often visited by VIPs. For some reason, even as a lowly flying officer, I seemed to get caught up in these affairs. On the morning of a visit from Lord Tedder, I happened to appear as defending officer in a hopeless court martial. Afterwards I had to explain myself to the great man over a pre-lunch drink in the mess; he was very correct and a little dry. Then there was the visit of Marshal of the Royal Air Force Sir Sholto Douglas, now head of BOAR. This was particularly important for our commanding officer, Group Captain Favell, because he'd been a staff officer on Sholto Douglas's staff during the war. Unfortunately it fell to me to be orderly officer of the station on the day of the visit. I decided that the best stratagem was to make myself as smart as possible, complete with orderly officer's armband in place, and go to the kitchens of the airmen's mess. I reasoned that the entourage was bound to visit there, inspect the food and ask the fatuous question, 'Any complaints?' So I asked the question first and familiarized myself with the kitchen layout and the fairly grim menu of the day. I then waited and sure enough, round came the entourage, Douglas to the fore, chin thrusting proudly ahead. I saluted in front of cauldrons seething with bully beef stew. The cooks were all correctly placed; likewise, the stew and the orderly officer. The entourage satisfied itself that all was well and, to my immense relief, wheeled off to its next port of call.

The most forbidding visitor was Air Commandant Felicity Hanbury Williams, head of the WAAF. She arrived in her own Dakota with her staff, a buxom bevy of lady squadron leaders. I asked to interview her for *Wing*, our now well-established station magazine. As a result, I had twenty minutes with her, desperately trying to make light of a ponderous conversation about the future of the WAAF. Dame Felicity was handsome, but slightly severe in both looks and manner. Her most intimidating feature was a twitch in her left eye which pulsed every forty-five seconds: an unintentional 'come hither' wink which made our conversation almost impossible, for me at any rate.

In October I got a fortnight's leave in the UK. This didn't go as planned. For a start, on the way back in a Dakota I was airsick for the first time in my life. And next day I was really ill, again experiencing the sickness and pain which had culminated in my embarrassing sick-leave in March of the previous year when I'd come on leave from 305 Squadron. This time, however, there was a bulge about three inches long just below my stomach on the right. An RAF doctor visited me and, within an hour, an ambulance whisked me off to St George's Hospital. There, a *svelte*, dark-suited specialist looked me over and coldly pronounced, 'I should think you've got a stinking appendix.' He removed it that very night; only just in time too, a few hours more and it would have burst. I woke up in a ward overlooking the Winged Victory and the Royal Artillery Memorial. The patient in the next bed was the doorman from the Mirabelle; another appendix case, he had put it about that I was a Spitfire pilot who had bailed out over Hyde Park and hurt himself badly on landing.

Back in Germany again, I began keenly to anticipate demobilization and three years at Oxford. Meanwhile the magazine's success had led to the recruitment of a full-time member of staff, a German girl called Eva Vahlenbreder. She was dark, swift and slight with a charming smile. During the war she'd been a draughtsman in a U-boat-yard and, as a result, she drew very neatly and was a dab hand at magazine layout. Eva and her family came from Danzig, and they'd walked to the Gutersloh area in the winter of 1944–5, pushing their worldly possessions in a pram. Towards Christmas, I and a navigator colleague from 305, John Nethercote, culled various festive goodies from the mess, including a bottle of brandy, as a present for Eva and her family. We then drove across the frozen landscape to the clutch of farmhouses where they lived together with other refugees. The authorities had had great difficulty in housing the influx of East German refugees who, like all such refugees, were far from popular with the locals. Eva, her parents and brother were all crammed into two spotless rooms. They lit a candle and sang *Silent Night* as we handed over the package which, given their penury, was far from just symbolic.

Our own Christmas marked my swan song as mess officer. A stickler for dramatic timing, I left decorating the mess hall until after breakfast on Christmas Day. As lunch was a cold buffet starring a whole roasted pig, we had the place to ourselves until evening. I had a giant tree all ready round the corner. This was duly installed, sparkling with the best set of lights that any RAF electrical department could possibly provide. I'd got the German carpenters to knock up numerous little wooden candle-holders so that there were lines of candles the length of the table on both sides. We lit them and turned out the main lights just before the doors were opened to one hundred and twenty officers and some thirty wives. Unfortunately my briefing on the dinner hadn't allowed for German literal-mindedness: I'd failed to specify that the little rolls of bacon and other trimmings for the turkey should be hot; they were startlingly raw. I passed this off as an old German tradition and the novelty added to the overall success of the evening.

Although I wasn't due for demob until late February, I went on leave again in early January and hoped to extend it so that I could get to Univ by the start of the Hilary Term on 11 January. On a very cold and frosty morning, I said goodbye to Gutersloh, Germany and the RAF and drove on slippery roads across the north of the Ruhr to the Hook, Harwich and home. My plan worked. I arrived at Univ just in time for the coldest UK winter since 1939–40 and in February I journeyed north to an RAF station near Preston to get myself demobbed.

I was glad to be leaving the RAF – and thrilled to be back at Oxford and getting on with the next stage in my life. However, as the years went by, I came to appreciate the imprint the service had made on me. True, my career wasn't much out of the ordinary but the experience left me with a lifelong attitude. I felt, and still feel, honoured and privileged to have been in the RAF. Each of the services has had its great triumph – the navy has Trafalgar and the army, Waterloo – but those are in the distant past; the RAF has the Battle of Britain which happened in my own lifetime; moreover, its heroes and survivors were still serving when I was in the RAF. The service was a living legend in the finest British tradition and, as John Terraine has written in his excellent history of the RAF, it bore much of the brunt of the war. It also epitomized British technology at its best with phenomena such as the Mosquito and radar. As a member of the service, I shared in the *élan* which comes from being on the winning team. I also drew, and continue to draw, great pride and satisfaction from my experiences in the RAF; feelings that I suspect may sadly have been denied to later generations.